The Challenge
of Interdependence

The Challenge
of Interdependence:

Mexico and the United States

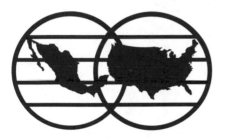

Report of the Bilateral Commission on the Future of United States– Mexican Relations

UNIVERSITY
PRESS OF
AMERICA

Lanham • New York • London

Copyright © 1989 by

University Press of America,® Inc.

4720 Boston Way
Lanham, MD 20706

3 Henrietta Street
London WC2E 8LU England

British Cataloging in Publication Information Available

Co-published by arrangement with the Bilateral Commission on the
Future of United States-Mexican Relations

ISBN 0–8191–7274–X (pbk. : alk. paper)
ISBN 0–8191–7273–1 (alk. paper)

Table of Contents

The Bilateral Commission on the Future of United States–Mexican Relations

COMMISSION MEMBERS*

Héctor Aguilar Camín
editor of the newsmagazine *Nexos*

Gilberto Borja
president of Grupo ICA

Yvonne Brathwaite Burke
partner in the law offices of Jones, Day, Reavis & Pogue, Los Angeles

Juan José Bremer
chairman of the foreign relations committee of the Mexican Chamber of Deputies

Fernando Canales Clariond
businessman from Monterrey

Henry Cisneros
mayor of San Antonio, Texas

Socorro Díaz
Mexican Senator from Colima

Lawrence S. Eagleburger
president of Kissinger Associates, Inc.

Ernesto Fernández Hurtado
director of Banco de Comercio

*With positions at time of appointment to Commission.

Executive Summary

The bilateral relationship between Mexico and the United States is becoming increasingly important to both countries. But an atmosphere of conflict and recrimination has been damaging the relationship, which both countries must make a concerted effort to improve.

The time is propitious to make this effort, as new Administrations are about to take office in both countries. Such an opportunity will not happen again in this century.

THE COMMISSION

The Bilateral Commission on the Future of United States-Mexican Relations is a group of private citizens who have been working over the last two years to reassess long-term patterns of change and continuity and to make recommendations for private leaders and public authorities in both countries.

Although an independent entity, the Commission has received expressions of encouragement from both the U.S. and Mexican governments.

Funded principally by the Ford Foundation, the Commission has solicited forty-eight papers from leading specialists. In addition, members have talked with current and former government officials, business leaders, and numerous other prominent figures in both countries.

All Commissioners agree with the spirit of the recommendations, which were decided by informal consensus, although not all Commissioners necessarily agree with every detail of every recommendation.

THE FUNDAMENTAL MESSAGE

Our fundamental message is twofold.

First, bilateral problems require bilateral approaches. *Unilateral actions cannot provide lasting solutions.* Not only does a bilateral approach assure full consideration of a problem; it also enhances the likelihood of finding a solution that *works.*

Second, the relationship is becoming increasingly complex and requires skillful *management,* not simplistic recipes. The two neighbors differ sharply in history, culture, political outlook, social organization, and economic development. But they also share common interests and are undergoing profound changes—within their societies and in the global arena. While asymmetry persists, the U.S. and Mexico are becoming increasingly interdependent. All these changes create problems. They also create opportunities— the challenge is to realize the full potential of the opportunities.

We have organized our report so as to highlight five of the most important issues we believe will face the two countries through the rest of this century. They are closely related with one another. For each we identify fundamental trends and assess realistic opportunities for bilateral cooperation.

ECONOMICS

New governments in both Mexico and the United States will soon begin coping with serious economic and financial problems.

The economic situations facing the two new governments are similar in several respects. Both nations are large debtors; both need to sustain economic growth mainly through exports in a world of growing protectionism; both need to attract substantial new investment; both are plagued with high government deficits and indebtedness. The differences, though, are greater. The U.S. is large and wealthy; Mexico is now a slowly developing country with a visibly declining standard of living.

For the United States, the challenges are to rebalance its economy and to redefine its role in the world. For more than forty years American leadership, finance, and commitment to open markets underpinned a dynamic, growing world economy. Now that leadership is in question, the U.S. has become the world's largest debtor nation, and free trade is under assault.

For Mexico, the challenge is to grow—with the benefits of growth shared by all its people. If the country's needs are to be met, the now stagnant economy must grow at annual rates of at least 6 percent.

GENERAL:

In a perfect world the two countries could address their challenges separately. But a 2,000-mile border and the interconnections of the two economies mean they must be faced simultaneously. From some perspectives this seems to make conflict almost inevitable.

To minimize such conflict economic solutions must be found in which both sides win or, at least, in which the number of losers is minimized and losers are compensated. This will require a framework that can address the whole range of sensitive issues—debt, trade, investment, and so on. As the larger and wealthier partner in the bilateral relationship, the U.S. must take the lead, not only in confronting its own structural weaknesses, but also in shielding Mexico to the extent possible from the repercussions of U.S. economic adjustments.

In this context, **the U.S. and Mexican governments** should together establish a cabinet-level binational economic commission which would:

- provide a high-level forum for permanent dialogue about macroeconomic policies between the two countries, and

- provide the two governments with an early warning mechanism to help reduce economic dislocations.

To assist its analysis and recommendations, this commission should seek the opinion of business and labor organizations and of academic specialists from both countries.

DEBT:

Unless the two countries succeed in working together to deal with Mexico's foreign debt on a sustainable basis, the bilateral relationship will not improve and may deteriorate. The unresolved debt overhang extracts excessive social, economic, and political costs from Mexico, limits the potential for commercial intercourse between the two countries, injects tension into the relationship, and—most important—affects the bases of social and political stability in Mexico.

For Mexico and other debtor countries aggressively pursuing structural economic adjustment programs, debt service obligations in the future should be designed *subject to their capacity to pay under conditions of growth*. Without growth, adjustment will not be sustained; without growth, resources for debt service will not be available.

Efforts should be made to accommodate this important conceptual change within the existing financial system. The U.S. government must play a creative facilitating role. For its part, the Mexican government should expand its debt-for-equity program, seek alternative market-based mechanisms for reducing the stock of existing debt, and continue to explore innovative financing proposals which could allow the country to tap new sources of finance. Since the foreign commercial banks account for such a large share of Mexico's foreign debt, they also must play a prominent role.

Therefore, **the incoming U.S. and Mexican Presidents**, in concert with other leaders, should invite a small group of international financial and political experts from the largest industrial countries and the major debt-impacted developing countries to undertake an examination of the debt crisis from a global perspective. The purpose of such a group would not be so much to discover new "solutions" to the debt crisis as to lay the basis for urgent political action.

Since matching debt service to payment capacity may or may not lead to either an absolute or relative reduction of the stock of existing debt, it might also be necessary to develop specific mechanisms to that end, possibly in conjunction with the World Bank.

TRADE:

If the debt issue has the potential to undermine U.S.-Mexican relations, increasing trade could be the cement which bonds the countries closer together. But here, too, is potential for conflict. Both countries are pursuing export-led growth and both countries need to contain the level of imports in order to service their foreign debt. The task facing the leaders of the two countries is to manage the conflicts, develop the complementarities, and leverage increasing bilateral trade into higher economic growth and more job creation.

Therefore, **leaders of Mexico and the U.S.** should adopt a two-step approach to their bilateral trade relationship, recognizing the necessary limitations that derive from the enormous economic disparities between the two nations. First, both countries should continue to agree to generalized trade concessions. Second, they should move promptly to free-trade agreements in all sectors where benefits from free trade may exist, especially industrial sectors. As these sectoral agreements mature (and as Mexico's economic liberalization advances), they may prove to be the building blocks for even more intense bilateral commercial cooperation.

INVESTMENT:

Both the U.S. and Mexico are badly in need of increasing investment. For the long run the urgency for Mexico is far greater, however, because its economy now lacks the productive base and infrastructure to compete effectively in the future.

The key to stimulating adequate investment flows is the creation of an environment conducive to profitable investment. Investors respond to the same incentives, regardless of nationality: freedom from excessive regulation, a stable policy environment, adequate rates of return, ready sources of financing, and good marketing opportunities. In all countries, however, including the United States, investment by foreigners raises questions about the control of national resources, the extent of foreign influence in domestic policymaking, and the ownership of national economic assets. Over the years, this has been particularly true in Mexico. Nevertheless, Mexico's precarious financial circumstances, the need to obtain current technologies, and the desire to assure better access to the U.S. market—especially through joint ventures—necessarily imply the need to encourage foreign investment.

Therefore, **the Mexican government** should adopt a more open and consistent policy for new foreign investment directed toward the export of manufactured goods, tourism, and in-bond and assembly industries; re-establish a debt-equity swap program in cases that are clearly beneficial for the country; and encourage foreign investment in projects that lead to prompt transfers of modern technology.

The two governments should establish a fast-track procedure to identify legal, administrative, fiscal, commercial, and patent issues that may pose obstacles to foreign investment; and adopt measures, consistent with their national policies, that reduce or eliminate those impediments.

IMMIGRATION

At the core of disagreements between Mexico and the United States about immigration are differing perceptions about the causes and consequences of Mexican illegal migration to the U.S. Mexicans stress the role of "pull" factors and the demand for migrant labor, and see U.S. employers (hungry for cheap labor) and U.S. consumers (wanting cheap goods and services) as the main beneficiaries. U.S. policymakers stress the "push" factors of unemployment and lack of opportunity, and see Mexican migrants and the Mexican economy as the main beneficiaries.

The Commission believes that, whether pushed or pulled, the workers face an essentially economic decision. Until the larger economic issues are squarely addressed, the pressure for migration will continue. Any bilateral policy must understand this reality. Legislation is at best a short-run mechanism for adjustment and regulation.

The key issue is the reduction of economic differentials between the two countries. Successful resolution of the problems of debt, trade, and investment constitutes a prerequisite for coping with the problem. This will take time, probably a generation. Meanwhile a number of shorter-run issues demand resolution.

The U.S. government should consider extension of the amnesty provisions under the Immigration Reform and Control Act of 1986 (IRCA), issue public reports on the full effects of that legislation, endorse the forthcoming U.N. resolution on the human rights of migratory workers, and uphold standards of civilized behavior toward migrants.

The Mexican government should forge a clear definition of its national interest regarding migration, stimulate employment in the major sending areas, and cooperate with U.S. authorities in insuring the human rights of migratory workers.

Both governments should work together to obtain an accurate count of the stock and flow of immigrants. They should undertake to reach a bilateral accord on migration, which should consider: a possible increase in the legal quotas of Mexican migration to the U.S., an agreement on the flow and treatment of "seasonal agricultural workers," the protection of migrants' human and labor rights, and the possibility of a long-run temporary worker program.

ILLICIT DRUGS

The production and consumption of illicit drugs is an international phenomenon with widespread, multiple consequences—including the social destructiveness of drug abuse on consumer populations; the stimulation of crime, violence, and lawlessness; and the poisoning of the international atmosphere.

Worldwide drug production and traffic have grown steadily during the past two decades, and particularly rapidly in the 1980s. On both sides of the U.S.-Mexican border, the drug traffic has expanded in quantitative terms (levels of demand, supply, and economic volume) as well as qualitative ones (effects of drug production and consumption on social, cultural, economic and political structures).

Supply and demand are interrelated aspects of a single market. Therefore, producer and consumer countries must share responsibility for dealing with the challenge. As long as efforts to control supply are not accompanied by efforts to control demand, there will always be an overriding economic incentive to produce drugs—somewhere—and to transport and distribute them to consumers.

The United States accounts for the largest and most dynamic market for illicit drugs in the world. Mexico has become the single most important source of drugs for the U.S. market, but this has not always been true. The cultivation and production of illicit drugs have shifted during the postwar period. After one source shuts down another replaces it. What remains constant is the presence of demand.

The U.S. government should recognize that demand within the U.S. is the driving force for production and traffic in Mexico; forge an adequately funded long-term policy of education, prevention, and treatment, as well as law enforcement; eradicate illicit drug production in the U.S.; and allocate its limited resources to combatting the most dangerous drugs (cocaine and heroin).

The Mexican government should concentrate law enforcement on large traffickers (not peasants); focus primarily on heroin and cocaine; strengthen drug abuse education and prevention; and provide economic alternatives for farmers now relying on illicit drug crops for their livelihood.

Both governments should increase support for multilateral drug control efforts; lower the level of rhetoric; establish a joint mechanism for regular consultation and collaboration on drug control issues; and work together to create a model for collaboration between producer and consumer countries.

FOREIGN POLICY

The content of a country's external policy depends upon its relative position in the world, upon the evolution of its history, and upon its aspirations for the future. It is therefore understandable that the foreign policies of Mexico and the United States do not always agree. The issue is whether the two countries can understand their differences, manage them constructively, and expand their points of agreement.

The differences in outlook are in fact striking—so striking that the Commission's report sets forth two separate views of international affairs, one North American and one Mexican. These profoundly different perceptions have motivated U.S. and Mexican foreign relations in the postwar era and, as such, have led to disagreements over such issues as Central America. But they should not be allowed to obscure the bedrock fact that the two countries share interests and aspirations that transcend the differences—and provide the basis for new collaboration.

First, Mexico and the United States share one of the longest borders in the world, which has proven to be one of the most important and lasting areas of agreement. The handling of the border presents a worthy model for other parts of the world—and for other aspects of the U.S.-Mexican relationship.

Second, each country has a direct and growing stake in the economic strength of the other—a special convergence of interests that will endure until and beyond the end of this century. These new challenges will exceed the capacity of either government acting alone.

Third, the international arena is undergoing important transformations. The Intermediate Nuclear Force (INF) treaty of late 1987 may herald a truly new phase in East-West relations. Within Latin America, the transition from military dictatorship to electoral democracy in major countries offers new possibilities for constructive cooperation at the regional level.

If a new collaboration is to work, both countries must learn to accept the reality that controversy will result from foreign policy disagreement; that there is a difference between disagreement and sanction—which we regard as inappropriate and counterproductive; and that foreign policy differences must be prevented from contaminating the bilateral relationship. Both countries must respect the right of the other to disagree. What changes should be made to enhance the likelihood of achieving a new collaboration?

Both countries would be advised to consider amending the manner of their discourse. Without compromising its interests and principles, the United States must learn to work with more prudence and subtlety with Mexico, recognizing that Mexico has its own national interests and rational objectives. Without compromising its interests and principles, Mexico needs to look with greater understanding on the global nature of the U.S. role and on the limitations and complications that position imposes on the conduct of U.S. foreign policy. Mexico could, as well, take greater advantage of opportunities deriving from its relationship with the United States by using the impressive legions of Mexicans who know the idiom and style of the United States in a more vigorous effort to bring Mexico's interests and needs to the attention of American policymakers.

The Commission has formed a series of recommendations to promote more effective interaction and communication between the two governments:

The U.S. government should create a high-level position of coordinator for U.S. policy toward Mexico; appoint individuals of stature to key positions with regard to Mexico; strengthen communication between the legislative branches of the two governments (in particular the U.S.-Mexican parliamentary group); and appoint an outside advisory group to consult on a regular basis with key U.S. government decisionmakers on Mexico.

The Mexican government should create a "specialized cabinet" for foreign affairs; strengthen the role and resources of the Mexican Embassy in Washington; strengthen the roles and resources of consulates in key U.S. cities; and promote dialogue between the Mexican and U.S. legislatures.

Both governments should work to create more formal mechanisms to energize, channel, and advance their mutual interests:

- The presidential summit should assume more substantive meaning, along with regular meetings between the foreign ministers and other high officials of the two countries.

- The permanent cabinet-level binational economic commission (recommended above) can also become an important channel for addressing foreign policy differences.

- A binational authority on border affairs should be established. In keeping with the exercise of national sovereignty, this organization could assume regulatory responsibility for matters of common concern and undertake the management of carefully specified activities (such as environment, customs, and transborder infrastructure projects).

Both countries should together take the lead in promoting new multilateral approaches to regional issues. A first step is to initiate a frank and open dialogue on the concept of regional security. The Commission believes that regional security involves not only military/strategic concerns, but must also encompass questions of socioeconomic development. In this regard, the Commission also believes that there is a strong convergence of national interests between Mexico and the U.S. Both countries oppose the installation of long-range missiles in the hemisphere, both look forward to the early and peaceful resolution of contemporary conflicts in Central America and the Caribbean.

Institutionally, Mexico and the U.S. should together promote a meaningful reinvigoration of the Organization of American States (OAS). They should also promote informal *ad hoc* mechanisms for international cooperation (as Mexico has already done with other nations of the region). In the long run, hemispheric security might be best served by a series of interlocking and regional networks: those closest to the problems will be in the best position to find workable solutions.

EDUCATION AND PUBLIC OPINION

The problems of economic interdependence, migration, drugs and foreign policy pose serious and enduring challenges for the management of the bilateral relationship. These issues are needlessly complicated, however, by cultural stereotypes that cloud public understanding, by ignorance and misperception that affect policymakers and the media as well as ordinary citizens, by the failure to inform and educate, and by the dearth of scholars and researchers needed to produce new knowledge and expert analysis.

The future shape of the bilateral relationship between Mexico and the United States is being determined, to a large degree, by the magnitude and quality of the cultural relations between our two peoples. The future is now being shaped:

- by the information and images available in the media;
- by what our children are taught (or not taught) in school;
- by the number and quality of cooperative contacts among individual citizens, private institutions, and public agencies of the two countries;
- by the extent to which the people of the two countries are coming to know about and learn to respect each other's cultural and scientific achievements;
- by the investment each country is making in training and employing scholars and experts on the history, economy, politics, culture, and society of the other.

All these dimensions are in urgent need of improvement.

EDUCATION:

Both countries should increase and improve primary-, secondary-, and university-level teaching about each other. Efforts should include curricular reform, exchanges of educators, study-abroad seminars, expanded field trips, and greater support for university outreach programs.

U.S. authorities should create national and regional clearing-houses to develop inventories of curricular and extracurricular materials on Mexico for use by schools, and develop special supplementary teaching materials to combat negative cultural stereotypes.

NEWS COVERAGE:

A concerted effort is needed to provide U.S. media personnel with more intimate knowledge of Mexican society, culture, and politics. This should include exchanges of personnel between news organizations, development of a source to provide English translations of Mexican news and commentary, private and public agency efforts to provide more continuous and instantaneous information sources to the U.S. media.

The Mexican government should undertake a deliberate effort to promote understanding among policymaking officials of U.S. and international media expectations.

Both countries should develop specialized outreach programs and workshops directed to editors and journalists.

ENTERTAINMENT MEDIA:

U.S. public educational television programs, including entertainment and cultural features as well as news, should be made more accessible to the Mexican public; cultural programming and news coverage from Mexico should be made more accessible in the U.S. In addition, independent studies should be undertaken to assist the U.S. film and television industries in avoiding unwarranted assaults on the sensitivities of Mexican and other Hispanic audiences.

EXPERTISE AND CULTURAL EXCHANGE:

The United States and Mexico have failed to invest adequately in the development of the expertise needed to produce and disseminate knowledge about the other.

A major expansion is needed of training and research centers on the United States in Mexico and on Mexico in the United States, coupled with national programs of support for graduate training and postdoctoral research—funded by the two governments, alone or in collaboration, and by public agencies and private initiatives in the two countries.

Also needed is a non-governmental binational U.S.-Mexican Council for Advanced Research to facilitate a wide range of scholarly collaborations and exchanges.

Further, the two countries should form a partnership in the area of science and technology—through such institutions as the National Science Foundation and the National Academy of Sciences—and strengthen the Mixed Commission on Science and Technology.

Finally, and most important, **both governments** should work to implement, expand, and develop the recent Bilateral Agreement on Cultural Exchange and Scientific Cooperation between Mexico and the United States.

*   *   *   *

We urge representatives of Mexico and the United States to focus on both the *nature* and *potential* of the relationship. Even as they grapple with immediate problems, they should do so in the context of a long-run view of national interests. The U.S.-Mexican relationship is constantly evolving; as the bilateral agenda changes, there will be a need for continual evaluation and innovation in the policy process.

Collaboration demands more than good will. It demands a willingness to discard preconceptions and to search for innovations. Working together and respecting each other, Mexico and the United States can create a remarkable future.

The Challenge
of Interdependence:
Mexico and the United States

Report of the Bilateral Commission
on the Future of United States-
Mexican Relations

Introductory Statement

An atmosphere of conflict and recrimination surrounds the relationship between the United States and Mexico. This atmosphere is damaging the bilateral relationship at the very time when each country is becoming increasingly important to the other. Opportunities to further the interests of each, and of both, are being lost.

The problems will not disappear. Things are likely to get only worse by themselves.

The United States and Mexico must make a deliberate effort to improve the bilateral relationship, and they must do so now.

The time is propitious. New Administrations are about to take office in both countries. These new governments will be in a position to revise longstanding assumptions, reassess the importance of the relationship in light of long-term trends and national interests, and alter their modes of dealing with each other. Mexico and the United States have a remarkable opportunity for improving their relationship—an opportunity they will not have again in this century.

THE COMMISSION

The Bilateral Commission on the Future of United States-Mexican Relations is a group of private citizens who have come together to consider how they might contribute to the improvement of the relationship. Formally announced in September 1986, during the final two years of the Administrations of Presidents Miguel de la Madrid in Mexico and Ronald Reagan in the United States, the Commission elected to undertake a vigorous assessment of long-term patterns of change and continuity in U.S.-Mexican relations. Looking ahead into the 1990s, the Commission agreed to formulate recommendations for private leaders and public authorities in both countries. In particular, the Commission undertook to search out areas of bilateral agreement, to explore common ground, and to formulate ideas that would simultaneously serve the mutual interests of both nations.

The Commission has received approval and encouragement from both the United States and Mexican governments, including expressions of support from Bernardo Sepúlveda Amor, the Mexican Secretary of Foreign Relations, and George Shultz, the U.S. Secretary of State.

The Commission nonetheless remains a private, independent undertaking. It is representative of leading currents in the public and intellectual life of both countries, and many of its members have held—or still hold—official positions of importance. Commissioners have taken part as individuals, not as representatives of their countries or of other organizations to which they might belong.

Throughout its work the Commission has focused its central attention on the *bilateral relationship*, not on the internal affairs of either nation. We have thus undertaken to avoid both the appearance and the fact of interference in one another's domestic affairs. Our goal here is not to pass judgment on the past or even the present; it is to offer a prescription for the future.

Members of the Commission have engaged in hundreds of hours of intensive discussion. Meeting behind closed doors, we have exchanged our views on a wide range of issues. We have spoken with candor and frankness. We have formed friendships and developed mutual respect. We have learned much from one another.

This experience has enabled us to reach decisions on recommendations by informal consensus, rather than by rigid, formal vote. Obviously, no such consensus can be reached without a willingness on all sides to share in a process of give and take. This has not always been easy.

And not all Commission members in fact agree with every detail of every recommendation, or with every statement in the text. We all agree with the spirit of the recommendations, however, and with the importance of our earnest attempt to achieve a consensus report. On specific points of disagreement, Commissioners have been invited to submit individual statements; the result appears in Appendix V.

THE METHOD

The findings and recommendations of the Commission appear in this book-length report, produced for public consumption in both the United States and Mexico. Its length stands in recognition of the complexity of the bilateral relationship and of our awareness that simplistic solutions are not solutions at all. Its simultaneous publication in both countries reflects our conviction that any real improvement in the relationship depends in equal measure on efforts from both sides of the border.

To prepare for its task the Bilateral Commission has conducted a two-year program of study and research. Meeting at regular intervals at various sites in Mexico and the U.S., we have talked with current and former government officials—cabinet members, diplomats, bureaucrats, governors, legislators, mayors, border agents and police authorities. We have heard from leaders of the business and labor communities in both countries. We have received statements from journalists, artists, social activists and local figures. A roster of all these witnesses appears in Appendix IV of this report.

We commissioned a total of forty-eight papers by leading outside specialists. Appendix II gives a listing of these papers. Presented to the Commission at a series of two-day workshops, these papers provided much of the background information that appears in this report, though they do not necessarily reflect the views of the Commission. A selected number of them will be published as a separate collection in the coming months.

THE MESSAGE

As our title suggests, we urge both nations to confront "the challenge of interdependence." By focusing on "interdependence" we seek to draw attention to the *interconnectedness* of the two societies. What happens in one country has an impact on the other, and our national destinies are consequently linked to one another. This connection runs in both directions although, as we indicate in Chapter 1, interdependence does not signify parity: asymmetry remains a basic feature of the relationship.

From this same standpoint, we also mean to emphasize the importance of taking bilateral approaches to bilateral problems. *Unilateral actions cannot, in our view, provide lasting answers to bilateral questions.*

What we really advocate is an approach. Even if the bilateral agenda undergoes change, and the specific themes we explore become less (or more) important in the years ahead, we believe that the U.S.-Mexican relationship in the 1990s will require bilateral treatment. Not only does a bilateral focus assure full consideration of the question at hand; it also enhances the likelihood of policy success. Precisely because of their bilateral orientation, we are confident that our recommendations will work.

The U.S.-Mexican relationship requires skilled and thoughtful *management*, not simplistic recipes. We caution against excesses of optimism or despair. Underlying social and cultural differences will always exist between the two nations, and there will sometimes be differences in national interest and policy. But opportunities for collaboration and support will also occur, and we believe there exists at this moment exceptional potential for meaningful consultation and positive cooperation. We look on the future with hope.

The complexity of the relationship constitutes a major theme of our report. The two nations have become more and more interdependent. What happens in one country affects the other directly, and both are undergoing profound changes—in society, politics, and economics. Both countries are also confronting profound changes in the global arena. All these changes create new problems. But they also create new opportunities—the challenge is to realize the full potential of these opportunities.

THE ISSUES

The key issues involved in the relationship tend to be interrelated. They resist instant solution; each requires an integrated and sustained series of policy measures. We deal in this report with the five of the most difficult and enduring issues we believe will face the two countries in the 1990s:

- economics
  (especially trade, investment, and debt)
- migration
  (especially the impact of recent U.S. legislation and projected future trends)
- drugs
  (consumption, production, and trafficking)
- inter-state relations
  (especially differences over foreign policy)
- education and public opinion
  (especially the inculcation of stereotypes through the schools and the mass media).

For each of these broad themes we identify fundamental trends that are bound to persist through to the end of this century; assess realistic opportunities for bilateral cooperation; and offer policy recommendations to leaders in the public and private sectors of the two countries.

ACKNOWLEDGEMENTS

We offer thanks to all those groups and individuals who have assisted the work of the Bilateral Commission. In addition to the authors and experts listed in Appendices II and IV, we acknowledge the contributions of our special panel of academic consultants: Jorge A. Bustamante, John H. Coatsworth, Wayne A. Cornelius, William Glade, Guadalupe González, Cassio Luiselli, Carlos Rico, and Marta Tienda. Alan Stoga and Mathea Falco helped in the shaping and drafting of chapters two and four.

The Commission members wish to express their deep appreciation for the efforts of the staff directors: Rosario Green and Peter Smith. Their responsibilities—to pull together a large and dedicated staff, to organize the researches contributed by an army of experts, to draft the report, and to arrange our numerous meetings throughout Mexico and the United States—would have defeated ordinary mortals. They brought to our efforts a full measure of expertise, wisdom, energy—and patience. They and their colleagues—Lee Dewey, Andrea Elimelekh, Faye Engelmayer, Julia Hirst, Juan Manuel Martínez Nava, Lourdes Melgar, Esther Rocha,

Blanca Salgado, Gerardo Santos, Arturo Sarukhan, Felicity Skidmore—performed minor miracles to insure that the Commission could complete its appointed task and issue this report. We are deeply grateful.

We owe special recognition to the Ford Foundation, our principal source of financial support. William D. Carmichael, Stephen Cox, Teresa Schriever, and David Winder all played instrumental roles in the project. And we offer heartfelt thanks to the Foundation president, Franklin A. Thomas, whose visionary leadership gave us both the incentive and the opportunity to carry on with this whole endeavor.

Mexico City
Washington, D.C.
November 1988

1

The Nature
of the Relationship

The relationship between Mexico and the United States has no counterpart anywhere in the world. Nowhere else do two close neighbors reflect such sharp differences or share such common interests. Imbued with dissimilar cultural legacies, Mexico and the U.S. have traversed divergent historical paths. One is rich, the other not. They have forged contrasting models of social organization. They speak different languages and follow different customs. And they have constructed distinct perspectives on the international arena. This is a remarkable juxtaposition of societies, one that vividly illustrates the gap between the developed and the developing worlds.

But Mexico and the United States share common interests— including a 2,000-mile border—and for this reason the relationship is steadily gaining importance. As both societies undergo rapid change they are exerting increasing influence upon each other— economically, socially, politically, and diplomatically. As international realities become ever more complex, so does the bilateral relation, and the two countries need each other all the more. *Each has an abiding interest in the wellbeing of the other.*

A special opportunity to improve the quality of the relationship exists at this moment, with new governments coming to power in both countries. In order to realize this potential, however, the countries must overcome the burdens of a long and difficult past.

To take full measure of the challenge ahead, we briefly trace in this chapter the development of our two societies, the differences between them, and the complex and sometimes painful ways that they have come together. We first focus on contrasting historical and cultural legacies of the two nations; we then examine the history of U.S.-Mexican relations; we move on to analyze some persisting features of the contemporary relationship; and, finally, we outline some recent changes that have altered the nature of the relationship, including the role of public opinion.

HISTORIC LEGACIES

Mexico and the United States embarked on separate historical paths from the moment of their founding. Contemporary Mexico, like the rest of Spanish America, resulted from colonial *conquest;* North America emerged mainly from a process of *settlement.* The society of sixteenth-century Spain, energetically approaching its imperial zenith, bequeathed two powerful forces on the New World: the feudalistic pretensions of the conquerors themselves and the absolutist aspirations of the monarchy. The puritans and planters who emigrated from seventeenth-century England, by contrast, carried with them the seeds of a political liberalism that would flourish and develop in the absence of a feudal establishment. Eager to establish monopolistic control over its newfound wealth, the Spanish crown would impose an imperial bureaucracy over its holdings in America; untempted by any such windfall, British authorities would rely essentially on commerce, not control, and they granted their colonists considerable autonomy in matters of local governance.

MEXICO: CONQUEST TO REVOLUTION

Native Indian societies constructed major theocratic civilizations in what is now Mexico long before the arrival of the Spaniards. Archaeological evidence offers compelling testimony to their cultural, political, and military achievements, and to their advanced knowledge in mathematics, astronomy, medicine, and architecture. During the fourteenth century A.D. the Aztecs founded Tenochtitlán, the site of present-day Mexico City, as the capital of a vast and flourishing empire that extended its control over neighboring peoples and lands.

In the late fifteenth and early sixteenth centuries came the discovery of America and the arrival of the Spaniards, led by Hernán Cortés. The intentions of the *conquistadores*, as Bernal Díaz del Castillo said in his memorable phrase, were "to serve God and the King and also to get rich, such as gentlemen should do in life."[1] Cortés enlisted the support of Tlaxcala and other communities that chafed under Aztec control. He used his Indian mistress, Doña Malinche, to portray himself as saviour and protector. He played upon Indian fears that he was exacting revenge on behalf of an angry god, Quetzalcoatl. Finally, he laid siege to Tenochtitlán and took the city in 1521. This victory allowed the Spaniards to impose total change—on the political, economic, and social system— beginning with the destruction of religious temples and the annihilation of leaders within the indigenous society, especially the military and clerical aristocracy.

The Spanish crown promptly set out to assert political control over its newly conquered territories. Joining forces with the Church, the "Catholic kings"—Ferdinand and Isabella—and their successors created an elaborate and effective bureaucracy that combined centralism with flexibility, hierarchy with pragmatism. Local officials possessed considerable discretion over practical matters, as shown by their occasional responses to royal decrees—*obedezco pero no cumplo* (roughly, "I accept your authority but will not execute this law").[2] But lines of power were strictly vertical, and ultimate authority resided in the crown.

> New Spain was an intricate tapestry of influences, powers, and jurisdictions. Facing the political and juridical power of the Viceroy and the courts [*audiencia*] was the moral and religious authority of the Archbishop of Mexico. The Archbishop, in turn, had a serious rival in the bishop of Puebla, the other principal city. And they both had to face the powerful religious orders.[3]

1. Bernal Díaz del Castillo, *Historia verdadera de la Conquista de la Nueva España*, fifth edition (Madrid: Espasa-Calpe, 1982), p. 27.
2. José Ignacio Rubio Mañé, *El virreinato: Introducción al estudio de los virreyes de Nueva España, 1535-1746*, vol. I (México: Fondo de Cultura Económica, 1955).
3. Octavio Paz, *Sor Juana Inés de la Cruz o las trampas de la fe*, third edition (México: Fondo de Cultura Económica, 1983), pp. 51-52.

During the seventeenth and eighteenth centuries New Spain continued to expand. Conquerors, priests, and settlers reached to and beyond the city of San Francisco, now part of the American West, and as far south as Panama. The Philippines also came within its jurisdiction.

The viceregal economy was supported by the labor of the Indians. The natives worked almost incessantly—in mines, in fields, in factories and sweatshops—under conditions of cruel exploitation. The conquest and subsequent diseases led to a precipitous reduction in the size of the Indian population.

One of the distinctive features of Spanish colonization, however, was the idea of incorporating indigenous elements into the social order. This commitment stemmed from philosophical, humanistic, and religious outlooks of sixteenth-century Spain. Partly in response to demographic realities, too, Spaniards intermingled with Indian women to produce a mixed-blood category known as *mestizos*. Accounting for perhaps one-quarter of the population of New Spain by the late eighteenth century, *mestizos* came to reflect— and to promote—a commitment to racial inclusiveness. In subsequent eras, the *mestizo* population would become the dominant element in Mexican society and comprise a defining feature of the national self-image.

The highly centralized state in New Spain protected social privilege and established a complex network of separate jurisdictions. There were specific laws for the religious orders and the Church; others for *encomenderos* (Spaniards entrusted with control of Indians), merchants, miners, artisans; still others for the congregations and the brotherhoods. Indian communities received special protection under the Laws of the Indies. Special statutes applied to other ethnic groups in colonial society: blacks, mulattos, mixed-blood *mestizos*, and whites (themselves composed of two groups: *peninsulares*, whites born in Spain, and *criollos*, whites born in the New World). Most of these groups had no political representation. The dominant bureaucratic apparatus was in the hands of *peninsulares*, and New Spain did not experience the Spanish form of parliamentary representation known as the Cortes.

The *criollos* eventually rose up to challenge the supremacy of the *peninsulares*. When in 1808 Napoleon forced King Ferdinand VII of Spain to abdicate, the creoles banded together in defense of Spanish sovereignty, and it was only a matter of time before they would claim it for themselves. After a decade of bloody and often brutal war in which *mestizos* came to play a crucial part, Mexico achieved its independence in 1821.

The fighting left the country in disorder and decay. The economy was in a shambles. Spaniards had taken their capital abroad. The gold and silver mines, once the pride of Spain's overseas empire, had fallen into disrepair, and the textile industry had hit hard times. There were very few jobs—and a great deal of unemployment. But the most challenging task for the country was the quest for political organization. As a distinguished Mexican historian has pointed out, this would become a tragedy lasting more than half a century.[4]

In conflict were two distinct social orders: the colonial system, with its semifeudal characteristics, not fully eliminated by the fact of independence; and a new vision, secular and liberal and modern, not fully implanted by the fact of independence. This ambiguity has led to characterization of early nineteenth-century Mexico as "the fluctuating society."[5]

The old colonial order found defenders among the Church, high military officers, and the landholding aristocracy—all of whom sought to maintain or expand their traditional privileges, to restrict freedom, and to uphold a centralized state (preferably a monarchy). The new liberal order drew support from the middle sectors, including lesser-rank officers and the lower clergy, who sought to abolish privilege and to establish the supremacy of civil authority within a federal and republican polity.

This ideological conflict was profound, resulting in frequent military clashes, in political instability, and at times in virtual chaos. During the 40-year period from 1821 to 1860 Mexico had at least 50 separate presidencies, each one lasting an average of less than one year; 35 of these regimes were led by army officers. The period saw the promulgation of a federalist constitution in 1824, centralist revisions in 1836 and 1843, and new federalist initiatives in 1847 and 1857.

The struggle between liberals and conservatives began to move toward resolution in the 1850s, when the liberals gained a temporary triumph with the Revolution of Ayutla. They called a

4. Daniel Cosío Villegas, *Historia moderna de México, La República restaurada: vida política*, third edition (México: Editorial Hermes, 1973), p. 45.
5. Jesús Reyes Heroles, *El liberalismo mexicano*, vol. II (*La sociedad fluctuante*) (México: Universidad Nacional Autónoma de México, 1958), p. xii; and Juan Felipe Leal, *La burguesía mexicana y el estado mexicano*, fifth edition (México: El Caballito, 1972), p. 49.

constitutional convention in 1857 and, under their leader Benito Juárez, imposed a series of laws that came to be known as *La Reforma*.

Conservatives launched a counterattack in 1858. During a six-year civil war they gained support from the French empire and in 1864 they imported a European monarch, Maximilian von Hapsburg of Austria. Not surprisingly, this maneuver aroused strong nationalist sentiments. Juárez led a successful overthrow of the empire and a court sentenced Maximilian and two leading Mexican conservatives to execution in 1867.

Aside from witnessing political instability and internal conflict, the nineteenth century was a period of profound transformation in the political culture of Mexico. Liberal ideas assaulted archaic socioeconomic structures, promoted the modernization of the country, and greatly enriched the political and cultural spirit of the nation.

The liberals consolidated power under Juárez until his death in 1872. A few years later General Porfirio Díaz, also a liberal, seized the presidency through another military coup.

Díaz remained in power from 1877 to 1911 and summarized his credo in two slogans: "Peace, Order, and Progress," and "Administration over Politics" (*Poca Política y Mucha Administración*). Díaz managed to create a broad ruling coalition in keeping with prevailing social and economic realities. At the peak of his system were the *haciendas*, vast stretches of land owned by a small number of families, a cadre that came to constitute an authentic landed aristocracy.

Díaz and his advisers actively promoted an economic growth. Government policies stimulated agriculture, mining, commerce, and incipient industrialization, and for these purposes encouraged foreign investment as well. European capital was the first to meet with special favor; then came the Americans. Foreign trade increased ninefold between 1877 and 1910, and the United States became Mexico's leading trade partner.

The Mexican Revolution erupted in 1910. Peasants, workers, middle-sector people from the cities and the countryside joined together in protest against their political and social exclusion from the *Porfiriato* of Díaz. Theirs would become the first great social revolution of the twentieth century. The Constitution of 1917 would define political and social rights for the people as well as the basis for political organization.

Distribution of land to the peasants, the right for workers to organize and strike, the principle of an eight-hour day, access to public education—these were some of the major achievements of the revolutionary cause. Others included assumption by the nation of ultimate ownership of all land, water, and subsoil deposits, thus establishing the basis for land distribution and for oil nationalization. Article 27 of the Constitution, moreover, stipulated that foreign propertyowners as well as nationals must submit to the laws of Mexico. Some of these revolutionary measures became matters of serious concern to foreign owners and investors. The government of the United States took action as a result.

The Revolution marked a significant advance in Mexico's struggle with its complex colonial legacy. It established the basis for a political system that would bring order and stability to national life. It gave full expression to the needs and aspirations of the common masses. It would, as a result, become the touchstone of national identity. And it would bring order to the management of foreign relations.

During the century-long period from independence to the Revolution, Mexico was struggling to resolve crucial domestic issues. But it was not allowed to do so in peace. Throughout the period, Mexico had to face frequent threats and even attacks from other countries—England, France, and (as we shall see) the United States. Mexico's international posture was essentially defensive—a continuing attempt to sustain the nation's integrity and sovereignty in the face of external pressure. This tradition has left its mark on contemporary diplomacy.

THE UNITED STATES:
PROVIDENTIAL MISSION TO GOOD NEIGHBORHOOD

Just as the Spanish monarchy imposed its political will through imperial fiat, so did English settlers express their political will through experimentation. Even after the achievement of independence from Great Britain, in a sharp series of battles from 1776 to 1783, there was more continuity than change in political affairs. And as the founding fathers gave shape to their young republic, they embarked upon a particularly bold experiment—the creation of a democracy—on which they proceeded with considerable uncertainty. As the history of the Greek city-states had shown, all secular communities had flourished and decayed; all had a beginning and end; and democracies had shown themselves to be especially vulnerable to the temptations of absolutist rule. Even after the nation's leaders had discarded the Articles of Confederation in favor of a new Constitution in 1787, doubts continued to linger. As one observer would declare in 1809: "Can any man who looks upon the state of public virtue in this country . . . believe that this confederated republic is to last forever?"[6]

Along with this feeling of uncertainty, New England puritans and their descendants espoused the fervent conviction that providential will had given them a sacred mission. We are as a City upon a Hill, as John Winthrop had said in 1630, with the eyes of all the world upon us. The very magnitude of their tribulations confirmed their sense of special calling: God would not impose such drastic trials without some higher purpose. It was in the New World that God's kingdom would come. As Jonathan Edwards proclaimed, "the Latter-Day Glory is probably to begin in America."[7] A voice in the wilderness, America would be a beacon to the world.

This idea of spiritual mission combined with precepts of liberal thinking to create a theory of political democracy. As individuals exercised the freedom of their will in matters theological, so should they be able to express themselves in the political arena. There would be no room for monarchy or hereditary privilege. Once admitted to the community, all individuals shared equal rights and opportunities. In time the United States would have to face up to massive contradictions within its own society. One was the displacement and near-eradication of the native Indians (which meant there would be hardly any *mestizos*). Another was the establishment of slavery, elimination of which would require the bitter Civil War of the 1860s. Yet another was the position of women, who would take another half century to obtain the right to vote.

Despite such contradictions, the American ideals of political democracy and social opportunity continued to provide great inspiration. Generations of hardy frontiersmen—soldiers and hunters at first, then ranchers and farmers—came forward to settle and develop the lands of the west. Late in the nineteenth century, massive numbers of Europeans—Irish, Italians, Germans, Poles, and

6. Quoted in Arthur M. Schlesinger, Jr., *The Cycles of American History* (Boston: Houghton Mifflin, 1986), p. 7; in this insightful book see especially chapter 1, "The Theory of America: Experiment or Destiny?"

7. Ibid., p. 13.

others—brought their cultures, their spirits, and their energies to U.S. society. Between 1880 and 1900 approximately 9 million immigrants came to American shores, bringing the total population of the country up to 76 million. Ethnic differences created occasional frictions, but for the most part American society became a "melting pot." The key to integration was mobility. As opportunity beckoned, American folklore centered on the theme of rags-to-riches success. At the core of U.S. society was steadfast belief in the American Dream.

At the same time, a remarkable combination of natural and human resources created the basis for rapid economic development. As a country, the United States possessed fertile plains, extensive rivers, deep harbors, precious metals, industrial minerals. And as a people, America unleashed powerful creative energy through the idea of equal opportunity. Technological innovation flourished; the adaptation of electricity as a source of light and power in the 1870s would prove especially important. The U.S. constructed transcontinental railroads, built industrial empires, and embarked on a period of extraordinary economic growth. The volume of manufacturing swelled by 240 percent between 1880 and 1900, during which time the production of steel grew nearly tenfold. "Twenty-five years after the death of Lincoln, America had become, in the quantity and value of her products, the first manufacturing nation in the world," historians Charles and Mary Beard have written. "What England had accomplished in a hundred years, the United States had achieved in half the time."[8]

Almost inevitably, this rapid transformation produced social dislocations. Demonstrations and strikes by organized labor erupted in violence in the 1880s and 90s. Farmers lamented the eclipse of the frontier, resented the roles of middlemen in the newly commercialized system of agriculture, and created a populist movement. As Andrew Carnegie and others proclaimed the virtues of social Darwinism, such novelists as Mark Twain satirized "the gilded age," Edward Bellamy envisioned a utopian collective, and Upton Sinclair described life in the Chicago stockyards as a "jungle." Open criticism of this kind was a central ingredient in U.S. society, renewing and enriching the quality of public life. These

8. Quoted in Richard N. Current, T. Harry Williams, and Frank Friedel, *American History: A Survey*, third edition (New York: Alfred A. Knopf, 1971), p. 435.

challenges would ultimately find meaningful expression in the progressive movement of the early twentieth century, and they would lead to the enactment of significant reforms. Dissent proved to be a staple of democracy in the U.S.

With regard to the Americas, the articulation of national purpose first took form with the promulgation of the Monroe Doctrine in 1823. Partly aimed at czarist Russia's territorial claims in the American Northwest, the doctrine asserted that the American continents "are henceforth not to be considered as subject for future colonization by any European power." Also focusing upon an apparent design by the Holy Alliance to help Spain regain her former colonies, President Monroe warned against the reinstatement of monarchical rule:

> We owe it, therefore, to candor, and to the amicable relations existing between the United States and those powers, to declare that we should consider any attempt on their part to extend their political system to any portion of this hemisphere as dangerous to our peace and safety. ... we could not view any interposition for the purpose of oppressing [the newly independent nations], or controlling in any other manner their destiny, by any European power in any other light than as the manifestation of an unfriendly disposition toward the United States.[9]

Thus did the U.S. declare itself, in opposition to the absolutism and imperial designs of European powers, to be the guardian of independence throughout the hemisphere.

Westward expansion reinforced the U.S. sense of righteous purpose. As President James K. Polk contested Britain's claim to the Oregon territory in the mid-1840s, for example, a newspaper editor named John L. O'Sullivan invoked providential will. Blithely dismissing "all these antiquated materials of old black-letter international law," the *New York Morning News* asserted that the U.S. claim "is by the right of our manifest destiny to overspread and to possess the whole of the continent which Providence has given us for the development of the great experiment of liberty and federated self-government entrusted to us."[10] It was America's self-appointed mission to democratize the continent. According to the nineteenth-century notion of "manifest destiny," the moral ideal

9. Dexter Perkins, *A History of the Monroe Doctrine*, revised edition (Boston: Little Brown, 1963), p. 28.

10. Albert K. Weinberg, *Manifest Destiny: A Study of Nationalist Expansion in American History* (Baltimore: Johns Hopkins University Press, 1933), pp. 144-145.

of democracy was more relevant to the justice of the issue than the technical criteria of international law.

Half a century later the United States proceeded to expand and consolidate its influence throughout the Caribbean basin, dispatching troops to Cuba and the Philippines and acquiring a canal through Panama. In this context President Theodore Roosevelt proclaimed in 1904:

> Any country whose people conduct themselves well can count upon our hearty friendship. If a nation shows that it knows how to act with reasonable efficiency and decency in social and political matters, if it keeps order and pays its obligations, it need fear no interference from the United States. Chronic wrong-doing, or an impotence which results in a general loosening of the ties of society, may in America, as elsewhere, ultimately require intervention by some civilized nation, and in the western hemisphere the adherence of the United States to the Monroe Doctrine may force the United States, however reluctantly, in flagrant cases of such wrong-doing or impotence, to the exercise of an international police power.[11]

Known as the "Roosevelt Corollary" to the Monroe Doctrine, the rationale took on clear meaning: the U.S. could assert the right to intervene in Latin America.

By the early 1900s, the American sense of national destiny encouraged contradictory impulses. On the one hand, it gave rise to the notion that the United States was exceptional, superior, a truly chosen land whose political ideals and institutions could (by definition) never flourish anywhere else. This was an isolationist idea. On the other hand, this sense of uniqueness shaped and defined a political mission: to spread the gospel of democracy. This was an activist idea. Imbued with this conviction, many American leaders could not rest content with the construction of a working democracy at home. They were moreover charged to *extend* the virtues of this idea to other parts of the globe, to carry out the divine task of political civilization. This was, to them, not just a matter of preference; it was a sacred obligation.

The combination of idealism with pragmatism became a hallmark of U.S. foreign policy. Even Woodrow Wilson, who fervently believed in the virtues of democracy and peace, ended up dispatching marine contingents to various parts of Central America and

11. Quoted in Current et al., *American History*, pp. 579-580.

the Caribbean — including Mexico. (Characteristically, Wilson ascribed his foreign policies to the nation's higher calling: as he once proclaimed, "We have come to redeem the world by giving it liberty and justice.")[12] The pattern of intervention continued through the 1920s.

It was in 1933 that Franklin Delano Roosevelt proclaimed the Good Neighbor policy, the essence of which was non-intervention. The U.S. withdrew its forces from Nicaragua and elsewhere, lowered its diplomatic profile, promoted the idea of collective security, actively supported the strengthening of the inter-American community, and subscribed to the 1933 convention of Montevideo: "No state has the right to intervene in the internal or external affairs of another." As Secretary of State Cordell Hull explained, "the United States government is as much opposed as any other government to interference with the freedom, or sovereignty, or other internal affairs or processes of the governments of other nations."[13] The emphasis would be on collaboration and cooperation, not coercion; on multilateral agreements, not unilateral action.

National history and political culture thus bequeathed the United States with a very different outlook on the world from that of Mexico. Unencumbered by feudalistic traditions and blessed by bountiful natural resources, citizens and leaders in the United States could develop a cohesive society and stable institutions. U.S. citizens have taken justifiable pride in their country's role in World Wars I and II. Foreign policy would be for them a source of triumph, not a struggle for survival.

Clearly, these divergent historical experiences have created very different societies in Mexico and in the United States. It is vitally important for all to recognize these differences, to acknowledge their distinct qualities, and to cherish their respective contributions to modern civilization. We must learn to live with differences, not attempt to erase them.

Such historical overviews provide only an introduction, and a frame of reference, for the study and understanding of U.S.-Mexican relations. Because of this abbreviated presentation we have not been

---

12. Quoted in Schlesinger, *Cycles*, p. 54; and see chapter 3, "Foreign Policy and the American Character."

13. Bryce Wood, *The Making of the Good Neighbor Policy* (New York: W.W. Norton/Columbia University Press, 1967), p. 118.

able to include all the historical judgments of all Commissioners. We have merely attempted to highlight the most illustrative aspects of the differing national pasts.

THE BILATERAL RELATIONSHIP: CONFLICT TO COLLABORATION

What is now the bilateral relationship has evolved through a variety of stages from military confrontation to diplomatic negotiation. A first conflict arose over Texas. In the 1820s Mexican leaders permitted colonists, most of them slaveholding planters from the United States, to settle in the northeastern province known as Texas, then a largely unpopulated wilderness. Despite their agreement to accept Mexican citizenship, the colonists soon began chafing under Mexican rule. In 1836 they unilaterally declared their independence, thus unleashing a brief but brutal war. In 1837 the United States recognized Texas as a sovereign polity. And in 1845, after a series of complex maneuvers, it annexed the republic of Texas.

More was still to come. While North Americans claimed that the southern border of Texas extended to the Río Grande, Mexicans insisted that the limit should end, as it always had, at the Nueces River. In 1846 President Polk dispatched U.S. troops under General Zachary Taylor to the disputed area, in what many historians interpret as a deliberate move to provoke a fight. Polk then used Mexico's retaliation as an excuse to proclaim war. Despite the opposition of influential statesmen at home, including Illinois Congressman Abraham Lincoln and South Carolina's John C. Calhoun, Polk had the war that he sought.

It would change political geography. Taylor swept into the city of Monterrey, rebels in California took sides with the United States, and in 1847 American troops under General Winfield Scott advanced from Veracruz to Mexico City, seizing the capital after subduing the resistance of young Mexican cadets. The following year, in the Treaty of Guadalupe Hidalgo, Mexico was obliged to surrender a huge span of land—from New Mexico and Colorado to California, more than a million square miles—in exchange for a modest $15 million. Several years later the United States extended its holdings by obtaining an additional section of New Mexico and

Arizona through the Gadsden Purchase—a transaction remembered in Mexico for the application of U.S. pressure, and therefore known as "the imposition of La Mesilla" (el Tratado Impuesto de la Mesilla).

The result for the United States was the appropriation of ultimately prosperous land. From the California Gold Rush to construction of the transcontinental railroad and then beyond, development of this area would become one of the signal achievements of American society. In the short run, the Mexican War may well have exacerbated differences between North and South over the extension of slavery and thus helped bring on the Civil War. But in the long run, it did much to make the United States the country that it is today.

The consequence for Mexico was severe humiliation. It had endured the defeat of its troops, the occupation of its cities, and, all told, the loss of more than half its land. (See Map 1.) The shock wrought political havoc within the country, eventually prompting the already-noted installation of Archduke Maximilian of Austria as emperor of Mexico. And it led to agonized soul-searching for the nation as a whole.

Even today, Mexicans' recollections of these events is vivid and intense. More fervently than Americans "remember the Alamo," Mexicans are taught to remember the cadets who struggled vainly against Scott's troops in Mexico City. The official name for the conflict of 1846-48 provides a glimpse of the Mexican sense of injustice: it is, quite simply, "the war of the North American invasion."

The United States has not taken any territory from Mexico since 1853, but the American presence has been substantial nonetheless. In the 1870s Porfirio Díaz began imposing stability on Mexico and, after some initial tensions, the United States threw its full support to the Díaz regime. Economic ties between the countries flourished. By 1910, the centennial year of Mexico's declaration of independence, the United States was purchasing three-quarters of Mexican exports and American business had far surpassed Britain and France as the largest source of foreign investment in Mexico.

The outbreak of the Mexican Revolution took the U.S. unawares, but the American government soon resumed an active role. In 1912 the U.S. ambassador in Mexico City, Henry Lane Wilson, actively encouraged a plot to overthrow Francisco I. Madero, the political idealist whose denunciation of Díaz had triggered the revolution itself. Two years later President Woodrow Wilson (no relation of the Ambassador), frustrated in his attempt to undermine Madero's assassin, seized on the arrest of some U.S. sailors as a pretext to occupy the city of Tampico and the port of Veracruz. Characteristically, the high-minded Wilson intended to influence the outcome of the revolution: it was his goal, he is reported to have said, to teach Latin Americans how to elect good men. Wilson eventually managed to extricate himself from Veracruz, the occupation of which had served mainly to unite Mexico's competing factions against the Yankee invaders. But in 1916 he intervened again, this time responding to a border raid by General Francisco Villa with

1. TERRITORIAL CHANGES BETWEEN MEXICO AND THE UNITED STATES, 1836-53

a punitive expedition under General John J. Pershing. These two events prompted Mexican President Venustiano Carranza to formulate the "Carranza Doctrine" against foreign intervention.

Ultimately, the United States gave its support to the faction that triumphed in the revolution, but not without seeking to nullify some radical provisions in the Mexican Constitution of 1917— especially the assertion of state authority over subsoil rights, a clause which meant that the government could nationalize foreign-controlled oil fields, many of which were held by U.S. companies. This issue remained a bone of contention between the two countries for decades.

After the Mexican Revolution the bilateral agenda focused mainly on issues of foreign investment—and, especially, on petroleum. At the urging of U.S. oil interests, the Administration of Warren G. Harding withheld recognition from the postrevolutionary government of Alvaro Obregón because of unresolved disputes over practical interpretation of the constitutional clause asserting state ownership and control over subsoil rights. It was not until 1923 that the governments held the so-called "Bucareli talks," during which the U.S. agreed to extend diplomatic recognition— in exchange for a promise that Mexico would not seize oil lands held by foreign companies that had engaged in active drilling prior to 1917. Several years later Mexico proclaimed the "Estrada doctrine," denouncing the use of diplomatic recognition as an instrument of political intervention.

Petroleum remained an object of dispute. In the 1930s labor conflicts arose, partly because of the U.S. companies' discriminatory wage policies against Mexican laborers, and the oil companies resisted a series of court rulings in favor of the workers. In 1938 there came a thunderbolt: proclaiming the need to protect the country's patrimony, President Lázaro Cardenas nationalized the foreign firms and turned the exploitation of reserves over to a fledgling state agency, Petróleos Mexicanos (PEMEX). World War II broke out soon afterward. The companies, under pressure from the Allied governments (and U.S. President Roosevelt), eventually came to terms with the Mexican state, whose cooperation in the war Washington judged to be of overriding importance.

Resolution of this issue paved the way for extensive collaboration between the two countries during World War II. Mexico declared war on the Axis in 1942 and joined the Allied cause. A joint U.S.-Mexico commission acted to coordinate military action and to assure the training of Mexican officers in the United States. Mexico supplied the U.S. and the Allies with strategic materials— not the least of which was petroleum. A mutual conscription arrangement for resident aliens led to the incorporation of approximately 250,000 Mexican nationals in the U.S. armed forces; 14,000 of these men participated in combat, and 1,000 died in battle. As military mobilization led to a labor shortage in the U.S., the two governments in 1942 signed an agreement for the legal employment of temporary workers from Mexico, known in Spanish as the *braceros*. And within the hemisphere, Mexico played an important diplomatic role on behalf of the Allies.

The Allied victory ushered in a period of relative harmony in U.S.-Mexican relations, a time when many believed that the two countries were enjoying a "special relationship." The emergence of Mexico's postwar "economic miracle" provided ample opportunities for U.S. investors, and trade between the two countries flourished. The *bracero* agreement, initially a wartime measure, would stay in effect through 1964. And in reflection of this closeness, the chief executives of the two countries inaugurated a tradition of presidential summit meetings—starting with Roosevelt's visit to President Manuel Avila Camacho in 1943 and extending to the present day.

Disputes of these years were largely diplomatic. Upholding the principle of non-intervention, Mexico refused to support U.S. policies in Guatemala, Cuba, and the Dominican Republic. (We discuss these occasions in detail in Chapter 5.) These were significant issues, but leaders of the two countries were able to manage them in a spirit of mutual understanding.

The U.S. and Mexico continued to maintain a working partnership. Perhaps the high point came in 1964, when the United States returned to Mexico the Chamizal, a section of land that had fallen into dispute after the Río Grande changed its course. (Mexico had won an arbitration on this point in 1903.) But in 1964 the U.S. also terminated the *bracero* agreement, which Mexico would have preferred to prolong—an incident that did not lead to much public objection because of the initiation of the *maquiladora* program for in-bond industries in the border region. The low point of the decade came in 1969, when President Gustavo Díaz Ordaz protested that "Operation Intercept"—a blunt instrument against the narcotics trade—led to the interruption of social and commercial traffic in the border area. For the most part, however, interaction between the two countries was smooth.

What happened to this "special relationship"? Why has there been so much acrimony since the 1970s? To approach this question we now turn to an examination of structural features of the relationship itself.

THE BILATERAL RELATIONSHIP: CONTEMPORARY CHARACTERISTICS

History and contiguity have imbued the relationship between Mexico and the United States with peculiar characteristics and inescapable realities. We focus here on four such features: asymmetry, conflicts of interest, diplomatic limitations, and cultural differences.

Asymmetry. The United States is bigger, stronger, and richer than Mexico and has been ever since the mid-nineteenth century (though not before). The United States has about three times the population of Mexico, fifteen times the gross national product (GNP), and an overwhelming military superiority. The United States accounts for about two-thirds of Mexico's trade, whereas trade with Mexico makes up only between 3 and 6 percent of international transactions for the U.S. Under these conditions bargaining tends to be unequal; such discrepancies pervade the entire relationship.

Conflicts of interest. What is good for Mexico is not always good for the United States and vice versa (or, more precisely, what is good for certain interests in Mexico is not always good for certain interests in the United States). With regard to commerce, the United States and Mexico have conventional buyer-seller disputes and those deriving from different levels of development. For instance, the United States would like to purchase large amounts of Mexican oil at the lowest possible price; Mexico wants to reserve much of its petroleum for domestic development, to avoid long-term dependence on a single purchaser, and to fetch the highest possible price for exported oil. Such differences can be resolved through negotiation even after the contemporary market glut disappears, but they will not disappear altogether. They are part and parcel of the commercial connection.

This simple observation suggests that there will necessarily continue to be some differences of interest between Mexico and the United States. It is impossible to eliminate bilateral disagreement altogether. In this regard it might be useful to make a distinction between two types of conflict — that which is unavoidable, as a logical expression of differences in interests; and that which is unnecessary, usually as the result of human error (poor communication, miscalculation, or misunderstanding). A reasonable goal for policymakers is to recognize this crucial difference, to *minimize* unnecessary conflict and to learn to *manage* the unavoidable kind.

Diplomatic limitations. Government-to-government negotiations cannot resolve all key bilateral issues in a definitive manner. This is due in part to the nature of the issues—like migration, which responds to socioeconomic stimuli and stoutly resists official regulation. The blunt truth is that, in many areas, intersocietal exchange will simply overwhelm the plausible reach of intergovernment accords. The powers of both governments are limited.

An additional constraint on diplomatic negotiation derives from diversity and contradictions in policymaking, particularly in the United States, where multitudinous government agencies, each with its own perspective and constituency (including almost all departments of the executive branch plus both houses of Congress), take part in the policy process. This situation contrasts sharply with the decisionmaking process in Mexico, where presidential will generally prevails.

Cultural differences. Divergent value systems and discordant senses of history pervade the relationship between the two countries. North Americans look to the future while Mexicans remain aware of the past. As the philosopher-poet Octavio Paz once said: "North Americans consider the world to be something that can be perfected, while we [Mexicans] consider it to be something that can be redeemed."[14]

This is not an ornamental flourish. It has crucial implications, because it helps define what the two countries consider to be normal. For the United States, the customary standard for evalu-

14. *The Labyrinth of Solitude: Life and Thought in Mexico,* translated by Lysander Kemp (New York: Grove Press, 1961), p. 24.

ation has been the very recent past—especially the halcyon years
after World War II, when the United States was the world's dominant power and Mexico was the junior partner in an apparently
satisfactory "special relationship." Any departure from this baseline
represented undesirable abnormality. For Americans, harmony has
been the norm.

For Mexico, the standard for evaluation is the full sweep of
history. Intense concern with the past has bred a deep-seated suspicion of the United States. Mexicans recall with bitterness the
nineteenth-century disputes over Texas and the military invasion
that led to the loss of half the nation's territory. They remember
United States interventions in the Mexican Revolution, American
suspicions about the constitution of 1917, and strident opposition
to the nationalization of oil in 1938. For Mexicans, conflict and contention are the norm.

Furthermore, many Mexicans tend to assume that the exercise
of power reflects rational intentions. Events do not happen by mistake; they happen because those in power bring them about. In the
bilateral context this often translates into a conviction that United
States actions toward Mexico are orchestrated, not coincidental;
deliberate, not accidental; organized, not spontaneous. It is widely
believed in Mexico City, for instance, that hostile congressional
hearings and unfavorable newspaper stories constitute integral
parts of coordinated conspiracies to harass and "destabilize"
Mexico. Americans shake their heads in disbelief.

The Mexican presumption of intentionality adds yet another burden to negotiation: diplomats are expected to account for an
enormous range of actions and activities, including the rambunc-
tiousness of journalists and legislators. Needless to say, this difference in elemental beliefs can impede mutual comprehension
within the general public as well.

THE BILATERAL RELATIONSHIP:
RECENT TRANSFORMATIONS

Such longstanding divergences between the two countries can
produce misunderstandings that strain the bilateral relationship.
But they do not explain the marked deterioration of the relationship in recent years. What has happened to exacerbate the
problems?

It is not just a matter of diplomatic clumsiness or ideological zealousness, though such factors undoubtedly intensify bilateral pressures. We think that the ultimate cause of the problem lies in the failure—on both sides of the border—to analyze and appreciate the significance of long-run transitions that have imbued the relationship with a new and singular degree of *volatility* and *unpredictability*.

One basic change is the *expansion of the bilateral agenda*. There are so many interconnections between the two countries—trade, investment, energy, debt, migration, drugs, Central America—that there is likely to be disputation over something almost all the time. But it is impossible to know where specific conflicts may emerge, and this makes it hard to manage the relationship. It also means that a harmonious partnership will require a constant process of adjustment, readjustment, and negotiation.

Another change is the *shifting locus of decisionmaking*, especially in the United States. For bureaucratic reasons, it is difficult for the United States government to devise and apply a consistent policy toward Mexico. And as the range of bilateral issues expands, the cast of characters constantly increases. The conduct of bilateral affairs no longer belongs to diplomatic experts alone; it is now affected by bankers, investors, newscasters, and a host of other newly interested groups.

This process is especially conspicuous when issues undergo "domestication" within the U.S. The Simpson-Rodino (originally Simpson-Mazzoli) immigration bill and its ultimate disposition were determined largely by domestic considerations: its postponement in 1984 was in part due to presidential campaign politics, and its eventual approval in 1986 may have borne some relationship to an imminent congressional election. Decisions affecting Mexico are not only dispersed throughout a massive Washington bureaucracy; to an increasing degree, they are also reflective of public opinion.

A third long-run change is the alteration and *complication of the international arena*, in which Mexico is seeking a new role. The world system has not only become multipolar instead of bipolar; it has also become a multilayered system, with the emergence of an intermediate stratum between great powers and small countries. It seems safe to assume that Mexico's position as a middle-range power and "newly industrializing country" (NIC) will increase during and beyond the 1990s. The global system is becoming more diversified rather than less, and nations like Mexico, Brazil, India, Argentina and South Korea will have growing opportunities to exert influence and prestige on the regional level.

Central America provides a case in point. Whatever the outcome of regional peace proposals, it would have been utterly impossible to imagine the Contadora initiative during the 1950s or even the 1960s. Neither Mexico nor its partners (Colombia, Panama, Venezuela) would have contemplated such a move. This long-run change in power relationships will undoubtedly persist— and could create a potential source of continuing friction between Mexico and the United States, although the Commission believes that in the long run there will need to be more such initiatives in the interests of both countries.

A fourth source of volatility comes from the fact that the United States-Mexican relationship is itself becoming *more and more dependent on trends and forces throughout the world.* A mutually beneficial commercial relationship will require, for example, sustained economic growth throughout the world. A major conflagration in the Middle East and any consequent shutdown of oil exports would have serious repercussions for Mexico and the United States. The positions that Argentina and Brazil take regarding their debt obligations will have major implications for Mexico's connection with its United States creditors.

The point is so obvious that it is often overlooked: the bilateral relationship between Mexico and the United States does not exist in a vacuum, and it is increasingly subject to a growing variety of external influences. By the same token, positive changes in the international arena can have a constructive impact on the relationship.

Fifth, and perhaps most important of all, *the U.S. and Mexico have become increasingly interdependent.* The fate of Mexico has long been tied to that of its neighbor to the north. What is new is the extent to which the U.S. now depends on Mexico. The most controversial issues of the 1980s—debt, finance, trade, migration, narcotics—all serve to emphasize this point. As subsequent chapters show, these highly visible issues have two related features in common. First, in one form or another, they will persist for some time: none of them will go away. Second, they demonstrate the realities of "inter dependence." They all illustrate the absence of unilateral control: over economics, borders, even social customs.

THE ROLE OF PUBLIC OPINION

Public opinion has emerged as a major factor in the conduct of U.S.-Mexican relations. As the countries have become more important to each other, issues in the relationship have aroused substantial degrees of public concern. The persistence of stereotypes has hampered mutual understanding and set limits on options available to policymakers. Popular attitudes in both nations reveal considerable ambivalence about the other, but the existence of positive feelings nonetheless provides a basis for improved comprehension and new cooperation.

In the United States, the public at large believes that Mexico is important: in one recent poll, over three-quarters of the general respondents and over 95 percent of a leadership subsample agreed that the U.S. had a "vital interest" in Mexico. Americans also express friendship toward Mexico. On a subjective indicator of favorable feeling, U.S. respondents have given Mexico consistently high ratings—behind only Canada, Britain, West Germany, and Japan. In another survey, an overwhelming 83 percent said they feel friendly toward "the people of Mexico."

At the same time, the U.S. public shows little respect for Mexican institutions. Respondents express frequent concern about drug trafficking, poverty, and corruption. In a 1986 poll, 69 percent expressed the conviction that Mexico was "poorly governed." As a rule, Americans are quick to criticize political systems different from their own, and public judgment of Mexico in the 1980s appears to have struck a deeply responsive chord.

As for Mexicans, it is commonly said they possess a love-hate attitude toward the United States. We urge refinement of that view. Public-opinion polls on this subject are scarce, but the ones that exist generally reveal a profound appreciation for the institutions and accomplishments of U.S. society. One survey showed that 48 percent of the Mexican respondents expressed a "favorable" opinion of the government of the U.S. A total of 78 percent expressed admiration for U.S. technology and economic achievements. At the same time, most respondents showed a preference for their own country's cultural values, especially the emphasis on family and children. Admiration for the U.S. does not mean loss of national pride.

The most common Mexican criticism of the United States has to do not with American society but with U.S. foreign policy. Of those

Mexicans who registered reasons for disapproval of the U.S. in one recent poll, over 38 percent focused on foreign policy questions (nuclear arms, intervention, and so on); a similar proportion cited drug abuse and violent crime. Another 10 percent of the critics expressed unhappiness with U.S. attempts to restrict the flow of migrants.

What is striking, in fact, is the range of concern about the state of the relationship itself. To compare national profiles on this issue, Table 1-1 assembles data from responses on more or less similar questions in surveys taken in 1986 in the two countries. Three-quarters of the American respondents characterized U.S.-Mexican relations as "friendly" or "very friendly," and only 1 percent expressed a strong sense that they were "very unfriendly." In Mexico, only 7 percent described the relationship as "very friendly," compared with 20 percent of the U.S. respondents; 59 percent thought it was "friendly," and nearly one-third described the rela-

TABLE 1-1.   PUBLIC PERCEPTIONS OF U.S.-MEXICAN RELATIONS

	Evaluations by Americans	Evaluations by Mexicans
Close/very friendly	20%	7%
Friendly	55	59
Not friendly/unfriendly	17	30
Very unfriendly	1	3
Not sure	7	—
	100%	100%

SOURCE: Harris Survey Press Release 44 (August 11, 1986); *New York Times*, November 17, 1986.

tionship as "unfriendly" or "very unfriendly." The data convey mixed messages: first, there is considerable optimism and good will within both countries; second, Mexicans clearly show much more anxiety about the state of the relationship than do Americans. And if Mexicans seem to be unduly apprehensive, the U.S. public seems a bit cavalier.

In significant ways, the always complex relationship between Mexico and the United States has thus undergone profound and important changes. It has moved from historical conflict to diplomatic collaboration to contemporary consternation. Recent transformations have added new concerns and complications—and created new opportunities as well. After a long and difficult past, the U.S. and Mexico face an encouraging future.

2

Economics: Debt, Trade, and Investment

Mexico and the United States are approaching crossroads in their economic histories as well as in their bilateral economic relations. New governments in both countries will soon begin coping with serious economic and financial problems. The new Mexican government will inherit a strategy that in recent years has begun to be implemented; unfortunately, a U.S. strategy is only beginning to emerge.

The economic situations that will confront the two new governments are similar in several important respects. Both are large debtors; both face the urgent need to sustain economic growth, mostly through exports in a world of growing protectionism; both need to attract substantial amounts of new investment; both are plagued with excessively high government deficits and indebtedness. The differences, though, are greater. The U.S. is one of the largest and wealthiest countries, while Mexico is now a slowly developing country with a visibly declining standard of living. Even though Mexico has the thirteenth-largest economy in the world, Mexican per capita income is one-eighth of that of the United States.

During the 1980s the differences have widened. The U.S. has controlled inflation and created millions of new jobs. Mexico has generated triple-digit inflation and has been unable to create enough jobs for its rapidly growing labor force. U.S. savings are inadequate and the economy is overleveraged. While Mexican personal savings are high, lack of confidence in the peso and the underdeveloped capital market retard investment. The U.S. economy is integrated into global markets for capital, goods, technology and information; Mexico barely participates in these markets. Mexico's income distribution is heavily skewed: the top quartile of the population receives 20 times the per capita income of the bottom 20 percent. In the U.S. the ratio is 9.5 to 1.

The U.S. economy has grown by more than 20 percent in real terms since the start of the decade, while Mexico—starting from a much lower base of development and with a higher rate of population growth—has grown only 7 percent. Combined with the country's population growth, this had led to a decline in Mexican per capita income of 10.5 percent during the past seven years.

For the United States, the challenges of the next years are to rebalance its economy and to redefine its role in the world economic system. For more than forty years American leadership, finance, and commitments to open markets underpinned a dynamic, growing world economy. Now that leadership is in question, the U.S. has become the world's largest debtor nation, and free trade is widely under assault. Were these circumstances to continue, the U.S. might not long remain the wellspring of the global reserve currency and the benefits which have flowed from the dollar's pre-eminence would disappear.

For Mexico, the challenge is to grow—with the benefits of growth shared by all its people—despite the legacy of past policy miscalculations and an uncertain international environment. If the country's needs are to be met, the now stagnant economy must grow at annual rates of at least 6 percent. Only such growth rates will allow the creation of profits and jobs sufficient to reduce the temptation to migrate elsewhere (a theme we shall explore in Chapter 3) and to improve the distribution of income.

In a perfect world these challenges facing the two countries could be addressed separately. But the realities of a 2,000-mile border and the already intertwined nature of the two economies mean they must be faced simultaneously. From some perspectives this seems to make conflict almost inevitable. Mexicans see their country's external debt as one of the principal blocks to growth—and U.S. institutions are the country's largest creditors. The United States must reduce its trade deficit—to a significant degree by curtailing imports—at the same time that Mexico needs to continue to expand exports, especially to the U.S.

The U.S. is by far Mexico's largest trading partner and economic developments in the United States deeply affect Mexican economic performance. Too often Americans are ignorant of basic Mexican economic and political facts, and consequently imagine the relationship to be one in which Mexicans unfairly benefit from their proximity to the U.S. They do not recognize that it may be in the United States' own interest to change its economic policies to moderate their impact on Mexico. Many Mexicans resent the advice and criticism that periodically emanate from the U.S. In the past there has been a reluctance to accept U.S. investment and almost an expectation that U.S. companies and policymakers would seek to exploit Mexico. Even sound economic counsel or proposals for commercial cooperation are sometimes rejected if labelled "Made in the U.S.A." In practical terms, the consequence is that two of the solutions to Mexico's debt and development crisis—increased bilateral trade and investment—too often become opportunities for conflict. Some Americans see growing Mexican exports and increasing U.S. investment in Mexico as taking jobs from the U.S.; some Mexicans see criticism of their export push as an effort to make the debt crisis permanent and fear that liberalization of their economy would lead to domination by the U.S.

To minimize conflict—and its destructive consequences for the bilateral relationship—economic solutions must be found in which both sides win or, at least, in which the number of losers is minimized and losers are compensated. Inevitably, this will require a framework in which the whole range of sensitive issues—trade, debt, growth, investment, and so on—can be addressed. These pieces could provide opportunities for skillful and farsighted politicians to design the elements of a new bilateral economic relationship. The goal of such a relationship would be to maximize economic growth and opportunity in both countries. The means would be through policies informed by a full understanding of the linkages among various issues.

Such emphasis on the interconnections among issues would not obviate the need for structural economic reforms in both countries. Mexico needs to encourage investment from both foreign and domestic sources; the U.S. needs to save more and to increase its productivity. Both countries need to reduce their fiscal deficits. This approach has the promise of creating an environment conducive to mutually beneficial problem-solving.

THE MEXICAN ECONOMY AT THE END OF THE 1980s

During the 1980s Mexico—one of the world's largest debtors and one of the largest oil exporters—has had to cope with a debt crisis, an oil crisis, and a volatile world and domestic financial environment.

There has been a succession of oil policies, economic programs, and debt restructurings and refinancings, but the economy remains burdened by the legacy of earlier policy miscalculations. Policymakers seem to be confronted with a Hobbesian choice between stagflation and stop/go economic growth with hyper-inflation. The former erodes real living standards; the latter creates uncertainties which destroy investors' confidence; both limit the country's ability to develop.

Mexico has the potential to solve its economic problems. In Mexico there is a skilled and modern industrial class, though one gravely hurt by the crisis; there is a national consensus on the need to formulate new and alternative economic strategies; there are industrial groups that are relatively strong, despite the debt burden, and increasingly self-confident about their ability to penetrate export markets. The country is now following more realistic, market-oriented economic policies. And Mexico has shown that its business, labor, and government leaders have the maturity to seek common objectives through coordinated efforts. Such are the necessary ingredients for a drive toward modernization. Recent attempts to liberate productive capacity point in a promising direction, but the unbalanced growth of the 1970s and the debt crisis of the 1980s have left the economy mired in stagflation.

Mexico's problem has three dimensions: first, existing economic constraints; second, a difficult international economic environment; and, third, the social and political costs of coping with the legacies of the past.

CONSTRAINTS

The sheer size of Mexico's debt and debt burden is one of the most serious constraints. At the end of 1987, total debt was estimated at $107.6 billion, equal to 76 percent of Gross Domestic Product (GDP). (See Table 2-3.) Interest payments were about 6 percent of GDP. Although each of these numbers represents an improvement from peak levels of recent years, the debt burden alone is almost enough to stifle growth. On reasonable estimates, the ratio of interest payments to exports is likely to stabilize above 25 percent during the next six years, and scheduled amortization would raise the total debt service ratio to more than 50 percent in the early 1990s. These are high by any standard. In view of Mexico's growing difficulty in servicing the debt, its negotiations with creditor banks acquire crucial significance.

A counterpart to the foreign debt has been the massive capital flight of the past decade. Capital flight between 1976 and 1987 was in the tens of billions of dollars. These outflows not only inflated the foreign debt numbers, but undercut productive investment.

There is another dimension to the country's debt problem: the massive accumulation of domestic indebtedness fed by large public sector deficits. Interest on the public sector's domestic debt was equal to 15.2 percent of GDP in 1987; total public sector interest payments were almost 20 percent of GDP, which consumed more than three-quarters of total public sector expenditures.

It is important to recognize the changes that have occurred in the government's fiscal position since the onset of the crisis. The overall public sector borrowing requirement has increased precipitously, more than doubling from around 8 percent in 1980 to approximately 16 percent in 1986 and 1987. Such a huge deficit does not reflect the government's efforts to control spending and increase

TABLE 2-1. MEXICO'S PUBLIC SECTOR DEFICIT
(AS % OF GPD)

	1982	1983	1984	1985	1986	1987	1988[a]
Overall public sector borrowing requirement	16.9	8.6	8.5	9.6	16.0	15.8	9.9
Primary balance[b]	-3.5	4.8	5.5	3.9	2.2	4.9	8.3
Interest payments[c]	12.0	13.0	12.6	11.9	17.0	20.0	18.2[d]

a. Projected. Before the government's Economic Solidarity Pact, the overall deficit was expected to be 18.5% with a primary surplus of 5.4%.

b. Overall borrowing requirement less interest payments, adjusted for accounting differences.

c. Domestic plus foreign.

d. Estimated.

SOURCE: Bank of Mexico.

revenues; the deterioration was totally accounted for by increased interest payments. In 1980 the so-called "primary" deficit of the public sector—which excludes only interest payments—was over 3 percent of GDP; in 1987 this figure—by then a positive balance— was in surplus by nearly 5 percent of GDP. Although new initiatives are required to reduce unnecessary expenditures, this surplus is a good measure of the efforts of the government to raise revenues and control expenditures as well as a good measure of the drag which has resulted from excessive borrowing. This inevitably complicates the adjustment process and frustrates the government's policy efforts to generate growth. In 1987, for example, interest payments on public sector debt, domestic and foreign, came to approximately 20 percent of GDP, including more than 15 percent of GDP on domestic public debt denominated in pesos.

The sheer magnitude of the domestic debt and the decision to maintain positive real interest rates (to discourage capital flight) create a policy dilemma. The large overall deficit itself produces further increments to debt and, hence, more interest obligations. In such circumstances, inflationary pressures are extremely difficult to contain without recession. But unless they are contained, the economic and political underpinnings of structural reform would sooner or later be destroyed.

The effects of the debt burden are compounded by the legacy of the import substitution strategy which the government followed during most of the postwar period. Many public and private sector companies have survived only because they were until recently effectively protected from foreign or domestic competition. Most of these companies are effectively cut off from world-class technologies and industrial processes and are, hence, unable to use Mexico's natural advantages of an abundant labor force, favorable geographic location, and substantial energy resources to compete effectively in world markets.

In an historic break with Mexico's past, the government has been aggressively taking apart this protective shell. The decision in 1986 to join GATT (the General Agreement on Trade and Tariffs), the elimination of most quantitative trade restrictions, the shift to and the lowering of tariffs, the devaluation of the peso, the increase in foreign investment, and the practical elimination of price controls are beginning to open the economy to foreign competition.

After the Mexican stock market crash in October 1987—the Mexican market fell even before the sharp drop on Wall Street—

some opponents of these policies demanded their reversal. Instead, the government announced a new stabilization effort, the Economic Solidarity Pact, designed principally to bring down Mexico's unprecedented triple-digit inflation. The Pact had several principal elements: a social pact among labor, business, and government; a strengthening of public sector finances (designed to reduce the overall public sector deficit by almost 6 percentage points of GDP, compared to 1987, and to increase the non-interest or primary surplus to more than 8 percent of GDP); a credit squeeze; a greater opening of the economy to foreign competition; controlled increases in wages and administered prices. Within the framework of the Pact, Mexico has accelerated the liberation of its trade regime from the already aggressive pace implied by its GATT commitments.

In early 1988 this politically courageous program began to work. Inflation fell precipitously and foreign exchange reserves remained at historically high levels. Most observers nonetheless agree that there is a long way to go. The Mexican economy today is under-capitalized, overindebted, and inflation prone, without much of the technology or economic infrastructure needed for satisfactory growth and development.

THE ENVIRONMENT

Since the onset of the debt crisis, Mexico has been buffeted by a difficult world environment. Historically high real interest rates added to the debt burden; falling oil prices cut revenues; slow world economic growth limited the expansion of non-oil exports. Reflecting the collapse of oil prices, inflation abroad and the sharp drop of the peso, Mexico's terms of trade—temporarily bolstered by the oil boom of the late 1970s—fell abruptly after 1980-81. By 1987, Mexican exports that earlier had earned enough to buy $1.00 worth of imported goods at the beginning of the decade could buy only half as much.

The specter of increasing protectionism, especially in the United States (which is Mexico's largest market), but also in Europe and Japan (which should also be targets of Mexico's export drive), has cast a shadow upon the country's economic strategy. Nevertheless, non-oil exports to the U.S. have increased from $3.5 billion in 1980 to an estimated $10.4 billion in 1987.

Mexican export growth might have been even more dynamic, but for U.S. trade restraints, especially in steel, textiles, and sugar.

These are each industries in which Mexico enjoys considerable cost advantages over U.S. producers, but in which restrictions, bilateral or multilateral, prevent Mexican companies from competing on a fair basis.

Nevertheless, the extent to which the U.S. economy has been open to Mexican products is a mixed blessing. The unexpectedly long U.S. economic expansion and the recent decline in the value of the dollar have allowed Mexican entrepreneurs to survive the collapse of domestic demand and has provided Mexico with a source of foreign exchange, growth, and, in a limited way, job creation. At the same time, Mexican exporters have not had to develop the infrastructure for trading beyond North America. The practical result is that the Mexican economy is becoming more vulnerable not only to increased protectionism or a cyclical slowdown in the United States, but to the effects of the U.S. structural adjustment (higher exports, slower growing domestic demand than overall growth and, eventually, lower imports) which is now under way.

THE COSTS

Mexicans themselves are bearing much of the cost of reforming their economy. The economy has grown little in real terms during the presidential term which began in 1982. Inflation has imposed a vicious burden on the unprotected sectors of the economy. Real consumption per capita has dropped more than 15 percent since 1980. Real wages have fallen sharply since 1982, although some of this must have been made up by an expansion of non-wage incomes. Total employment has stagnated while the labor force has been growing at 3.6 percent per annum. The gap between available jobs and available workers has led to increased outmigration, massive underemployment and wastage of human resources. Finally, the costs of the adjustment have fallen unevenly: wage earners have lost about one-fifth of their share in GNP and unskilled workers have lost more jobs than skilled workers. The result is that extreme poverty has increased.

The opening of the economy, which can help lay the foundation for future growth, creates winners and losers among businesses, too. Companies which are flexible and entrepreneurial enough to

TABLE 2-2. MEXICAN REAL GROWTH DURING THE 1980S
(ANNUAL % GROWTH RATES)

	1982	1983	1984	1985	1986	1987	1980-1987[a]
Gross Domestic Product	-0.6	-4.2	3.6	2.6	-4.0	1.4[b]	6.8
Per Capita Gross Domestic Product	-3.2	-6.6	1.0	0.0	-6.3	-1.0[b]	-10.5

[a]Cumulative variation.

[b]Preliminary.

Source: Economic Commission on Latin America (CEPAL).

reorient production to international standards and to find markets have been quite successful; others have had to contract their operations or have failed altogether.

These costs, however inevitable, may threaten to erode the political basis for continued economic reform. But further reforms, building on the base already established, are essential to recreate the possibility of sustained growth. The result is a dilemma: without growth, the politics of economic reform could become unmanageable, but growth cannot be achieved without further reform.

THE FUTURE

Mexico's economic strategy must be aimed at long-term, sustainable economic and social development as measured by positive per capita income growth with maximum employment creation. The incoming government will inherit several important advantages as well as disadvantages in its uphill effort to achieve this goal:

- The outgoing administration's efforts to open the economy to foreign trade, to price competition, and to market forces, generally, as well as the underlying improvement in the country's fiscal position, are gradually making at least parts of the economy more competitive;

- The balance of payments has been responding positively to more realistic economic policies;

- The volume of foreign debt has fallen in 1988, because of repayments by the private sector and debt swap programs;
- The Economic Solidarity Pact has reduced inflation dramatically.

Nevertheless, based on recent experience and in the context of a troubled global economy, Mexico will be hard-pressed to grow fast enough to absorb its rapidly expanding labor force over the next several years without an extraordinary effort. Indeed, the failure to eliminate inflation as well as the burden of foreign debt service appear likely to constrain the country to slower than desirable growth. Moreover, the continuing weakness of investment—between the end of 1981 and the end of 1986 the Bank of Mexico's index of gross fixed investment fell 45 percent—means Mexico's infrastructure and productive base have been seriously eroded. As a share of GDP, investment has steadily fallen during the 1980s, to well under 20 percent at present.

The challenge of overcoming these constraints cannot be met by returning to the pre-1982 import substitution strategy. The recent commercial opening appears to be an appropriate strategy, though there need to be complementary policies in support of national industry with objectives established by the government.

Mexico faces an urgent need to increase domestic savings, to keep them in the country, and to channel them toward productive investments especially in the export sector. Although the level of internal savings is fairly high by international standards, it is not sufficient. Mexico should aim to raise the proportion of GDP which goes to productive investment to at least 26 percent. While this represents an ambitious target, it is necessary in order to realize real GPD growth rates of 6 percent annually—which are necessary to accommodate the country's medium-term social and development requirements. Mexico needs dramatic increases in both industrial and infrastructural investment—including ports, highways, railroads and other facilities required to support growing levels of economic activity. Such an investment-intensive strategy invariably has been followed by countries that have achieved rapid increases in productivity, exports, and standard of living.

Without the cooperation and active participation of foreign creditors, investors, and governments, even this will not succeed. On reasonable forecasts, Mexico would need net external financing totalling at least $15 to $20 billion over the next six years. Given the reluctance of commercial banks to increase their loans on a voluntary basis, most of this would have to be in the form of borrowings from multilateral development banks, new trade credits, or so-called "concerted" lending from the commercial banks. There is a dilemma, however. Although Mexico will not be able to grow without access to these funds, Mexico would not be able to service such a large increment of debt at market interest rates. Ways must be found to minimize the amount of new debt flows relative to new direct investment flows and to contain the cost of new debt— as well as to reduce the existing debt service burden. Partial success has already come from the use of various market processes—debt-equity swaps, the renegotiation of private sector debt and other creative debt refinancing programs—but the future will require additional instruments.

The task for Mexico's leaders is to define a strategy that can achieve the social and economic goals the country urgently demands—sustained growth in income and employment, as well as increased living standards for those who have been left behind— while reducing the vulnerability to external shocks and the reliance on foreign debt. Under the best of circumstances, this will be an extraordinarily difficult challenge.

THE U.S. ECONOMY AT THE END OF THE 1980s

The new U.S. President, like his Mexican counterpart, will face daunting challenges in his effort to steer the U.S. economy on a path of sustained non-inflationary growth. The outgoing Administration leaves office with a mixed economic legacy. On the positive side:

- Creation of 15 million new jobs since 1980, at a time when European employment was stagnating;
- A start on the revival of the U.S. manufacturing sector—which is beginning to make important parts of U.S. industry again competitive in world markets, as evidenced by rapidly increasing U.S. exports;
- An economic expansion which continues to set records for longevity.

On the negative side:

- Accumulation of around $500 billion in net foreign liabilities, which has eroded the traditional surplus on services in the balance of payments;
- A dramatic increase in the gross indebtedness of the federal government to $2.6 trillion, which has resulted in net interest payments equal to almost 15 percent of federal spending and more than 3 percent of Gross National Product;
- Still massive trade, current account, and federal budget deficits;
- Steady reduction in the savings rate which, as a share of disposable personal income, has fallen from 7.5 percent in 1981 to 3.2 percent in 1987;
- Sharply increased financial market volatility and erosion of confidence in the dollar as the key international reserve currency;
- A sharply reduced ability to manage future economic shocks without being forced into recession; and
- A weakening of the international trading system as evidenced by the rise in managed and, especially in agriculture, subsidized trade.

The United States shifted from being the largest creditor nation in 1981 to being the largest debtor nation in 1985. This affects Mexico and other developing nations in several ways. First, the U.S. not only ceases to be a source of capital but becomes a large user of global capital. Second, the cost of capital is raised to all borrowers. Third, the debtor status of the U.S. inevitably erodes the country's international leadership role, making the global economic system more crisis prone. And fourth, as for any debtor, the need to service its debt creates an imperative for the U.S. to improve its commercial account, which could imperil developing countries' own export drives.

Unlike Mexico's external debt, which consists largely of term loans from commercial banks and official agencies, U.S. foreign liabilities include large-scale foreign ownership of domestic stocks, corporate bonds, and government securities; foreign investment in plants, equipment, and real estate; and foreign deposits in U.S. banks. Much of this is highly volatile, sensitive to short-run shifts in financial market conditions and in perceptions of the quality of economic management. Thus, the U.S. not only needs to finance the continuing deficit on current account (which in 1988 means that net foreign liabilities are growing by around $130 billion or so), but must prevent capital already in the country from flowing out. In practical terms this excessive dependence on foreign capital means that real interest rates must remain high, reducing the flexibility of policymakers.

The combination of lower private savings and larger budget deficits has also contributed to keeping interest rates high. A decade ago the general government deficit (i.e., the federal, state, and local governments combined) amounted to about 10 percent of net private savings; the balance was available to finance investment. Today the general government deficit consumes two-thirds of net private savings, inevitably raising the cost of funds to private sector investors who must compete for the remainder.

The growing dependence on foreign capital sources and the widely perceived slippage of the U.S. position in the global economy have unleashed strong nationalist and protectionist forces within the country. These are evidenced in the new trade legislation which potentially imposes significant new burdens on U.S. trading partners, and in a steadily rising share of U.S. imports subject to some kind of restriction. Both raise doubts about long-standing U.S. commitments to open markets.

Partly because of the dramatic devaluation of the dollar (which has lost more than half its value against major currencies since early 1985), and partly because of a sometimes painful industrial restructuring process which is beginning to bear fruit, U.S. exports are booming. In 1988 exports are likely to be around one-third greater in value terms than in 1986. Indeed, the export sector provided around one-third of the growth in the U.S. economy in 1987 and is likely to produce one-half of the growth in 1988.

It may be almost as difficult for the rest of the world to cope with an improvement in the U.S. balance of payments position, however, as it is to deal with continuing massive deficits. A reasonable objective of the new President should be to reach current account balance during the next Administration in order to stop the growth in foreign debt. To do so would require that Gross National Product grows considerably faster than domestic demand, with production for export growing faster than production for domestic consumption. This, in turn, implies slower growth or even stagnation in U.S. living standards, but faster growth in consumption abroad, especially in Germany and Japan where domestic demand would have to grow faster than production. Such a shift would require a sharp increase in growth of U.S. manufacturing output, which, because of capacity constraints already evident, would require large capital investments. Realizing those investments would require lower interest rates, lower federal budget deficits, and higher savings.

Even if all these conditions could be achieved so that the deficits gradually fall and foreign indebtedness gradually stops growing, U.S. net foreign debt could reach as much as $900 billion by the end of 1991.

An alternative scenario—faster reduction in the deficit and smaller growth of the debt—would seem to require a further dramatic fall in the value of the dollar accompanied by a deep recession. This scenario would probably introduce massive dislocations in the global economy and set the stage for a 1930s-style round of competitive protectionism and, sooner or later, a 1930s-style depression.

One of the keys to avoiding the latter alternative—which would be as disastrous for Mexico as for the U.S.—is the development of a consensus economic adjustment strategy within the U.S. This would include bipartisan initiatives: to reduce the federal budget deficit, to renew U.S. industrial competitiveness, to avoid more protectionism, and to stimulate higher savings and investment.

The other key to avoiding a repeat of the economic disasters of the 1930s is development of a cohesive global strategy among the major industrial and developing countries. Unfortunately, the quality of the policy dialogue among the major industrial countries has been poor in recent years and the policy dialogue between major developed and developing countries is virtually non-existent. There is no international consensus on whether the United States is on a path that will lead, sooner or later, to more stable global economic conditions; hence, there is no consensus on the degree of economic and financial risk which the United States' industrial allies can realistically assume to help stabilize the world economy. This raises the probability of a severe recession during the next several years.

THE LONG RUN

Until the U.S. addresses the fundamental financial and economic imbalances that exist, the economic system will be increasingly crisis prone, other industrial countries will be reluctant to accept U.S. leadership, international financial institutions will become less effective, trade tensions will rise, and global growth will be lowered. Economic pressures on Mexico will rise and only an extraordinary binational effort to insulate Mexico from these forces would allow achievement of even its minimal growth objectives.

Inevitably, though, the U.S. will finally achieve a new equilibrium. The intertwined U.S. problems of inadequate savings, high deficits, and excessive indebtedness will be resolved. Whether smoothly or abruptly—through conscious acts of economic statesmanship or the heavy-handed weight of market forces—the U.S. will move to a surplus on external trade.

Once that occurs, the U.S. should be well situated to achieve renewed economic growth. The benefits of the ongoing industrial restructuring, an extremely sophisticated and deep financial market, the sheer size of the domestic marketplace, and a skilled labor force (albeit one which requires large investments in continuing education and retraining) should position the U.S. to take advantage of newly energized entrepreneurial forces and emerging technologies. The U.S. is so firmly embedded in the global flow of technology that it will immediately benefit from advancements in telecommunications, computer technology, new materials, biogenetics, and other industries. This could lay the basis for a new period of international or regional economic growth. In either case, Mexico should benefit.

However, progress to an era of renewed economic expansion will be difficult. As the larger and wealthier partner in the bilateral relationship, the U.S. must take the lead, not only in addressing its own structural weaknesses, but in shielding Mexico to the extent possible from the repercussions of U.S. economic adjustments. This effort should be undertaken in the recognition that U.S. national interests are served by a healthy Mexican economy.

The Commission recommends establishment of a cabinet-level binational economic commission.

The commission would have two major tasks:

- First, to provide a high-level forum which promotes permanent dialogue about macroeconomic policies between the two countries, paying particular attention to the examination of policies which impact on each other's economic prospects;

- Second, to provide the two governments with an early warning mechanism which could reduce economic dislocations by allowing officials to anticipate policy changes in the two countries.

Such a dialogue now exists only sporadically; the U.S. has much more intimate policy discussions with its northern neighbor as well as with other industrial countries. The absence of such exchanges can lead to the imposition of policies which unintentionally damage each other's economic interests and complicates crisis management.

To assist its analyses and recommendations, this commission should seek the opinions of business and labor organizations and of academic specialists from both countries.

DEBT

Unless the two countries succeed in working together to deal with Mexico's foreign debt on a sustainable basis, the bilateral relationship will not improve and may deteriorate. The unresolved debt overhang extracts excessive social, economic, and political costs from Mexico, limits the potential for commercial intercourse between the countries (by limiting Mexico's ability to buy U.S. produced goods), imparts an unsustainably high level of tension into the relationship, and affects the bases of social and political stability in Mexico.

Mexico has succeeded in rescheduling its public sector debt, reducing spreads on interest rates, and eliminating significant amounts of private sector indebtedness. Early in 1988, the country offered to swap bonds backed by U.S. government securities (purchased by the Mexican government with some of its reserves) for discounted commercial bank loans in an effort to reduce the overall volume of debt. The operation was only marginally successful, since most commercial banks were unwilling to recognize actual losses and to replace the discounted loans with bonds

TABLE 2-3. MEXICAN DEBT OUTSTANDING
($ BILLIONS, END YEAR)

	1981	1982	1983	1984	1985	1986	1987[a]
Total debt	77.3	91.2	94.2	94.8	97.6	102.4	107.6
Official creditors	10.8	13.8	13.6	14.5	17.5	22.4	27.5
Commercial banks	58.1	67.3	71.0	72.9	73.1	73.8	74.7
U.S. banks	21.8	24.3	25.4	25.8	24.4	23.5	22.4
Non-banks	8.4	10.1	9.5	7.3	7.0	6.3	5.4

[a]Preliminary.

Note: At mid-1988 Mexican financial officials indicated that total debt had declined to the $100-$103 billion level reflecting repayments of private sector debt (some of which may have occurred in 1987), the debt-equity program, and the swap operation described in the text.

SOURCE: Institute of International Finance.

that still carried Mexican interest rate risk. Nevertheless, the initiative was important because it was part of an effort to reduce the absolute level of indebtedness—a significant shift in the country's debt strategy.

Mexico's debt level and debt service burden are simply too high in relation to the size of the economy and the growth of export earnings. At the start of the decade, debt was equal to less than one-third of GNP; in 1988 it is around 70 percent. Because of the surge in exports, the share of export revenues (from goods and services) devoted to interest payments has fallen from 35 percent to 27 percent, but these payments are still equal to around 6 percent of GDP. And total debt rose from $77 billion in 1981 to more than $100 billion at the end of 1987. (The debt data are provisional because of uncertainties about the level of private sector debt outstanding; the actual debt level in 1987 may have been several billion less than reported.) In 1988 there are indications that total debt outstanding is around the $100-103 billion level.

Unfortunately, much of this borrowing was not productive and did not generate the foreign exchange resources needed to finance debt service. It supported a level of consumption greater than that justified by the country's economic output. This resulted from the constant press of a young, rapidly expanding population (and, more particularly, labor force) which led to political and social pressures to keep consumption growing. As in the United States at present, the legacy of unsustainably rapid consumption growth financed with foreign debt inevitably is a period of slower growth—if only to service the debt.

PERCEPTIONS

Mexican observers maintain that the national elections of July 1988 revealed new currents in Mexican society, which have emerged in reaction to the economic crisis and to the challenge of democratic development. All political parties agree that the election results were an expression of a broad-based attitude of malaise and exhaustion. Popular discontent stemmed largely from the social costs of prolonged economic crisis.

Many Mexican policymakers and economists believe that the country's debt service burden is incompatible with return to adequate levels of growth, because it drains resources needed for investment. They are convinced that interest payments on the foreign debt at the level that has existed for the last three years, relative to the GDP (see Table 2-4), have not permitted—and will not permit—the Mexican economy to grow at adequate rates or to absorb the increasing labor force. Indeed, the coalition of leftist parties in the 1988 elections proposed a unilateral debt moratorium as one of its most important campaign planks.

There is also widespread belief in Mexico that present secondary market values for the country's debt (recent quotes are around 50 cents per dollar) represent the real economic value of these loans and that Mexico should benefit from this discount. Some government officials have indicated that reducing the value of at least some of Mexico's commercial debt to the discounted levels is a cornerstone of the country's international financial policy. However, there is little agreement on how to realize the discounts.

Finally, there seems to be a widely held view that confrontation with creditors is more likely to lead to economic hardship than to economic recovery. From this perspective, continuing uncertainties about Mexico's attitude towards its debt and its creditors inhibit foreign and domestic investment, encourage new capital flight, prevent the repatriation of previous flight capital, and preclude the resumption of new capital flows. In short, failure to put the debt on a sustainable basis undercuts efforts to finance and to achieve renewed growth.

TABLE 2-4. MEXICAN DEBT INDICATORS

	1981	1982	1983	1984	1985	1986	1987[a]
Total Debt ($ billions)	77	91	94	95	98	102	108
as % of GDP	31	53	63	54	53	79	76
as % of exports[b]	284	332	331	295	332	439	366
Interest Payments ($ billions)	9	12	10	12	10	8	8
as % of GDP	4	7	7	7	6	6	6
as % of exports[b]	35	44	36	36	35	36	27
Net Resource Flow[c]							
as % of GDP	-6	-3	3	5	4	3	1

a. Preliminary.

b. Of goods and services.

c. Defined as net interest payments minus net foreign investment and net borrowing from public or private sources; a positive figure indicates an outflow.

SOURCE: Institute of International Finance.

There is less of a consensus within the U.S. on the issue of developing country debt, or, more particularly, Mexico's debt problem. Since the onset of the debt crisis in 1982, the U.S. Administration and the Congress have insisted that private creditors should undertake the bulk of rescheduling and refinancing since they had extended the largest share of the debt. This meant that the principal thrust of economic and financial adjustment programs was aimed at reestablishing borrower credibility in financial markets; countries were supposed to adjust their policies so that they could eventually return to the markets to resume their borrowing. The U.S. government has also insisted that each country's situation be addressed on its merits, that the principal vehicles for official intervention should be multilateral, and that officially sanctioned stabilization programs should be at the heart of each country's recovery program.

Treasury Secretary James A. Baker III introduced an important new element in 1985 when he recognized that debtor countries would have to grow both to service their debts and to sustain structural adjustment efforts. At the same time, however, although Secretary Baker expressed the hope that, in addition to the commercial banks, the World Bank would become an important source of new funds, it quickly became clear to most observers that the amount of new money available to developing countries within the accepted debt management framework would be inadequate to finance growth as well as to sustain debt service. Perhaps more importantly, Baker also argued that industrial country growth would have to be sustained above 3 percent and real interest rates would have to fall, conditions which have not generally been met in recent years.

The U.S. banks, accounting for almost one-third of Mexico's commercial bank debt, have taken a lead role in negotiating financial restructurings with Mexico. Along with other creditor banks, they have lowered the margins they charge on loans, extended new credits, refinanced (and, in the process, reduced) private sector debt, sustained trade finance facilities, lengthened the terms of maturing loans, and built up loan loss reserves (on average equal to around 30 percent of principal value) against outstanding loans to Mexico, as well as other developing countries. The large creditor banks have generally not been willing to sell public sector loans at a discount, however, or to allow Mexico to repurchase its loans at a market discount rate.

Some leading American financiers, legislators, and analysts have gone a step further. They seem to accept the Mexican contention that a reduction in debt and debt service is essential to restoring Mexico's financial and economic health and that the public sector in creditor countries should play a role in easing the impact of this reduction on the commercial banks. However, this approach, although motivated in part by a desire to restore the financial soundness of the banks and in part by an effort to stimulate the purchasing power of potential markets for U.S. exports, has evoked little resonance in the Administration, the Federal Reserve, or the Congress. There is also considerable concern that it would be difficult to establish a special facility for Mexico not available to other key debtors.

Finally, discussion of "Mexico's debt problem" runs counter to the longstanding U.S. government assumption that the debt issue, although needing to be addressed on a case-by-case basis, must be viewed in a multilateral context. In practice, the U.S. government has resisted the argument that any special relationship justified a predominantly bilateral approach to a country's debt problem.

The differing perspectives of debtor and creditor come together in a shared recognition that the underlying value of the debt would be enhanced by more manageable debt service levels, both because the certainty of debt service payments would improve and because renewed growth (assuming the proper mix of economic policies) would generate the resources needed to make interest and principal payments.

This immediately raises the question of how losses on existing debt would be shared and what impact such losses would have on future capital flows. With regard to the former, a sort of market process is already available: if banks realize losses on Mexican debt, they receive tax credits which effectively spread some of the cost across the whole universe of taxpayers. But the absorption of these costs by shareholders in the banks and the fiscal systems of the creditor countries does not—but could—translate into a reduction of service payments for the debtor countries. Because commercial banks show little present inclination to return to voluntary lending, the issue of new private debt flows is somewhat moot. Nevertheless, Mexico clearly will need access to new debt financing in the future to cover current account deficits generated by more rapid rates of economic expansion.

STEPS FORWARD

The Commissioners believe that creditor countries must come to a clearer understanding of the current situation in Mexico. A new way must be found for Mexico to restore its productive potential and achieve rates of growth sufficient to satisfy its social needs, while fulfilling its financial obligations. The most fundamental responsibilities of Mexican authorities are attending to the material needs of their citizens and maintaining the political stability of their country. Thus, it is essential to agree upon levels of debt payment (interest as well as principal) consistent with Mexico's capacity to pay under conditions of growth. Otherwise the country will not have the resources needed to service its debt and, at the same time, to achieve the necessary rate of economic growth.

Achieving these conditions in the future will require recognition of several principles:

- Solution—or even sustainable management—of Mexico's debt problem requires both public and private efforts, and the U.S. government will need to play a leading role. However, the debt crisis cannot be solved solely on a bilateral basis.

- Mexican debt-service payments cannot exceed the country's capacity to pay, even in periods during which external circumstances may deteriorate, and must be defined in the context of the country's need for growth.

- Mexico should continue its efforts at constructive negotiation with its creditors.

- The private creditor banks cannot be expected to solve the problem by themselves, but are an integral part of any program to make debt service more consistent with faster economic growth.

- Throughout, Mexico will in its own national self-interest need to adopt appropriate macroeconomic policies and to continue structural reforms and the liberalization of its productive forces: sustained economic reform is an essential precondition to making any financial initiative successful.

- Market processes and banking practices which reduce the volume of debt, and hence debt service, need to be encouraged and expanded; this may require regulatory, tax and accounting changes for the benefit of both the creditors and the debtors.

- Mexico will need to have access to net new capital flows, if economic development and growth are to be restarted. If official and voluntary private lending are inadequate, then governments and international financial institutions should strongly encourage the banks to provide additional new loans.

Admittedly, "capacity to pay," though critical, is an elusive concept. We understand it to mean the financial resources available for debt service consistent with adequate rates of economic growth—for Mexico in the coming years this means averaging 6 percent per year—supplemented by foreign investment and prudent levels of new borrowing.

The Commission recommends that, for Mexico and other debtor countries aggressively pursuing structural economic adjustment programs, debt service obligations in the future

should be designed subject to their capacity to pay under conditions of growth.

Without growth, adjustment will not be sustained; without growth, resources for debt service will not be available.

Efforts should be made to accommodate this important conceptual change within the existing financial system. The U.S. government must play a creative facilitating role: supporting more generous financing of the international financial institutions, liberalizing commercial bank regulations with regard to the treatment of sovereign debts, and encouraging innovative financial schemes which could lead to the reduction of debt and debt service. In particular, the U.S. Congress should act quickly on the World Bank's request for a General Capital Increase and the U.S. executive and legislative bodies should support more innovative uses of the Bank's loan and guarantee authorities.

For its part, the Mexican government should expand its debt-for-equity program and continue to explore innovative financing proposals which could allow the country to tap new sources of finance.

Since the foreign commercial banks account for such a large share of Mexico's foreign debt, they also must play a prominent role in any effort to make the debt service burden more compatible with return to adequate rates of economic growth. In their own interests, the banks should remove contractual obligations which restrict Mexico's ability to repurchase its own debt and consider interest capitalization as a partial alternative to new "concerted" lending. Further, the banks should be prepared to make new loans to Mexico in support of commercially viable investments that save or generate foreign exchange.

Mexican Commissioners strongly encourage foreign commercial banks to offer to sell portions of their Mexican loan portfolios on an annual basis, so long as Mexico meets its contractual obligations.

All members of the Commission believe that the social costs to Mexico and other developing countries of fulfilling their financial obligations under current conditions must be taken fully into account; if those costs and the urgency of the situation are ignored, powerful pressures could soon put the political and social stability of such countries to a serious test. It is in the interest of both debtor and creditor nations to avoid this.

The Commission recommends that the incoming U.S. and Mexican Presidents, in concert with other leaders, invite a small group of international financial and political experts from the largest industrial countries and the major debt-impacted developing countries to undertake an examination of the debt crisis from a global perspective.

This group should be asked to propose concrete near-term actions with respect to the debt issue to be undertaken by public and private creditors and debtors to reduce the risk of a global economic downturn and, more particularly, to achieve adequate economic growth in the developing world. The purpose of such a group would not be as much to discover new "solutions" to the debt crisis as to lay the basis for urgent political action.

Since matching debt service to payment capacity may or may not lead to either an absolute or relative reduction of the stock of existing debt, it might in addition be necessary to develop specific mechanisms to achieve debt reduction through market forces. In this context, we have examined several alternative proposals which could accomplish this and commend them for consideration by the expert group as well as by the incoming Mexican and U.S. Presidents:

- A facility could be established within the World Bank to purchase, at market values, the foreign debt of Mexico and other highly indebted countries in comparable circumstances. The purpose of such a facility would be to capture and pass on to the debtor the prevailing market discount.

- Mexico could widen its efforts to substitute all or part of its current debt by a reduced debt at negotiated values, supported by institutional guarantees—if available—or high-quality financial instruments (like zero-coupon U.S. government bonds) covering both principal and interest.

- Mexico could consider establishing a sinking fund for debt repurchase, with funds additional to those devoted to servicing the debt, in order to benefit from the reduced values of its debt in the market.

There is an urgent need to turn the corrosive impact of the debt crisis on bilateral relations into a positive force for closer cooperation and to lay the basis for faster economic growth. Under present prospects, the risk of deterioration is high, in economic as well as political terms. Failure to resolve the debt crisis would seriously damage economic prospects for both countries, as well as the bilateral relationship.

TRADE

If the debt issue has the potential to undermine U.S.-Mexican relations, increasing trade could be the cement which bonds the countries closer together. But here, too, is potential for conflict. Both countries are pursuing export-led growth and both countries need to contain the level of imports in order to service their foreign debt. Yet, as demonstrated by the impressive growth of Mexico's in-bond and assembly industries, increasing U.S. investment in Mexico, and the expanding incidence of joint ventures and technology exchanges, the two economies are complementary in important ways. Mexico has a large and increasingly skilled labor force, with low wages in relation to the U.S., and substantial energy resources; the U.S. has important technological and managerial assets, a sophisticated exporting infrastructure and, of course, a huge domestic market.

The task facing the leaders of the two countries is to manage the conflicts, develop the complementarities, and leverage increasing bilateral trade into higher economic growth and more job creation.

MEXICO-U.S. TRADE FLOWS

Since 1970, foreign trade has become increasingly important to both Mexico and the United States. First because of the development of the oil sector and later because of the recession and debt-crisis-induced export boom, Mexico's ratio of combined exports and imports to GDP rose from under 10 percent in 1970 to almost 40 percent in 1987. For the much larger U.S. economy, there was a smaller, but still significant, change: total trade as a share of GDP rose from 8.8 percent in 1972 to 22 percent in 1987, particularly because of import growth. This shift made foreign trade more important to the economy's overall health than it had been since the start of the postwar period.

The increasing dependence of the U.S. economy on imports, particularly during the 1980s, reflected the huge increase in the federal deficit; inadequate domestic savings; the sharp rise in the dollar's international value; the damage to the U.S. manufacturing sector done by low productivity, high and growing labor costs, and underinvestment; and the rapid growth of consumption. Between 1980 and 1987 import growth and penetration were extremely rapid: imports rose from $250 billion to $410 billion. At the same time, U.S. exports first fell sharply, and then began to recover rapidly in 1987 and 1988.

There is little evidence that increasing foreign protectionism contributed to the growing U.S. trade deficit. Yet because of the massive trade deficit now slowly receding, the inherent lags between economic reality and political perception, the vagaries of the political calendar, and some highly visible examples of protectionism in particular markets such as Japan, claims of unfair competition and protectionist rhetoric are widespread in the U.S.

Mexican trade developments have also been uneven in recent years. In the 1970s, the oil boom led to rapid growth in export revenues and import expenditures. In the early 1980s, the onset of the debt crisis dramatically reduced imports—from $24 billion in 1981 to $9 billion in 1983, according to Mexican statistics—leading to a large trade surplus from 1982 onward. The debt-crisis-induced recession led domestic manufacturers to shift their focus from the domestic to the international market which, along with new export-oriented government policies, laid the basis for strong growth in non-oil exports. A brief recovery of domestic demand for Mexican products slowed the growth of non-oil exports in 1985, and the collapse of oil prices reduced petroleum revenues sharply in 1986 and 1987. Nevertheless, total exports have exceeded $20 billion in five of the last six years while imports have yet to approach the 1980-81 levels. In addition, the composition of exports has shifted from an excessive reliance on oil to a diversified base including a range of manufactured products. The share of manufactured exports rose from about 22 percent of total exports in 1980 to almost 48 percent in 1987.

Bilateral trade has also grown and changed. On Mexican data, the persistent balance in favor of the U.S. shifted abruptly to a Mexican surplus in 1982; during 1982-1987, the surplus totalled almost $30 billion. This shift was accounted for not only by an important increase in non-oil exports—more than three quarters

TABLE 2-5. U.S.-MEXICAN BILATERAL TRADE
($ MILLIONS)

	Mexican Exports		Mexican Imports	Trade Balance
	Total	Non-oil		
1971	911	911	1,478	-507
1972	1,118	1,118	1,722	-604
1973	1,318	1,318	2,277	-959
1974	1,703	1,671	3,779	-2,076
1975	1,668	1,330	4,108	-2,440
1976	2,111	1,693	3,790	-1,689
1977	2,738	1,882	3,660	-822
1978	4,057	2,495	4,628	-571
1979	6,252	3,085	7,540	-1,288
1980	9,982	3,501	12,155	-2,173
1981	10,530	4,121	15,859	-5,330
1982	11,116	3,834	8,909	2,207
1983	12,973	4,186	4,921	8,052
1984	14,125	5,475	7,388	6,737
1985	13,146	5,187	8,907	4,239
1986	10,603	8,068	7,392	3,211
1987[a]	13,326	10,500[b]	7,878	5,448

Note: Bilateral trade includes Mexican exports to and imports from the U.S.
[a]Provisional.
[b]Estimated.
SOURCE: Ministry of Commerce, Mexico.

of the increase in such exports has gone to the U.S. market in recent years—but also by a significant reduction in Mexico's import of U.S.-produced capital goods, intermediate products and raw materials.

For Mexico, the United States accounted for 60 percent of exports and 65 percent of imports during the last six years, by far the country's largest trading partner. While Mexico continued to account for a far more modest share of U.S. exports and imports (5.6 percent of each, although Mexico is the third largest trading partner of the U.S.) the composition of trade changed noticeably. In 1986 and 1987, Mexico for the first time recorded surpluses in non-petroleum trade with the U.S. Mexican exports to the U.S.

increasingly include finished automobiles, automotive parts, electronics, manufactured iron and steel products, and other complex industrial products.

Rapid growth of Mexico's in-bond and assembly industries has also been an important feature of the bilateral commercial relationships in recent years. The number of such plants has grown from 629, employing 173,100 workers, in 1983, to 1000, employing 335,000 workers, in 1987. Net foreign exchange earnings also rose (although not as dramatically, because of the fall of the peso) from $0.8 billion in 1983 to $1.6 billion in 1987. At the same time, the composition of these industries has changed as more automotive parts, electronics and machinery companies have established in-bond plants.

These in-bond and assembly operations are significant for their contributions to training and employment, at a time when job creation in the rest of the economy has been weak, as well as to foreign exchange earnings at a time when increasing revenues has become a top national priority. In addition, they help to improve both countries' competitiveness *vis-à-vis* the rest of the world. Unfortunately, there has been little backward linkage into the Mexican economy: only 2 percent of the total value of all components used in the production-sharing plants are of Mexican origin. In the future, however, it is likely that such in-bond industries will encourage further industrial development.

Because they combine low wages, tax advantages and—in many cases—modern technology, the export potential of in-bond and assemply industries beyond the U.S. market is considerable. Unfortunately, little has been done so far to penetrate other markets.

TRADE POLICIES

Until the mid-1980s, Mexico essentially pursued an import substitution development model, with domestic industry well protected by tariffs and, especially, non-tariff barriers. Indicative planning, regulation of key sectors, reservation of certain activities to Mexican investors, subsidies, price controls, quantitative trade restrictions, and limits on foreign investment all were used to develop as closed an economy as possible. The oil- and debt-induced boom of the 1970s permitted this strategy to survive long after its economic justification had passed. Mexican analysts now recognize that the overprotected economy which evolved during the past several decades was ill-prepared to cope with the economic shocks of the 1980s.

Under the pressure of those shocks, Mexican economic policy from 1982 to 1985 fluctuated widely. Periods of adjustment alternated with periods of unsustainable stimulus, and trade liberalization was pursued with varying degrees of intensity. Beginning in 1986, however, the country adopted a more realistic exchange rate policy, abolished most price controls, sold or closed many state-owned enterprises, eliminated quantitative restrictions on imports in favor of a tariff based system, reduced tariffs, and scheduled the phasing out of most remaining non-tariff import barriers. All these actions were made more effective by the decision to join GATT, which had long been opposed within important circles of Mexican political life because it symbolized a much-feared opening of the economy to global competition and because it posed a material threat to specific industrial sectors.

The decision to join GATT, which is still being implemented, was a watershed in the country's trade policy. It ratified the shift from an import-substitution to an export-oriented development model. Despite continued resistance by some Mexicans—including some long-established foreign companies which have prospered under protection—the change seems to be widely viewed as irreversible.

In contrast to Mexico's strong movement toward an open trade regime, protectionist forces have been gaining momentum in the United States. Rapid increases in import penetration, unsustainably high levels of imports, and adjustment problems in key sectors (like automobiles and agriculture) have made many U.S. politicians, government bureaucrats, and businessmen more receptive to managed trade. This has raised questions about the depth of the U.S. commitment to open markets that sustained the postwar trading system.

Nevertheless, the U.S. has reaffirmed its rhetorical commitment to free trade and has taken the lead in launching a new multilateral trade negotiation, the Uruguay Round. At U.S. insistence, these negotiations focus not only on traditional tariff cutting, but also on reducing protection which affects trade in agriculture and services, on barriers to investment, and on strengthening the GATT itself. In addition, the U.S. is making a strong effort, bilaterally as well as multilaterally, to improve the protection of intellectual property.

However, in recent years the U.S. has undertaken a series of policies that run counter to the spirit and practice of free trade. These include launching an unprecedented number of administrative trade actions, encouraging the depreciation of the dollar to promote exports, legislating duties which violated GATT strictures (e.g., a differential tax on imported versus domestically produced crude oil), negotiating a series of so-called "voluntary" import quotas, reducing the benefits of special tariff programs for developing countries (i.e., the Generalized System of Preferences), increasing export subsidies (especially in agriculture), and negotiating market-sharing arrangements (e.g., semiconductors with the Japanese). As was often argued when various protectionist measures were being implemented, these actions may have prevented even more dramatic departures from the country's historical commitment to free trade. But, on balance, the record of the 1980s shows a shift toward managed trade.

The United States has also departed from its traditional insistence on multilateralism in its trading regime to negotiate bilateral free trade agreements with Canada and with Israel. Both are aimed at creating essentially free trade in goods and services on a bilateral basis. In addition, the Canadian agreement includes provisions covering investment flows. The agreements as negotiated are consistent with GATT commitments, but could also provide the building blocks for a reorientation of U.S. commercial policy away from the traditional commitment to globalism if future Presidents and Congresses become more protectionist—perhaps in reaction to growing European and Japanese restrictions.

The Israeli agreement includes special provisions reflecting the large asymmetries between the U.S. and Israeli industrial sectors. One of the most important distinguishing features of that agreement is an infant industry section which allows Israel to impose higher tariffs to protect emerging industries, provided production does not exceed ten percent of that country's base-year imports from the U.S. These special tariffs are designed to be phased out over time.

We do not believe that the agreement between the United States and Canada is a suitable framework for trade relations between the United States and Mexico. Unlike Canada, Mexico could not be expected to eliminate all tariffs and export subsidies quickly. More importantly, Mexico is unlikely to be able soon to bind itself to eliminate the differences in domestic and export energy prices, agree to national treatment for foreign investment and services, or totally foreswear safeguards, investment-related performance requirements, and the use of government procurement as a development instrument.

While the U.S.-Israeli free trade agreement is a more appropriate model for two countries at different stages of development, we believe Mexico and the U.S. should pursue a different approach to stimulating bilateral trade relations. To this we now turn.

BILATERAL TRADE RELATIONS

For most of the postwar period, Mexican-U.S. commercial relations developed without a formal governmental framework and, indeed, without excessive friction, partly because of the relatively low absolute level of trade flows. This changed, especially during the 1980s, as trade grew and trade complaints proliferated. In 1984, Mexican exports representing more than $500 million in value were submitted to investigation because of actions brought under U.S. trade laws. Disputes over textiles, fisheries, subsidies and countervailing duties, and the protection of the patent rights of research intensive industries operating in Mexico became increasingly pointed as Mexico's domestic economic situation deteriorated and U.S. trade policy—as practiced—became more protectionist.

In 1985 the two governments took an important first step toward building a framework to address these issues in a joint public statement recognizing the growing importance of bilateral trade and investment flows. At that time, the governments reached agreement to make it more difficult for U.S. companies to seek redress from Mexican competition (by applying to Mexico the so-called "injury test") in return for a commitment to phase out subsidies. The immediate practical result was to reduce the number of petitions for countervailing duties against Mexican exports, although in the perception of many Mexican analysts and businessmen the continuing threat of increasing U.S. protectionism had a deleterious effect on trade.

In 1987 the governments took a further step, announcing a framework for bilateral trade negotiations and dispute settlement. Unlike the agreement between Canada and the U.S., which reduces actual trade barriers, this accord is a general statement of principles emphasizing the importance of an "open and predictable environment for international trade and investment." Somewhat more concretely, it points toward procedures for dispute settlement and increased bilateral consultations, and establishes an urgent agenda for discussions including textiles, agriculture, steel, electronics, investment, services, and intellectual property.

For Mexico, willingness to discuss foreign investment was a significant reaffirmation of its commitment to open the economy yet further. For the U.S., the agreement was an effort to regularize the historically sporadic attention which it has paid to Mexico and, more particularly, to trade and investment issues between the two countries.

THE FUTURE

The goal of Mexican and U.S. trade policies should be increased trade and growth. For this to be realized, the starting point must be a firm commitment by both countries to freer trade. During the next years, short-run economic and political forces may work against more open markets, especially in the U.S.

Thus, the Commission recommends that both incoming governments reaffirm their intention to pursue the freest possible trading relationships.

Without a vision of how the two economies might interact in the long term, the possibility of increasing trade tensions and disruption will remain high. The urgent need for the United States to redress its continuing trade deficit further increases the likelihood of conflict. Since the U.S. must move toward a sustainable balance on its external accounts, increasing exports and containing imports will become a key national priority. Inevitably, this risks colliding with Mexico's own equally essential export drive.

In the past Mexicans have been understandably reluctant to reduce trade barriers since their industry was oriented toward the domestic market under an umbrella of high tariffs. But the devaluation of the U.S. dollar in international markets, the decline of the peso *vis-à-vis* the dollar, and the now-accepted notion that only accelerated export growth can produce much needed foreign-exchange receipts convinced Mexicans that their national industries both could and should take advantage of opportunities in international markets.

By the same token, a number of U.S. firms will probably find that, by locating supporting production operations in Mexico, they can compete more successfully—not only in the U.S. but also in third markets. To realize this opportunity, tariffs on exports from Mexico to the U.S. will need to be reduced.

The Commission recommends that the leaders of both countries adopt a two-step approach to their bilateral trade relationship, recognizing the necessary limitations that derive from the enormous economic disparities between the two countries. First, the countries should continue to agree to generalized trade concessions. Second, they should move promptly to free-trade agreements in all sectors where benefits from free trade may exist, especially in industrial sectors.

This would in the long run establish a *de facto* limited bilateral free trade agreement.

Increasing binational sectoral development is already a key element of the Mexican and U.S. economic relationship. But more can be done: more sectors should be covered and more aggressive reduction of tariff and non-tariff barriers should be pursued. A key element of such cooperation would be the programmed elimination of tariffs, in particular sectors, as rapidly as possible. As these sectoral agreements mature (and as Mexico's economic liberalization advances), they may prove to be the building blocks for even more intense bilateral commercial cooperation.

Finally, it is important to emphasize that the goal is not economic integration. The goal is economic growth and job creation.

The world trading system seems headed for change. The 1980s have been a decade of increasing government management of international trade; the ongoing Uruguay GATT Round is designed to reverse that trend as well as to extend greater trading freedoms to services, investment, and agriculture. Mexico seems prepared for a successful conclusion to the next GATT negotiations, and the country certainly has the potential to benefit from more globalized free trade if it is able to make major adjustments in its economy. An enhanced trading relationship with the United States would lead to mutual benefits for both countries in any event, and it would better position Mexico to benefit from its own comparative advantages and equip it for an even more significant role in the world economy.

INVESTMENT

Both the U.S. and Mexico are badly in need of increasing investment, and both must in the short run reach out to foreign investors to find adequate financing. For the long run the urgency for
Mexico is far greater, however: the combination of a stagnant
economy and several years of investment shortfall means the
economy lacks the productive base and infrastructure to compete
effectively in the future.

Simply put, the key to stimulating adequate investment flows
is the creation of an environment conducive to profitable investment. Domestic investment will always be more important than
foreign investment in volume terms. But investors respond to the
same incentives, regardless of nationality. Freedom from excessive
regulation, a stable policy environment, adequate rates of return,
ready sources of financing, and good marketing opportunities will
encourage investors. In all countries, however, including the United
States, investments by foreigners are sources of political sensitivity. They raise questions about the control of national resources,
the extent of foreign influence in domestic policymaking, and the
ownership of national economic assets. Over the years, this has been
particularly true in Mexico, which has excluded foreigners from
certain sectors (e.g., petroleum) and has by law limited the degree
of foreign investment in particular economic enterprises.

Nevertheless, Mexico's precarious financial circumstances, the
need to obtain current technologies, and the desire to assure better access to the U.S. market—especially through joint ventures—
necessarily imply the need to encourage foreign investment.

INVESTMENT DATA

Net direct-investment flows into Mexico averaged $600 million
per year during 1982-86, according to balance of payments statistics. In 1987, direct investment was a record $3.2 billion, reflecting
in part the effects of the government's debt-equity swap program.
Investment approvals, which generally are greater than actual
realized investments, exceeded $7 billion last year. In future years,
net investment inflows in excess of $1.5 billion per year will be
necessary in light of the unavailability—and undesirability—of
massive new foreign debt financing.

Unfortunately, there are significant differences in how the two countries account for direct investment flows. According to U.S. data, at the end of 1986 the book value of U.S. direct investment in Mexico was $4.8 billion, almost entirely in manufacturing. According to Mexican data, however, cumulative direct investment by U.S. firms in Mexico was $11 billion through 1986 and, on a preliminary basis, $13.7 billion through 1987—out of total foreign investments of $20.9 billion.

CHANGING ATTITUDES

Regardless of the data, no one argues against the proposition that Mexico needs a significant increase in investment both in infrastructure and in the productive sectors. Until recent years, the judgment within Mexico has strongly been that the great bulk of the needed investment must be of domestic origin. Now, however, there is increasing recognition that foreign investment is an effective instrument for penetrating foreign markets, for improving efficiency, and for attracting and absorbing modern technology.

Despite the weaknesses of the Mexican economy in general and of the balance of payments in particular, there is broad agreement within Mexico that the country cannot afford a totally open investment regime, if only because of the potential weight of dividend and other remittances on limited foreign exchange resources. Mexican law establishes the basis for public sector intervention in the economy, including the regulation of foreign investment, and reserves certain sectors for public ownership (petroleum, electricity and banking). Constitutionally mandated objectives include integrated development, the maintenance of national sovereignty, and the promotion of a more equitable distribution of income and wealth. A strong sense exists in Mexico that uninhibited foreign investment could frustrate the achievement of these national goals. In addition, the traditional fear persists that foreign companies might dominate politically and socially sensitive sectors of the economy.

On the U.S. side, criticism is strong of Mexican reluctance to embrace wholeheartedly foreign investment as an important, if partial, antidote to the debt and development crisis. Mexican fears of U.S. domination are perceived to be excessive; instead, U.S. observers emphasize the risk that Mexico is opting out of the global technological revolution through its ambivalence toward foreign investment which threatens to relegate the economy to permanent second- or third-class status.

In practice, of course, the dichotomy is not so stark: Mexico has steadily liberalized the treatment offered to foreign investors and, as a consequence, has seen a marked rise in investment proposals, approvals, and realized projects. The government's stabilization efforts recognize the pivotal role which the private sector must play in Mexico's economic recovery; as a result, the overall investment climate is becoming better.

The present government has interpreted existing laws that regulate investment in a more accommodating way and, in some cases, has authorized 100 percent foreign ownership. Moreover, government programs to privatize and streamline public enterprises and to encourage private sector debt rescheduling or repayment have improved the investment environment.

CONSTRAINTS

Nevertheless, problems remain. There is the perception that lack of confidence in the constancy and predictability of the interpretation of Mexico's laws and regulations affecting investment, and particularly foreign investment, remains an obstacle to greater investment levels and faster economic growth. It would be advisable to move from a system of bureaucratic discretion and exceptions to one where national and foreign investors have clearly defined rights and obligations embedded in the law. A more secure, more predictable, more transparent system would promote private investment and, possibly, the repatriation of flight capital.

Investors also need protection for their products and processes. Without such protection—without modernized patent and trademark laws—entrepreneurs will be unwilling to introduce up-to-date technology into Mexico. Disputes over such intellectual property issues have bedeviled U.S. and Mexican negotiators, but there now seems to be growing awareness in Mexico of the benefits which full protection of intellectual property would confer on national or foreign investors.

The availability of finance is also a serious constraint on attracting new investment. The debt overhang, the seemingly endless renegotiations and reschedulings, and the certainty that the debt strategy will change—without any clear indication of when and how: all inhibit new investment flows. Resolution of the debt crisis is almost a precondition to inducing adequate investment. But one mechanism that could help in the meanwhile is a debt-for-equity swap program through which investors buy existing bank loans at a discount and then use the discounted loans to finance equity investments. In practice, the debtor country government usually shares the discount with the investor. Several Latin countries are using swap programs to reduce the volume of their external indebtedness and to attract new investments. Mexico has used such a program but partially suspended it because it seemed to fail to induce investments that would otherwise not have been made and because of anticipated inflationary consequences.

Another constraint affecting new investment in Mexico is the specter of U.S. protectionism (mentioned earlier). The long-winded debate over new trade legislation in the U.S. raised fears that parts of the U.S. market might be closed to Mexican producers. And even though the final trade bill signed into law by President Reagan was less protectionist than it might have been, those parts of the law that make it harder to export to the U.S. inevitably reduce the attractiveness of Mexican-based investments designed to produce for the U.S. market.

THE FUTURE

The combination of a more secure legal framework, a more open economy, continued access to the U.S. market, and the availability of low-cost labor would assure Mexico of adequate foreign capital inflows. Given the magnitude of obstacles, however, Mexico is unlikely to be confronted by what seems to be a serious fear of some of its citizens—excessive influence of foreign investment—and both countries should make efforts to promote increased capital flows.

The Commission recommends:

- **The Mexican government should adopt a more open and consistent policy for new foreign investment directed for the most part toward the export of manufactured goods, tourism, and in-bond and assembly industries, with a right for investors to participate in domestic markets;**

- Mexico should re-establish a debt-equity swap program in cases that are clearly beneficial for the country;

- Mexico should encourage foreign investment in projects that lead to prompt transfers of modern technology;

- The two governments should establish a fast-track procedure to identify legal, administrative, fiscal, commercial, and patent issues that may pose obstacles to foreign investment; and each should adopt measures consistent with their national policies that reduce or eliminate those impediments.

Some observers believe that Mexico should reassess its reluctance to permit 100 percent foreign ownership by law, as opposed to by bureaucratically sanctioned exception. This is thought to be a source of economic inefficiency and to reduce the country's growth potential. Because of history, market size, deep-rooted suspicion of the United States and other real or perceived constraints, however, such a radical departure from longstanding practice is unlikely soon.

The Commission recommends that the incoming Mexican President initiate a long-term exploration of some of the country's policies regarding foreign investment, keeping in mind relevant aspects of the national interest.

Such a study should include joint ventures and shared investment as well as the possible definition of criteria for 100 percent foreign ownership (except in strategic activities and services in the public and private sectors reserved for Mexican ownership).

Achieving such goals will be facilitated by the evolving complexity of investment relationships. Direct ownership is now eschewed by many multinational investors in favor of more subtle linkages including joint ventures, licensing agreements, technology transfer agreements, franchising, co-production, management agreements, turnkey contracts, subcontracting and service contracts. U.S. and Mexican law and practice must be refined to allow entrepreneurs to develop the most productive relationships possible; private entrepreneurs must become more skillful in combining market access, technology, labor costs and skills, management, research, marketing, and distribution in packages which benefit both countries.

CONCLUSIONS AND RECOMMENDATIONS

Without a positive, shared vision of the future, bilateral economic relations will increasingly become occasions for conflict instead of cooperation and growth. The problems facing the two countries are enormous—almost overwhelming—and could easily overcome the good intentions which exist on both sides of the border. If they do, however, both sides will lose. U.S. bankers would see their loans go bad; U.S. exporters would lose markets; U.S. entrepreneurs would lose the advantages offered through cooperative development. On the Mexican side, producers would be cut off from their most attractive market; growth would falter and not enough jobs would be created; the country would forge improvements in its people's standard of living that could potentially flow from improved access to advanced technology and the enormous U.S. market. These conditions could lead to social instability.

The risks—and costs—of conflict would be high. Fortunately, the gains from cooperation could be even higher: both the United States and Mexico would grow faster if the bilateral relationship evolves in a positive direction.

The incoming Presidents will have to articulate a new framework within which the debt crisis can be moved to resolution, Mexico's stagnant economy can be restarted, the U.S. economic restructuring can proceed without damaging Mexico's own recovery, trade and investment flows can increase, and shared or complementary commercial opportunities can be exploited. Recognition of the linkages among these issues is essential: progress in one area is dependent on progress in all other areas.

But recognition of the importance of these issues to both countries is even more essential. In the past the bilateral economic relationship has suffered in part because of the erratic attention which these issues have received.

The Commission's recommendations are intended to overcome that legacy and to suggest elements of such a new framework. We have proposed that:

- The incoming Presidents, along with other leaders, should invite an international group of financial and political experts from developed and developing countries to propose concrete near-term actions to move the debt crisis toward resolution.

- The two countries should establish a permanent, cabinet-level binational economic commission to promote dialogue about macroeconomic policies, to serve as an early warning mechanism, and to incorporate the advice of the private sectors in national policymaking.

- Mexico should continue on its economic course of liberating the productive forces of the country at a more accelerated rate.

- The U.S. government must play a more aggressive role in creating a new debt management strategy for Mexico and other debtor countries which recognizes that their debt service obligations must be related to their capacity to pay. Elements of this strategy would include providing more generous financing of the international financial institutions, liberalizing commercial bank regulations with regard to the treatment of sovereign debt, and encouraging innovative financial schemes— including more creative uses of the World Bank's loan authorities.

- The Mexican government should continue to work constructively with its creditors, enlarge its debt-for-equity program, explore innovative financing proposals which could reduce the volume of debt and debt service, and seek new sources of finance.

- Both governments should urge creditor banks to take fuller advantage of market processes and banking practices which reduce debt service and to undertake new lending programs when appropriate.

- Both governments must recognize the need for increasing bilateral trade and investment flows as important ways to achieve their shared goals of faster economic growth and more rapid job creation.

- The U.S. should reaffirm its commitment to the freest possible trade regime and develop practical ways to reduce the impact of its own adjustments on bilateral trade and, hence, on investment in Mexico.

- The two governments should develop sectoral free-trade agreements where mutual benefits exist, especially in industrial sectors.

- Mexico should adopt a more open policy for new foreign investment, especially in manufactured exports, tourism, and assembly and in-bond industries, with a right for investors to participate in domestic markets, and should encourage investment in projects that attract transfers of modern technology.

- The incoming Mexican government should conduct a long-term review of some of its policies regarding foreign investment.

- The two governments should establish a fast-track procedure to identify and remove impediments to investors in their legal and administrative systems—including tax, trade, patent and trademark policies—in their respective jurisdictions and in accordance with their national interests.

These recommendations call for a bold break with the past. Their implementation will require both statesmanship and courage. To attempt less would not only be unworthy; it would also be predetermined to fail.

3

The Process of Migration

International migration has occurred throughout history in nearly all parts of the world. During the nineteenth century vast waves of people left Europe in search of a better life in the Americas, settling in the United States and, in the southern hemisphere, in Argentina and Brazil. Migration has continued into the twentieth century and spread to all corners of the globe: Turkish workers have moved to Germany, Algerians to France, Commonwealth citizens to England, Salvadorans to Honduras, Colombians to Venezuela. Almost everywhere, the results have led to a mixed record of costs and benefits for sending and receiving countries, and migration has often become a serious source of political tension. Powerful anti-foreign sentiment has emerged in such diverse countries as the Federal Republic of Germany, France, Japan, Nigeria, Switzerland, and the United Kingdom.

Similarly, Mexican migration to the United States has on occasion led to misunderstandings and hostilities. At the core of disagreements between the two countries rest differing perceptions about the *causes* and *consequences* of Mexican immigration. U.S. policymakers tend to see the Mexican influx as a result of "push" factors deriving from unemployment and lack of opportunity; Mexicans usually stress the role of "pull" factors and the demand for migrant labor. U.S. officials often contend that immigration policy is a unilateral matter and sovereign right; Mexicans see it as a bilateral process that requires a bilateral policy.

Also in dispute is the distribution of benefits. Mexicans see U.S. employers as the main beneficiaries of the illegal stream who are hungry for cheap labor, and U.S. consumers who want cheaper goods and services. A common U.S. opinion contends that primary advantages accrue to the Mexican migrants, their communities of origin, and the Mexican economy as a whole.

As members of this Commission we believe that the first step toward the development of a productive approach to these issues is the establishment of a common understanding of the causes and consequences of Mexican migration to the United States. We think it is essential to acknowledge that the migration issue is rooted in complex historical, political, and social circumstances.

Although migration deals with the movement of people, and is a profoundly human story, we think it is ultimately driven by economic realities. Whether "pushed" by untenable conditions in Mexico or "pulled" by opportunities in the United States, workers face an essentially economic decision. It is about differentials in job-creation levels, job openings, and wage levels—differentials that constitute the calculation behind the decision to leave families and communities in search of a better living. Repeated patterns of migration can create social traditions as well, but the underlying forces are economic.

Policymakers have advanced many forms of immigration legislation over the years. They have proposed quotas, temporary worker permits, enforcement strategies, and now employer sanctions and amnesty. Until the larger economic realities are squarely addressed, however, the pressure for migration will continue.

Any bilateral policy on migration must be mindful of the economic context. Such legislation as the Immigration Reform and Control Act of 1986 (Simpson-Rodino) touches many aspects of the problem, but it is at best a short-run mechanism for adjustment and regulation. What has been missing from U.S. and Mexican attention to the migration issue is a concerted, long-term economic approach. It will probably take a quarter of a century to reduce the economic differentials between the two countries in a significant way.

This is the time to start. Chapter 2 has set forth a bold agenda on economics. This much should be clear: if Mexico does not achieve sustained economic growth, there will be continued and even increased pressure for migration. Regardless of legislation or consultative mechanisms, economic realities will dictate the success or failure of migration strategies. Dealing with the debt problem in such a way that allows job creation in Mexico, trade agreements that spur economic expansion in Mexico, investment strategies that encourage new industries—these are key variables in determining the intensity of migration.

We also believe it is important to make careful distinctions between at least three social categories:

1. *Mexican emigrants to the United States:* people born in Mexico who reside permanently in the U.S.

2. *Mexican migrant workers in the United States:* people born in Mexico who reside habitually in Mexico and seek temporary work in the U.S. (Specialists sometimes divide this group into "commuters," who shuttle back and forth on a regular basis; and "sojourners," who come for periods of several months at a time.)

3. *Mexican-origin citizens of the United States:* people of Mexican parentage or background born in the United States, usually known as Mexican-Americans or Chicanos. (This group is not the central focus of this chapter.)

Individuals in the first two categories may have come to the U.S. legally or illegally. Members of the last category may come from families that have been in the U.S. for several generations. Plainly enough, these are distinct social groupings; much of the confusion over the migration issue has stemmed from ignorance of these distinctions and from the blurring of these categories.

We begin with a historical survey of Mexican migration to the U.S. We then attempt to unravel essential features of the contemporary situation: push-pull factors, economic and social incentives, geographic and occupational destination. After that we review the policy record to date, including the Immigration Reform and Control Act of 1986, and we conclude with a series of recommendations.

HISTORICAL PERSPECTIVES

A broad overview of Mexican immigration reveals four distinct historical periods. The first, for nearly a century, was characterized by a liberal border policy and relatively unrestricted immigration

(1848-1930). The second showed a relatively "closed" border and strong anti-Mexican sentiment (1930-1941). Third was a generally liberal but inconsistent border policy (1942-1964). Finally, there was a period of gradually more restrictive immigration policy seasoned with selective enforcement of the law (1965 to the present). In a general sense, this ebb and flow pattern parallels changes in the U.S. economy: the greater the demand for Mexican labor, the more liberal the policy—and the greater the migratory flow.

From the turn of the century until the Great Depression, an informal "open border" policy toward Mexico provided U.S. employers with an immense pool of unskilled workers to accommodate seasonal and cyclical variations in labor demand, primarily in agriculture, mining, and construction industries. The reserve of Mexican labor was particularly valuable after immigration from Europe began to subside. Moreover, temporary labor shortages during World War I left a vacuum for seasonal agricultural labor and created immediate demand for Mexican workers. High unemployment and revolutionary upheaval added a decisive push factor as well, so there emerged a fairly good fit between supply and demand. Because the National Origins Act of 1924 was intended to exclude Chinese and Asian immigrants, Mexican immigration was allowed to continue throughout the 1920s—at least until the stock market crash of 1929.

Restrictions on Mexican immigration during the 1930s represented a direct consequence of the Great Depression. Not only did Mexican migration come to a screeching halt; widespread deportations and anti-Mexican sentiment led to a reversal of the flow. Approximately half a million Mexicans were deported to their country during the Depression years. Despite its unfortunate conclusion, this first migration cycle was significant in establishing migratory traditions within Mexican communities and, on the U.S. side, in demonstrating the economic advantages that derived from access to an unregulated, flexible, and inexpensive supply of labor.

World War II began a second cycle of Mexican immigration, but this time with quite different and, apparently, more enduring consequences. In response to labor shortages in agriculture resulting from the draft, the U.S. government in 1942 proposed a formal agreement to utilize Mexican workers. In contrast to the unregulated use of Mexican workers to offset labor shortfalls incurred during the First World War, experience compelled Mexico to seek protection for workers' rights. Formally legislated as U.S. Public

Law 45, but more popularly known as the *bracero* program, this temporary worker agreement between Mexico and the United States began as an emergency measure to replenish labor lost to the military draft.

Although Public Law 45 formally ended in 1947, the practice of importing Mexican laborers to work in agriculture on a seasonal basis continued informally—that is, without official regulation or binding agreements. In 1951 a new bilateral agreement and Public Law 78 reformalized the *bracero* program as a temporary solution to labor shortages resulting from the Korean conflict. Public Law 78 remained in effect well past the end of the Korean War, but the U.S. allowed the bilateral agreement to lapse in 1964.

Tensions have increased since the 1960s for a variety of reasons. First, in the early 1960s immigration from Mexico resurfaced as a major political issue against the backdrop of the Civil Rights movement, which exposed the discriminatory underpinnings of the admission quota system that had been established by the National Quota Act of 1924 and reaffirmed by the Immigration and Nationality Act of 1952. These criticisms provided the impetus for the sweeping reforms legislated in 1965 (discussed in more detail below). Although the quota laws of 1924 and 1952 were the first apparent attempts to regulate the number of admissions, Mexicans were largely exempted from their regulations. It was the 1965 legislation that acquired special significance for its restrictive impact on Mexican migration.

MEASURING THE LEGAL FLOWS

Table 3-1 places legal Mexican immigration in a historical perspective. One column presents the absolute number of legal Mexican immigrants admitted each decade since 1900, and the other expresses the Mexican stream as a percentage of all immigrants admitted in each period. Both the absolute and relative numbers clearly show the growing momentum of Mexican immigration over the past 30 to 35 years. The upward surge was particularly pronounced during the 1950s, a period of relative prosperity in both Mexico and the U.S., when Mexicans doubled their share of all legal immigrants from roughly 6 to 12 percent.

The Mexican proportion of all legal immigrants rose more gradually during the 1960s and 1970s, but during this same period Mexico

TABLE 3-1. LEGAL MEXICAN IMMIGRATION, 1900-1985

Year	Number of Mexicans	Mexicans as %Total Admitted
1901-10	49,642	0.6
1911-20	219,004	3.8
1921-30	459,287	11.2
1931-40	22,319	4.2
1941-50	60,589	5.9
1951-60	299,811	11.9
1961-70	453,937	13.7
1971-80	640,294	14.2
1981-85	335,563	11.7

SOURCE: Immigration and Naturalization Service.

became the largest single source of immigrants to the U.S. This fact apparently did not go unnoticed; in 1976 Congress passed the Western Hemisphere Act, which extended the annual ceiling of 20,000 persons per country to the nations of Latin America. Over the very short term this amendment reduced the flow of legal immigrants from Mexico, but over the medium term (i.e., through 1985) this result was offset by a growth in the number of persons entering under preference categories "exempt" from numerical limitations.[1] As Table 3-2 demonstrates, the share of Mexican immigrants admitted under exempt (non-quota) categories rose from 32 percent of the total admitted in 1975 (prior to the Western Hemisphere Act) to approximately 66 percent of those who entered in 1985.

In 1985, 87 percent of Mexicans admitted under nonexempt "quota" visas qualified for the family reunification provisions. Only 13 percent of nonexempt visas were granted on the basis of occupational preferences, and of these only one-third were granted to principals; two-thirds were allotted to accompanying family members. At this pace there is reason to believe that the number of legal Mexican immigrants admitted during the 1980s will match,

1. The number of Mexicans legally admitted topped off at 101,000 in 1981, but fell 44 percent the following year. Since 1982, the annual number of Mexicans legally admitted has fluctuated between 56,000 and 61,000.

TABLE 3-2. LEGAL MEXICAN IMMIGRANTS ADMITTED
BY TYPE OF ADMISSION
(Selected Years 1947 to 1985)

	Quota		Non-Quota	
	Number	% of Total	Number	% of Total
1947	286	3.8	7,272	96.2
1950	174	2.6	6,570	97.4
1955	88	0.2	43,614	99.8
1960	150	0.5	32,558	99.5
1965	168	0.4	40,518	99.6
1970	27,267	60.8	17,554	39.2
1975	42,218	67.5	20,334	32.5
1980	24,831	43.8	31,849	56.2
1985	20,633	33.8	40,444	66.2

SOURCE: Immigration and Naturalization Service.

if not exceed, the size of the 1970s cohort.[2] There could well be another 700,000 legal arrivals during the decade of the 1990s.

Generally speaking, these historical trends serve to underline two major points. First, there has been—and continues to be—a significant volume of *legal* Mexican migration to the United States. Indeed, the inflow in the 1920s was just about as large as during the 1960s, and legal admissions have increased in the past two decades. Even in the absence of illegal migration, these flows would have a considerable impact on U.S. society. Not every Mexican worker is an "illegal alien."

Second, the recent upsurge in U.S. immigration, which began in earnest during the 1960s, has not been a uniquely Mexican phenomenon; immigration from virtually all regions increased appreciably in the aftermath of World War II (in fact, total U.S. immigration has increased by approximately one million additional persons per decade since 1950). Moreover, there has been a notable

2. If an additional 335,000 legal Mexican immigrants are admitted between 1986 and 1990, the absolute number admitted during the decade of the 1980s will be larger than that for the 1970s. This figure does not include those who might receive amnesty.

increase in the diversity of national origin of U.S.-bound migrants. Whereas immigrants from Europe predominated through the 1950s, Asian and Latin American migrants were the dominant regional groups after 1965. It may well be these changes in the composition of the migrant stream, as well as concerns about relative volume, that have helped to resurrect nativist sentiments and anti-migrant feelings within the U.S. public.

ESTIMATING THE ILLEGAL FLOWS

Parodoxically enough, these longstanding patterns of legal admission have both encouraged and facilitated the increase in *illegal* entries from Mexico since the 1960s. As restrictions on legal admission have tightened, many Mexicans have nonetheless inherited the idea of migration from their forebears and from community members. They have also been able to make use of extensive and well-established social networks that provide assistance in crossing the border and in finding jobs in the U.S.

The impact of these factors coincided with key changes in U.S. policy. First, the termination of the *bracero* program in 1964 shifted the movement of seasonal contract laborers from a predominantly regulated to a predominantly unregulated (undocumented) flow. This change consolidated a meaningful distinction between "legal" and "illegal" status. Second, the shift in U.S. immigration policy from emphasis on labor certification toward family reunification made it virtually impossible for unskilled Mexicans to enter the United States legally unless they were related to documented resident aliens or to U.S. citizens. This only increased the incentives for illegal migration.

Illegal immigration constitutes the most controversial aspect of the contemporary Mexican migrant stream, yet it is precisely this segment about which we know least. Recent scholarship provides compelling empirical evidence about the economic and demographic consequences of the illegal flow, but there remains a great deal of uncertainty over the *size* and the *growth* of the undocumented population in the U.S.

Demographers have reached fairly firm conclusions about the total *stock* of Mexicans in the United States at the beginning of this decade. There were perhaps 8.7 million people of Mexican origin (including Mexican-Americans) in 1980. Analyses of census data and other sources place the total size of the Mexican-origin *migrant* population, legal and illegal, around 2.5 million for that same year. Complementary estimates suggest that the stock of undocumented migrants from all countries ranged from 3.5 to 5 million, of which somewhat over half (55-60 percent) were estimated to be of Mexican origin. Around 1980, in other words, there were between 2 and 2.3 million undocumented migrants from Mexico in the United States.

There is no such consensus on the number of undocumented Mexicans in the United States in the late 1980s. Without new census figures, demographers have largely given up the task of estimation. The Statistical Analysis Branch of the U.S. Immigration and Naturalization Service has estimated that the size of this population may be between 2.5 and 4 million, with many observers leaning toward the upper end of this range. (Government officials often speak of 3.9 million.) The most remarkable fact is that we do not know how large the migrant population is; as a result, we cannot gauge the magnitude of the problem.

Nor is there any consensus about the *flow* of undocumented migrants.[3] It is generally agreed that the volume of illegal immigration increased markedly during the 1970s, but estimates of the pace of growth vary widely (and, some would argue, irresponsibly). One widely used estimate is 500,000 new entrants per year. This figure has no solid empirical basis, however, and it is not balanced with a comparable guesstimate of voluntary or involuntary departures.

Perhaps the most well-known assessment of trends comes from apprehensions of would-be migrants along the U.S.-Mexican border. The presumption is that the number of arrests provides a usable guide to the number of crossings. As Figure 3-1 indicates, apprehensions declined sharply in the late 1950s—during the heyday of the *bracero* program—and began a steady increase in the late 1960s. Aggregate apprehensions rose from approximately 345,000 in 1970 to over one million per year in the late 1970s and early 1980s, rising to more than 1.5 million in 1985 and 1986. The sense of a "rising tide" of immigrants emerges in clear and graphic form.

But as specialists have shown, apprehension statistics provide highly unreliable indications of migratory flows. They refer to

3. The distinction between *stocks* and *flows* causes confusion. Stock refers to the population in the United States at a particular point in time, whereas flows refer to movements back and forth across borders.

Figure 3-1.   Aliens Apprehended: Fiscal Years 1951-86

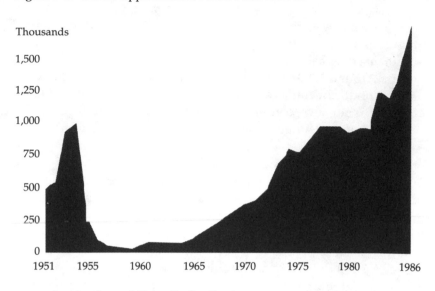

SOURCE: Immigration and Naturalization Service.

events—that is, to the number of arrests—and not to *people.* They make no allowance for multiple arrests (anecdotal evidence indicates that some individuals can be arrested more than once in the same day). They make no adjustment for voluntary returns to Mexico (while survey data indicate that the vast majority of migrants come only for temporary periods). And they are bound to respond to the varying intensity and magnitude of enforcement efforts by the U.S. Border Patrol.

Even at face value, apprehension figures challenge conventional wisdom. It is commonly asserted that there are two undetected crossings for each arrest: this, indeed, is the basic premise behind numerous policy pronouncements. But if this were true, there would have been at least 10 million undocumented migrants from Mexico in the United States in 1980—instead of the 2.0-2.3 million determined by analysts from the U.S. Census Bureau. Obviously something is grossly inaccurate. Part of the problem is that it is necessary to make allowance for the number of those who return to Mexico: the *net* inflow of migrants is generally assumed to be a good deal smaller than the *gross* inflow, although precise figures on this point do not exist.

Confusion around this issue leads us to believe that policymakers would be well advised to avoid the use of apprehension statistics as a guide to the flow of illegal migration—or, at the very least, to issue explicit caveats and qualifications along with the use of such data. And as we indicate below, we think the U.S. and Mexican governments should make joint efforts to obtain satisfactory estimates of the magnitude and composition of migratory stocks and flows.

Notwithstanding the imprecision of statistics, specialists agree that immigration from all sources has contributed an increasing share of demographic growth, rising from roughly 11 percent during the 1950s to 20 percent during the 1970s, but these rates are well below the comparable figures for the turn of the century—when immigration accounted for almost 40 percent of net population growth. And even now, the foreign-born population represents a significantly lower share of the total resident U.S. population, roughly 6 percent, than at the turn of the century, when immigrants comprised approximately 14 percent of the resident U.S. population. Nor does immigration account for most of the growth of the Mexican-origin population in the U.S. According to recent estimates net immigration from Mexico (legal and illegal) accounted for less than half the growth of the Mexican-origin population during the 1970s.[4]

CONTEMPORARY PATTERNS

Much of the bilateral tension between Mexico and the United States has stemmed from concerns and confusions about the flow of undocumented migrants. While there is widespread acknowledgement that the volume of undocumented immigration has risen during the 1970s and 1980s, there is less agreement about the causes or the effects of this increase. To disentangle these questions we now turn to several features of the contemporary scene: the economic incentives for migration, the social origins of the migrants, their paths of entry into the U.S., and their geographic and occupational destinations. We also touch upon the theme of assimilation into North American culture.

4. Although the Mexican-origin population is one of the fastest growing in the nation, this increase results largely from high fertility and the youthfulness of the population.

ECONOMIC INCENTIVES

For Mexico, the mid-1950s heralded the onset of what has come to be known as the "Mexican miracle." Aggregate economic growth fluctuated between 6 and 7 percent annually, inflation remained under 3 percent, fiscal and monetary policies provided an atmosphere of continuity and confidence. Thus Mexico enjoyed the benefits of its strategy of "stabilizing development."

Notwithstanding these accomplishments, Mexico's postwar policies of import-substitution industrialization entailed significant costs. Ironically enough, the rapid pace of economic growth may have distracted attention from issues of population growth. Even as the population was increasing at 3.2 to 3.5 percent per year, average economic growth rates of 6 to 7 percent yielded handsome gains in GDP per capita. It was not until the 1970s that Mexico adopted a national policy on population control. Efforts to curb demographic growth have been remarkably effective, bringing annual rates down to 2.2 to 2.5 percent a year, but this could not alleviate short-term pressures. As a result of the population boom in the 1960s and early 70s, Mexico has had about 750,000 to 1 million new entrants into the job market every year; its labor force is growing at one of the highest rates in the world, and will continue to do so for the next decade at least.

The strategy of "stabilizing development" also had distinctive features. Encouraged by import-substitution industrialization, manufacturing tended to be more capital-intensive than labor-intensive. This was especially true of the foreign sector, which owned one-half the 400 largest firms in Mexico and accounted for about 25 percent of total production. In other words, the expansion of the manufacturing sector did not create enough jobs to absorb the increase in the labor force, and a downturn in production in the early 1970s led to additional layoffs as well.

To offset these consequences the Mexican government furnished economic benefits and social programs to the urban working classes. Real wages rose on the order of 20-25 percent during the 1960s; price controls curtailed the retail cost of basic goods, including food; a series of subsidies, from retirement benefits to public transportation, upheld the standard of living for workers in the cities.

Some of these same policies wrought dislocation in the countryside. Prompted in part by the "green revolution" of the 1950s, agricultural production reached surplus levels in the early 1960s—and led to substantial exports. In this context the government opted to place strict ceilings on the price of corn and other staple goods. This held down the price of food in the cities but also led to a decline in production and employment in the rural sector. By the mid-1970s, according to some estimates, less than half of the economically active population in agriculture had full-time employment.

The petroleum boom of the late 1970s and early 80s prompted hopes for a return to prosperity. From 1978 through 1981 the Mexican economy resumed its place as one of the most dynamic in the world, with average annual growth rates of 8.4 percent, but disaster struck in 1982. Subsequent austerity programs of the Mexican government took a harsh toll on the country's working classes: real wages declined by 32 percent between 1981 and 1984 and unemployment swelled. As shown in Chapter 2, Mexico has suffered a prolonged state of economic crisis.

As a result of all these trends, Mexico has developed a large and growing labor force. Open unemployment from the 1960s to the 80s has hovered around 6 percent, but underemployment may have been as high as 40 percent. In other words, Mexico had a substantial number of *prospective migrants*. Whether they would actually move to the United States would depend, at least in part, on the availability of economic opportunities.

There have been strong "pull" factors at work within the U.S. Since the mid-1960s the U.S. economy has displayed uneven patterns of growth, showing some periods of brisk growth (1971-73) along with stagnation (1979-80, 1981-82) and moderate performance (1978-79, 1982-83). The rate of growth in labor productivity has for the most part declined, the level of "structural unemployment" has often been as high as 6 percent (compared to 3 percent in the past), and unemployment has been especially high among minority groups.

There have been two particularly notable trends in employment. First has been the decline of agricultural employment and the expansion of services (the manufacturing share of total employment has remained more or less stable). Second, especially apparent since the 1970s, has been the regional relocation of employment from the traditional high-wage areas in the industrial Northeast and Midwest to the historically low-wage Sunbelt states. These transformations occurred just as the baby-boom cohorts and large numbers of women entered the labor force, thus producing a glut in labor markets in some portions of the country.

Despite these changes in employment, the U.S. demand for Mexican labor has not undergone a decline since the 1960s. On the contrary, the demand has remained strong and even grown. This has been true for at least three reasons:

- first, substantial portions of the U.S. labor market have become "segmented"; in agriculture and in some other areas, Mexicans have taken jobs that U.S. citizens have spurned;

- second, Mexicans have acquired a reputation in many areas as a dependable, hard-working, reliable, and reasonably skilled labor force; this is especially true in areas where migrant workers have been active for more than one generation;

- third, Mexican labor is inexpensive; many migrants work at or below the minimum wage, and as a rule they are not in a position to mount collective action for wage increases.

Indeed, the wage differential is so large that many Mexicans might be tempted to seek jobs in the United States even with full employment at home. In the early 1970s the average minimum wage in California agriculture was nine times that in Mexico. By the mid-1980s, when the U.S. minimum wage was $3.35 per hour, the base minimum in Mexico was about 38 cents. By that same time average hourly pay in U.S. manufacturing was $13.46, compared with $1.37 per hour in Mexico (where the industrial minimum was 62 cents). In general the wage structure in the United States has been eight to ten times higher than in Mexico, with variations depending in part upon fluctuations in the rate of exchange.

SOCIAL ORIGINS

Economic factors, from wage differentials to labor demand, provide much of the explanation for the increase in Mexican migration to the U.S. during the 1970s. Equally important for understanding the growing momentum of Mexican immigration in recent times are the expanding *social* networks which have become increasingly more decisive in determining who migrates, for how long, and under what circumstances.

The role of tradition becomes plainly apparent from the fact that Mexican migrants to the U.S. have in past and present eras come from a relatively small number of "sending" communities. *About 70 percent of all Mexican migrants to the U.S. have come from only eight states out of the thirty-two within Mexico.* Together, these entities (Baja California, Chihuahua, Guanajuato, Guerrero, Jalisco, Michoacán, Sonora, and Zacatecas) accounted for only 27 percent of the national population in the 1980 census. And as shown by Map 2, they are located in the central as well as the northern zones of Mexico: indeed, the most substantial and continual patterns of emigration belong to Jalisco and Michoacán. The causes of these customs probably varied from place to place,[5] but the result is abundantly clear: specific communities within Mexico have built up their own traditions of migration, and these traditions exercise a crucial role in the present-day process.

Social factors are especially important because they mean that *cross-border flows will be less responsive to public policy and legislative statutes than in the past.* They also imply that recent and future migrants will live in concentrated areas, so the general impact of the Mexican "presence" will become ever more visible within U.S.-society.

Who are the migrants? Profiles describe them as young, typically in their early 20s; overwhelmingly male; and literate, to the extent that they have had some primary and/or secondary school, with about twice the educational level of the national average. Perhaps half are married, with dependents still in Mexico. Often the sons of agricultural workers, Mexican migrants tend to be from rural communities—but they are upwardly mobile as well. As one study has summarized, they are "neither from the lowest economic class nor from the highest. They are from somewhere in between, but generally nearer the bottom."[6]

They come from a variety of occupational backgrounds. According to one survey, 11.5 percent were agricultural laborers; almost twice that number, 22.4 percent, were semi-skilled urban workers;

5. One prominent reason was the layout of northbound railways in the late nineteenth century.
6. Harry E. Cross and James A. Sandos, *Across the Border: Rural Development in Mexico and Recent Migration to the United States* (Berkeley: Institute of Governmental Studies, University of California, 1981), p. 76.

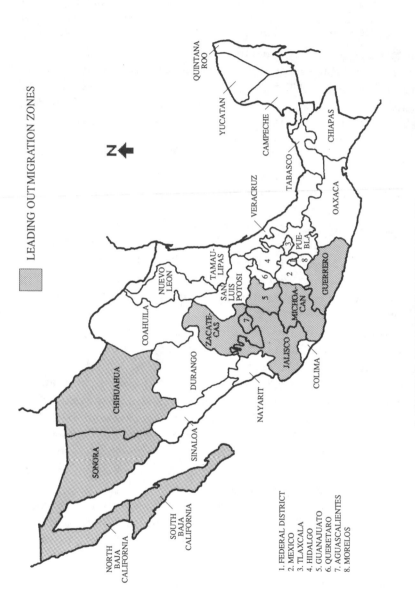

LEADING OUT MIGRATION ZONES

N

1. FEDERAL DISTRICT
2. MEXICO
3. TLAXCALA
4. HIDALGO
5. GUANAJUATO
6. QUERETARO
7. AGUASCALIENTES
8. MORELOS

2. REGIONAL SOURCES OF MEXICAN MIGRATION

and 23.8 percent were skilled workers. In other words, almost half (46.2 percent) spent their working lives in Mexico as skilled workers and artisans or as semi-skilled urban laborers. Only a fraction would qualify as *campesinos*.

PATHS OF ENTRY

It takes capital to migrate. The first requirement is getting to the border, which most do by public bus or train. Then they must decide how to cross. Most simply hike across, alone or with friends, usually under the cover of night. Constantly on the lookout for the Border Patrol, they must try to slip through without detection.

Those from traditional sending areas can usually rely upon the support and advice of an outpost community at or near the border itself. Perhaps one quarter of the undocumented migrants use hired agents, or *coyotes*, who help with the crossing itself and often find jobs as well; sometimes they provide false papers too. In the late 1970s the going rate was $250 to $350 per person; by the mid-1980s this had gone up to $500 and more, depending on the place of destination. This can be a difficult and dangerous process, as shown by the tragic incident of Mexican migrants who suffocated in a railroad boxcar in the summer heat of Texas in 1987.

The U.S. Border Patrol deploys its personnel at strategic points, using helicopters and searchlights to locate would-be entrants attempting to cross at night. Once caught, those without papers are usually processed and then released at some point near the area of their arrest—where they are free to try another crossing, sometimes even the same night. At the discretion of the arresting officer, because of possession of fraudulent papers or resistance to arrest or for any other reason, they can be detained. With the concurrence of a judge they can then be sentenced to 179-day terms in minimum-security prisons. At the end of this time they are deported once again to Mexico—where they can attempt to cross yet again.

These are trying circumstances both for the migrants and for the U.S. law enforcement officers—in the Border Patrol, in the INS, in the courts, and in local police departments. At times these officers have stepped in to protect migrants from abuse by *coyotes* or common thieves. But there have been complaints of unnecessary violence and mistreatment by federal and local law enforcement officers. Without casting any aspersion on the motivations of the law enforcement groups, most of whom do their job in a professional manner, we as members of this Commission wish to record our strong belief that international migrants—legal or illegal—continue to possess their elementary human rights. Crossing the border does not deprive them of their humanity.

Over time, the circumstances of illegal entry have undergone a significant change, as northward migration has become a deeply rooted social process. This evolution corresponds to a gradual but decisive shift in the *auspices* of migration. Recent arrivals come under a set of conditions that did not exist before. This change in the auspices of Mexican migration developed through two basic mechanisms: (1) the expansion of social networks in sending communities that broaden the base of prospective migrants; (2) the consolidation of social ties in destination communities that reproduce "daughter communities" in the United States and, in turn, serve as landing grounds for newer arrivals. (To take one example: the *municipio* of Aguililla, in the state of Michoacán, has 27,000 residents; approximately 7,000 people from this same community reside in Redwood City, California.)

This change in the auspices of migration has had several important effects. First, as we have already said, the Mexican migrant stream has become increasingly less responsive to legal "controls." This is because the social underpinnings of migration are more powerful in maintaining the flow than are legal proscriptions in stopping it. Second, it has tightened the links between sending and receiving communities; an economic downturn in a specific region of the United States could have a decisive impact on a local community in Mexico, for instance, especially because it could accelerate the cycle of return or circular migration. Third, it has increased the likelihood of long-term or permanent residence, since migrants can find extensive support systems within the United States.

For Mexico the greatest social effects of migration derive not from permanent departures, but from circular and return streams. Two types of counteracting effects stem from these flows. On the one hand, circular migration diffuses the idea of migration and increases its acceptability. On the other hand, the return of migrants who have accumulated substantial material resources after prolonged periods of U.S. residence can sharpen inequalities within the community, since the migrants are likely to have considerably more spending power than the stay-at-homes. There can be cultural consequences too, with the progressive "northernization" of villages in the Mexican countryside with long traditions of outmigration.

GEOGRAPHIC AND ECONOMIC DESTINATIONS

Mexican migrants have found their way to almost every part of the United States, but their historic concentration has been in the states of the Southwest. During the 1910s and 20s there was a strong stream that crossed through Texas and went up to the Upper Midwest, producing a large Mexican-origin community in Chicago and a number of settlements along the Wisconsin and Michigan coasts of Lake Superior. During the heyday of the *bracero* program, in the 1950s and early 60s, the most common destinations were agricultural areas of California and Texas. Since then there have been three concurrent tendencies: a preference for California, a return to Chicago and the Midwest, and a generalized dispersion throughout the U.S.

A survey of documented migrants in 1973-74 at two major crossing points, El Paso and Laredo, showed that about half expected to stay in Texas; about 15 percent were heading for Illinois, mainly Chicago, while 13 percent hoped to go to California; others were planning to go to the Upper Midwest, the Plains states, New York, Florida, and elsewhere. Because of its setting this survey no doubt overestimated the proportion of all migrants going to Texas and undercounted the share heading for California. But perhaps most strikingly, the vast majority of those interviewed was setting out not for agricultural areas but for urban communities: 73 percent were going to cities with more than 100,000 persons.

Since the 1960s the migrant workforce has found more diversified locations in the U.S. economy. Originally Mexican workers were recruited for agricultural jobs in the Southwest and, to a lesser extent, for jobs in mining and railroad construction. In recent decades Mexican workers have moved from a largely seasonal rural labor force to an urban underclass in a wide variety of regional locations. The increasing concentration of U.S. production in the Sunbelt, with its historically weak unions and low wage structure, provided special opportunities for Mexican workers. U.S. employers were quick to capitalize on these changes to maintain favorable profit margins.

The diversification of Mexican labor became especially apparent after the end of the *bracero* program. In recent years Mexican immigrants have sustained a gradual, but decisive move toward urban employment in response to growing labor demand in the competitive sectors of the U.S. economy. To illustrate the point, one recent study of metropolitan areas in California found 177 firms with at least 25 percent Mexican workers that produced more than 60 different types of goods and services. Most were small- or medium-sized operations, many as subcontractors in the most competitive sectors of the regional economy.

Plainly enough, declining demand in agriculture and the absence of wartime shortages during the 1970s and 80s have not eliminated the demand for Mexican workers. Quite the contrary: even as unemployment within the U.S. has undergone oscillations, the numbers of Mexican migrants have increased—and they have found durable niches within the U.S. economy. The demand for Mexican labor has become more diversified and, to all appearances, has steadily increased in volume.

The persistence of demand has not, however, led to much improvement in working conditions. Agricultural workers labor under the worst of circumstances—exposed to pesticides and sun, susceptible to injury, often deprived of the most basic sanitary facilities. Conditions in the cities are often nearly as poor. Undocumented migrants, especially, frequently labor in virtual sweatshops.

Nor does access to jobs bring access to social services. Undocumented workers have no access at all to disability or social-security benefits, despite the fact that they usually make contributions to those funds. Their children have the right to go to public schools— though most of them do not have children. They have uneven access to medical care and health services: about half the migrant population makes substantial use of community centers under the Migrant Health Program, in places where the MHP is readily available, but health care elsewhere is sharply limited. Access to publicly subsidized housing has also been uneven and has recently been challenged in the courts. All these subjects have generated considerable controversy.

Notwithstanding their employment opportunities, most migrant workers from Mexico seek to return to their homeland. This is especially true for the undocumented ones, who go to the United States in order to accumulate some capital in order to achieve opportunity and independence within their own communities. Leading experts are in agreement that, historically at least, the vast majority of Mexican migrants have been "sojourners," people who spend about six to eighteen months in the U.S. and then return to Mexico. Some make the trip more than once. We do not have firm statistics on the incidence of return trips to Mexico, and this would be a vital piece of information for policymaking. But the important point is this: *their ultimate destination usually lies at the point of origin in Mexico, not somewhere in the United States.*

For the most part the return home is a relatively smooth process, especially in communities with traditions of migration, though there is some evidence that migrants encounter difficulty becoming re-integrated into the local society. Having left their own communities in search of employment elsewhere, they are sometimes seen as disloyal opportunists. Having adopted alien customs, they are viewed as outcasts. And having experienced the temptations of modern consumerism, they are reluctant to re-establish permanent roots in underdeveloped communities. In general, however, the migrants find a welcome place back at home in Mexico.

ISSUES OF ASSIMILATION

For those who stay for long or indefinite periods in the United States, the changing auspices of Mexican migration have profound implications regarding social integration. Integration into the United States requires more substantial social and cultural adjustments of migrants than would their return to Mexico. Adaptation turns out to be much easier for temporary migrants who can avail themselves of the social supports provided by Mexican "daughter communities" and ethnic neighborhoods. Ironically, the proliferation of Mexican neighborhoods—which promote assimilation—has spawned resentment insofar as residential concentration is viewed as evidence that Mexican migrants cannot be integrated easily into U.S. society.

Fears about the cultural diversity and the potential sociopolitical problems produced by the "new immigration" have rekindled nativist sentiments within the U.S. toward Mexican migrants during the 1980s. Such feelings draw support from two broad generalizations. One is that recent immigrants, and particularly those who arrived after 1965, are less skilled than earlier arrivals, so they will presumably have a more difficult time acclimating to the U.S. labor market. A second assertion is that the proliferation of Mexican culture and the use of Spanish will lead to the dilution of Anglo-American culture.

But residential concentration does not necessarily indicate resistance to social integration. The Mexican-origin population in the U.S. displayed increasing residential dispersion during the 1960s, largely due to economic prosperity and occupational mobility. During the 1970s there was a return to residential concentration, mainly as a result of economic contraction and increased immigration. Growing attachment to ethnic ties and neighborhoods does not reveal the inability of Mexicans to adapt, but rather the persistence of personal attachments and a realistic assessment of their tentative acceptance in the United States.

Over time, there have emerged two basic forces—increasing volumes of migration and higher levels of residential segregation—that have increased the visibility of the Mexican presence in the United States. It is this heightened awareness that has, for the most part, created widespread worries about "silent invasions" and the "dilution" of mainstream American culture.

From this perspective, the appropriate question is not whether Mexican migrants can be integrated, but rather how much the growing Mexican presence strains tolerance for cultural diversity within American society. This issue is particularly acute in the Southwest and in border areas. A related question is how social intolerance may propagate economic inequality. Prejudice against Mexicans continues to block some channels of upward mobility. Detection and understanding of this problem becomes all the more complicated by the issue of timing, since the continuing arrival of new immigrants leaves a superficial impression of slow or limited economic mobility of the Mexican-origin population as a group.

As a matter of fact, generational patterns demonstrate that immigrants of Mexican origin undergo relatively full adaptation to U.S. society. With regard to marriage, for example, 13.3 percent of first-generation Mexican-origin men in one recent study married non-Hispanics; for the third generation the proportion was 36.2 percent, and for men of high occupational status the figure was 48.5 percent. For the third generation, the probability of marriage between a Mexican-American and an Anglo was higher than between a Mexican-American and either a first- or second-generation Mexican-American. Intermarriage has settled around the

50 percent mark in California; in upstate New York it has climbed over 90 percent.

Language follows a similar pattern. Among those born and raised in Mexico, 84 percent speak mostly Spanish at home. By the third generation, 84 percent speak mostly English at home. Indeed, many Mexican-Americans are monolingual in English by the third or fourth generation.

Occupational mobility tells a somewhat different story. Like other immigrants, Mexican-Americans make every effort to move up the economic ladder. A study of California, for instance, showed that 15 percent of the first generation of Mexican-Americans had white-collar jobs, compared with 27.4 percent of the second generation and 36.7 percent of the third. There is emerging a university-educated cadre of young Chicano professionals as the pattern of mobility continues.

Despite these similarities, the experience of Mexican immigrants differs from that of their European predecessors in at least four important ways. First, the European immigrants entered during a period of continuous labor demand, whereas the entry of Mexicans has encompassed more unstable economic climates, particularly during the post-World War II period. Second, while European immigration phased out over time, thereby permitting the forces of assimilation to obliterate cultural differences, Mexican immigration has not only continued—but also increased during a period of economic stagnation. Third, owing partly to the evolution of demand for unskilled labor and partly to hiring practices which defined some occupations as "Mexican jobs," Mexican origin and birthplace has become consolidated as an axis of the stratification regime. Fourth, European migrants were separated from their homelands by an enormous ocean; Mexicans can return fairly easily to their communities by land, and this leads to constant cultural replenishment.

COSTS OF MIGRATION

While Mexican citizens who migrate gain higher wages and some U.S. employers benefit from the availability of the migrant workforce, there are costs as well as other benefits for both nations.

There are important fiscal impacts in the United States. Recent research has shown the significant and growing costs for health care and social services to local governments. There is increasing doubt that local tax systems are structured adequately to capture revenues to offset the costs of such services. In local communities, this imbalance is a source of considerable tension and opposition to Mexican migration.

For Mexico, temporary emigration has represented something of a *solution* to the need for jobs in Mexico. It has provided employment, income, and a not-inconsiderable measure of foreign exchange (perhaps $1 to $1.5 billion per year). As one Mexican ex-President proclaimed: "It is not a crime to look for work, and I refuse to consider it as such."

But there have been costs for Mexico as well. One has been the absence of the some of the most energetic, audacious, and entrepreneurial members of the nation's work force; Mexicans would much prefer to have them employed in a revitalized Mexican economy. Another has been the reality of abuse and infringement upon human rights. Yet another has been the personal costs of migration: wives separated from husbands, children from fathers, for months and even years at a time. There has been, too, a collective psychological cost, a pained recognition that Mexico has not been able to provide satisfactory employment for its rising generations— and a sense of helplessness in the loss of sovereignty over citizens who cannot be well protected while in another land.

THE POLICY RECORD

Analysis of policy performance must necessarily focus on U.S. immigration measures. Neither the U.S. nor Mexico imposes restrictions on persons wishing to emigrate. Nor would we propose that they do so.

Within the U.S., changing social perceptions have exerted a strong influence on immigration policy. The succession of policy revisions over the last quarter century has clearly reflected the longstanding tendency in the United States to define Mexican migration as a problem of push factors or *supply*. Until the enactment of the Immigration Reform and Control Act in late 1986, none of the revisions in immigration policy sought to alter the *demand* for Mexican immigrant labor.

There is not much sign that any of these policies achieved their goals. Although the intent of the post-1965 revisions was to restrict the flow by changing the ground rules for legal entry, the Mexican stream has proven increasingly resilient. In large part this is because the revised admission guidelines were implemented after migratory traditions were well ensconced in the social structure of sending and receiving communities.

Diagnosis of the growing disparity between intended and unintended outcomes of policy measures must distinguish between *de jure* policies, which reflect a clear tendency toward increasingly more restrictive policies, and *de facto* policies, which involve the inconsistent enforcement of formal regulations. To prepare the foundations for our own policy recommendations, we now offer a brief assessment of policies to date.

THE SEEDS OF INCONSISTENCY

The history of intentional lenience begins with the exclusion of Mexicans from the literacy test requirement of 1917 because they were identified as a desirable labor source. It was for this same reason that they were excluded from the National Origins Acts of 1921 and 1924. Mexican workers proved to be quite valuable to make up the labor shortages encountered during World War I, and they could be easily deported when no longer needed.

After the deportations of the 1930s, *de facto* restrictions on Mexican workers and some other nationalities were eased. The *bracero* program is the best known policy initiative and, of course, the most pertinent with regard to Mexican immigration. During this same period the repeal of the Chinese Exclusion Act in 1943, the War Brides Act of 1946, and the Displaced Persons Acts of 1948 and 1950 also granted "qualified" easements in the admission of persons from non-European countries.

The McCarran-Walter Immigration Act of 1952 was significant for what it did and for what it did not do. By establishing a preference system which gave priority to prospective immigrants with special skills in short supply in the United States, it explicitly acknowledged the principle that immigration should be coordinated with labor demand in the United States. But the McCarran-Walter law did not abolish the discriminatory quota system legislated during the 1920s, despite the valiant efforts of President Harry Truman to convince the U.S. Congress otherwise.

U.S. policies also revealed internal contradictions. The most glaring inconsistency was, of course, the so-called "Texas Proviso" of 1952, which enabled growers in that state to hire undocumented field hands; in effect, the statute made it illegal to *be* an undocumented alien but not to *hire* one. More than any single aspect of U.S. immigration legislation, this provision exemplifies the main source of tension and misunderstanding between the two countries. Even in the face of anti-foreign public sentiment, the Texas Proviso implicitly acknowledged that some U.S. employers strongly desired Mexican labor.

Next came the immigration reforms of 1965. Passed in the midst of the Civil Rights movement, this legislation set the stage for dramatic changes in the size and composition of migrant streams. To abolish the discriminatory quota system, the 1965 amendments:

- provided for a more even distribution of visas between the eastern and western hemispheres;

- reordered priorities for visa preference categories, giving relatively greater explicit emphasis to family reunification over labor market considerations; and

- raised the number of visas allocated annually from 158,000 to 290,000 worldwide.

The issue of numerical limitation, and the manner in which it has been applied, is especially important for understanding the evolution of legal and illegal Mexican migration since that time. The 1965 reforms excluded several categories of people from the numerical limitations: spouses, unmarried minor children, and parents of U.S. citizens. Numerical ceilings were designated by region, with 170,000 allocated to the eastern hemisphere and 120,000 to the western hemisphere. In the original legislation a limit of 20,000 per country was imposed on the eastern hemisphere, while no specific ceiling was imposed on nations in the western hemisphere—at least not until 1976, when the 20,000 annual quota was extended to all countries. This reform had a particularly harsh impact on Mexico, which had already become the single largest source of migrants to the United States.

In effect, these measures increased the incentives for illegal Mexican migration to the U.S. As shown in Table 3-2, the volume of quota immigrants admitted from Mexico rose substantially during the 1960s and 1970s. After the extension of the 20,000 ceiling in 1976, the same table shows a subsequent and rapid increase in the number of non-quota admissions. This amendment further intensified the pressure on the Mexican visa backlog. By the late 1970s, illegal entry therefore became the main recourse for those seeking admission who were unrelated to U.S. citizens.

The efforts of the 1960s and 70s to clamp down on Mexican migration met with only limited success. For one thing, public sentiment would not permit the kind of flagrant racism that accompanied the deportation campaigns of the 1930s. Second, the 1965 amendments shifted the criteria for admission from labor certification to family reunification, and many Mexicans were able to take advantage of this opportunity. Third, the 1965 (and 1976) regulations were facing deeply embedded migratory traditions that generated their own momentum, partly independent of the economic and political forces that initiated them in the first place. Fourth, policies and practices with respect to Mexican migrants from World War I through the end of the *bracero* program led to the creation of structural demand for specifically Mexican labor in key sectors of the U.S. economy. Demand for Mexican workers continued in spite of legal restrictions.

SIMPSON-RODINO

Against this background, the Immigration Reform and Control Act of 1986 represents the culmination of a succession of attempts to implement tighter border controls. It major provisions are:

- economic sanctions against employers who knowingly hire undocumented aliens,
- permanent amnesty for undocumented workers who can prove continuous residence in the United States since any time prior to January 1, 1982, and
- partial amnesty for undocumented workers in the agricultural sector who worked for at least 90 consecutive days in the three consecutive years prior to May 1986 (SAW I) or during the year between May 1985 and May 1986 (SAW II); and a provision for the admission of "replenishment agricultural workers" (RAWs) in 1990-92.

This law is basically a response to the symptoms of an imprecisely defined problem and should not be viewed as a long-term strategy for managing the migration issue.

The ultimate success of the Simpson-Rodino legislation hinges on the prospects of the employer sanctions provisions in breaking the dependency of U.S. employers on Mexican migrant labor. With its grandfather clauses and its amnesty program, the 1986 legislation is the first to acknowledge officially that both *pull* and *push* factors have been responsible for the growth of Mexican migration.

Though its architects made strenuous efforts to satisfy a myriad of interest groups, they failed to obtain systematic input from one crucially interested party: Mexico. To be sure, they invited Mexican representatives to comment on the bill at various stages, but they also made it clear that adoption of the law would represent an act of U.S. sovereignty. Unwilling to give apparent endorsement to what they regarded as a unilateral reaction to a bilateral problem, Mexican authorities declined.

Simpson-Rodino is not likely to stem the tide of undocumented migration. The law relies to a substantial degree on voluntary compliance by employers. It is technically possible to comply with the rules—and still hire undocumented laborers. For instance, the statute obliges employers to request official papers but does not require them to verify the authenticity of documents: merely by inspecting the papers, employers can essentially satisfy their legal requirements. It is therefore possible for employees to be in violation of the law while their employers are not.

There is also not much indication that Simpson-Rodino will have a decisive impact on hiring practices. Interviews with employers offer preliminary evidence that they will continue with business as usual. Within nine months of enactment the government cited nearly 1600 employers for infractions of the law and issued fines totaling $250,000—for an average of just over $150 per firm. Plans to impose stricter fines after June 1, 1988 seem unlikely to make much practical difference. And there are limits, of course, on what the government can do: during 1988 the INS is expected to check hiring documents at only one-third of one percent of the nation's seven million employers.

Nor is the impact on migration self-evident. During 1987 U.S. officials frequently cited the reduction in the rate of Border Patrol apprehensions as evidence that Simpson-Rodino was having a major deterrent effect. We have already discussed the imperfections in the use of this indicator (redeployment of Border Patrol forces toward the interdiction of drugs instead of people could itself explain a significant part of any drop in these statistics). Taking the claims at face value, however, Figure 3-2 traces monthly levels of apprehensions along the U.S.-Mexican border from January 1981 through April 1988 (the latest available statistics as of this writing).

The data offer provocative insights. One clearly visible factor is the seasonal effect, which pushes apprehensions up in the spring, down in midsummer, slightly up in the fall and way down at year's end. Second is a slightly upward trend throughout the seven-year period, which could reflect a steady increase in the volume of migration—or the gradual strengthening of the Border Patrol throughout the 1980s. Third is the exceptionally high level of arrests

Figure 3-2. Monthly Apprehensions of Mexican Nationals along U.S.-Mexican Border, 1981-88

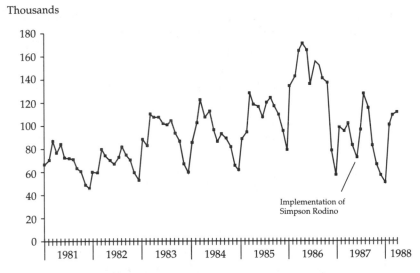

SOURCE: Data supplied by Statistical Analysis Branch, Immigration and Naturalization Service; figures show apprehensions by Border Patrol only.

in 1986, far above comparable levels for any previous year, which may indeed reflect the exacerbation of "push" factors during a time of especially acute economic crisis in Mexico.

As the figure shows, Simpson-Rodino took effect in May 1987. Anticipation and implementation of the law seem to have had a plainly deterrent effect during the spring and summer of the year, as would-be migrants struck an attitude of watchful waiting.

Apprehensions during the autumn cycle returned to their 1985 levels and soon surpassed those of previous years. In other words, potential migrants may have been watching and waiting from late 1986 to late 1987—and then they resumed their journeys north.

An alternative procedure for estimating migrant flows, developed at El Colegio de la Frontera Norte in Tijuana, makes a direct count of individuals preparing to traverse the most popular crossing point along the entire border, the Cañon Zapata. Photos taken at nightfall provide a clear analytical picture (reflected in Figure 3-3): monthly crossings for 1987 were lower than in 1986 from August through November, but in December 1987 they started to surpass the levels of a year before. The basic pattern coincides with the apprehension statistics. After potential migrants came to realize that there would not be any large-scale deportations, they began making up for lost time.

Preliminary evidence suggests that Simpson-Rodino may have exerted some change in the social composition of the migrant population. Studies by INS statisticians show that, as before, the Mexican arrivals are overwhelmingly young, male, and single. Nearly 20 percent are married, though only 6-to-7 percent have been travelling with family members. And in keeping with traditional patterns, most expect to stay in the U.S. for relatively short periods, predominantly as "sojourners."

Figure 3-3. Emigration from Mexico: Average Daily Counts in Cañon Zapata, August 1986-April 1988

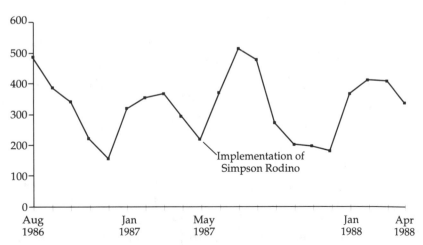

SOURCE: Jorge A. Bustamante, Proyecto Cañon Zapata, El Colegio de la Frontera Norte.

One new feature is increasing diversity in the regional origin of migrants. According to one survey in California, nearly 20 percent of the most recent arrivals came from the Mexico City metropolitan area, never a traditional sending community. This study also suggests that some of these migrants have been experiencing difficulty in finding regular, permanent jobs. Even so, they are reluctant to return to Mexico, partly out of fear that they will be unable to make it back into the United States. In a sense, they are feeling trapped in the U.S. As one expert has observed:

> To the extent that Simpson-Rodino has made the latest wave of undocumented migrants from Mexico and other countries less employable—at least in regular, long-term jobs with decent wages and some security—their lifetime loss of income-earning potential may have significant social consequences. Our interviews suggest that many of these people will become "trapped" in the U.S., accumulating debts, starting families here, or bringing dependents from Mexico. But their diminished earning prospects will limit the ability of these immigrant families to give their children the kind of education that they will need to achieve upward mobility in U.S. society. Through "immigration reform" legislation, the U.S. may finally succeed in creating the permanent underclass of illegal aliens that proponents of the 1986 law claimed it would eliminate.[7]

The second linchpin of the IRCA legislation is its legalization program. Despite good-faith efforts by the INS authorities, the final number of applicants for amnesty fell far below original expectations. The U.S. government anticipated as many as 3.9 million applications for permanent amnesty; by the May 4 deadline there had been only 1.7 million, 70 percent of them Mexican. The program was fairly successful in California and Texas, but much less effective in other regions of the country. According to the government's own figures, the program may have missed as many as two million qualified immigrants.

Like the employer sanctions, the amnesty provision contains contradictions that practically ensure its eventual failure. Many undocumented workers do not possess consistent documentation on their residence—almost as a matter of definition—and they have remained suspicious and afraid of U.S. legal authority. And for those who have qualified, the provision permits application for

7. Wayne A. Cornelius, "Impacts of the 1986 Immigration Reform and Control Act: A Second-Year Assessment," presentation to the Eighth Annual Briefing Session for Journalists (Center for U.S.-Mexican Studies, University of California, San Diego, June 1988), pp. 10-11; excerpted in the *Los Angeles Times*, July 3, 1988.

permanent resident status only after a succession of complicated steps. Temporary legal status must be followed by a second application for permanent resident status, at which time candidates must demonstrate competency in English and knowledge of U.S. laws and institutions. These are the conditions that are normally imposed only on aliens who apply for citizenship, not permanent resident status.

Moreover, there is no clear indication of what will happen to the undocumented migrants who came to the U.S. after January 1982, who have not worked in the agricultural sector, and who therefore do not qualify for any amnesty. We have no firm idea of how many there are, but estimates on recent inflows suggest that there must be at least one million Mexicans in this category. There is no reason to expect that they will simply go back home—especially in view of persisting economic difficulties in Mexico. Presumably they will be driven even further underground, subject to even greater exploitation.

We anticipate that U.S. demand for migrant labor will increase in the decade to come. According to official estimates the U.S. civilian labor force should grow from around 119 million in 1986 to 131.4 million in 1995, but the size of the male cohort age 16-24 years will actually shrink from 12.3 million to 10.6 million—an absolute decline of nearly 14 percent. And as Table 3-3 reveals, these are moderate projections; the decline for the entire age group (women included) could be as high as 3.8 million.

CONCLUSIONS AND
RECOMMENDATIONS

Let us begin with a recapitulation of some basic observations:

- migration pressures are the result of differentials in job creation levels, job openings, and wage levels from one side of the U.S.-Mexican border to the other;

- the flow of legal and undocumented migrants from Mexico to the United States responds to both push and pull factors;

- it is strongly resistant to governmental interventions;

- while the migrant workforce provides benefits to U.S. producers, there is growing evidence of the fiscal impact of the migrant workforce on social services and health care costs;

TABLE 3-3. SIZE AND GROWTH OF U.S. CIVILIAN LABOR FORCE: PROJECTIONS TO 1995 (MILLIONS)

| | 1982 | 1986 | Projections to 1995* | | |
			Low	Middle	High
Total, Age 16 and Over:	110.2	118.7	125.1	131.4	141.0
Men 16-24	13.0	12.3	10.0	10.6	11.3
Women 16-24	11.5	11.3	9.8	10.6	11.2
Total 16-24	24.5	23.6	19.8	21.1	22.5
Black and Other:					
16 and Over	14.1	15.6	17.9	19.0	21.4
Men 16-24	1.7	1.6	1.3	1.3	1.9
Women 16-24	1.5	1.6	1.5	1.5	1.8
Black and Other 16-24	3.2	3.2	2.8	2.8	3.7

*Based on differing assumptions about economic growth and employment.
SOURCE: Bureau of Labor Statistics, U.S. Department of Labor.

- Mexican policymakers would prefer to have migrant workers employed in a revitalized Mexican economy, thereby eliminating the human trauma and risks that characterize the process of illegal migration;

- massive and unregulated flows of migrants are problematic for both nations, but legal and agreed-upon levels of migration are advisable—and should be the subject of continuing bilateral discussion;

- the social and political tension that immigration sometimes creates can be ameliorated through a continuing bilateral policy dialogue.

As a general principle, we believe that the ultimate key to reasonable policies on migration lies in the achievement of solid and sustained economic growth in Mexico. Successful resolution of the problems of debt, trade, and investment—which we discuss in Chapter 2—constitutes a prerequisite for coping with the phenomenon of migration. Both countries have a profound interest in a steady increase in Mexico's capacity for productive employment. Even if a considerable portion of recent migrants entered the U.S.

as part of a social process, with longstanding communal patterns, there remains the possibility that massive flows in the future might consist largely of economic refugees in search of work. This would not be good for either country.

We do not recommend efforts to seal off the border between Mexico and the United States, which would not succeed in any case. Measures necessary to achieve this goal would probably require the militarization of the border, the adoption of national identity cards, the imposition of severe penalties on employers of undocumented workers and widespread deportation of undocumented migrants—measures not likely to be accepted by the American public.

For the United States government, the Commission recommends:

1.   Create a new application period for immigrants who might qualify for amnesty under the provisions of the current IRCA legislation;

2.   Consider the creation of a special "temporary amnesty" for those who entered the United States between January 1982 and November 1986 (when Simpson-Rodino was signed into law);

3.   Issue regular public reports on the full range of effects of the Simpson-Rodino legislation, and make these reports available to the binational interparliamentary meetings of U.S. and Mexican legislators;

4.   In keeping with national traditions, promptly and publicly endorse the forthcoming United Nations resolution on the human rights of migratory workers—and extend its provisions to all Mexican and other immigrants within the United States;

5.   Insure that public officers adhere to standards of civilized behavior toward migrants, and avoid physical or verbal abuse.

For the Mexican government, the Commission recommends:

1.   Forge a clear definition of the Mexican national interest regarding migration;

2.   Stimulate the creation of employment in the major sending areas, particularly those where outmigration is seen as contrary to the national interest;

3. **Cooperate with U.S. authorities in assuring faithful U.S. compliance with the U.N. convention on the human rights of migrant workers;**

4. **Actively collaborate with the U.S. government in the construction of a bilateral approach to immigration questions.**

For both the U.S. and Mexican governments, the Commission recommends:

1. **Work together to obtain an accurate quantitative count of the migrant population.**

Effective policy requires accurate information on the stocks and flows of migrants. The 1990 census year provides an excellent opportunity for such a joint endeavor.

2. **Undertake to reach a formal bilateral accord on migration.**

And with or without a formal accord, the two governments should adopt an explicitly bilateral approach to migration issues. The purposes of this accord should include:

*   consideration of a possible increase in the legal quotas for Mexican migration to the United States, in accordance with a clear understanding of the national interests of the two countries;

*   agreement on the flow and treatment of "seasonal agricultural workers," a group that has received special (but not fully defined) status under the IRCA legislation;

*   agreement on measures to protect the basic human and labor rights of the migrant population, including undocumented workers, and to assure reasonable working and living conditions; and, perhaps,

*   consideration of a long-run temporary worker program.

And as a basis for bilateral negotiation, it is essential that Mexico and the United States reach a common understanding of the causes and consequences of the problem. It is also essential for both governments to have a clear idea of national interests—of their own and of each other's. Any program for regulated labor migration must include satisfactory provisions for access to health and social services.

We realize that this is an imposing agenda, but we believe that a common agreement on such questions is desirable and necessary for both countries. An understanding on this issue would also remove a major obstacle to the long-term betterment of U.S.-Mexican relations.

4

The Problem of Drugs

The narcotics issue presents the United States and Mexico with a bitter paradox. On the one hand, it represents an area of the bilateral relationship where the national interests of both countries are in complete accord: both agree on the need to combat the illegal production, traffic, and use of drugs. On the other hand, the issue of narcotics control has been the source of repeated disagreements between the two countries, disagreements that not only have hindered joint efforts to combat drug abuse and traffic but also have had negative repercussions on the bilateral relationship as a whole.

The production and consumption of illicit drugs have become a major problem of the modern era. It is an international phenomenon with widespread, multiple consequences. From the perspective of the Bilateral Commission, we can identify three broad types of negative effects.

There is, first, the *social destructiveness* of drug abuse upon consumer populations. Drug abuse takes an enormous toll on individual addicts, their families and their communities. It constitutes a direct threat to personal and public health. Drug abuse takes a staggering collective toll as well: it reduces economic productivity, increases health care costs, and propagates violence and criminality. According to police reports, 39 percent of the murders in New York City in 1987 were drug related.

Local drug production often stimulates local consumption, as the rapid spread of heroin addiction in Pakistan and Thailand

113

demonstrate. The increasing abuse of marijuana and *bazuco* in Colombia provides a telling example within the Americas.[1] This pattern has not yet appeared in Mexico, although some studies suggest that drug abuse has increased in the last decade.

Second, there is the *political challenge* posed by the illicit drug traffic. From cultivation to consumption, illegal drugs tend to stimulate crime, violence, and lawlessness. The economic and paramilitary power of organized trafficking networks represents an overt challenge to legitimate authority. This has become most apparent in Colombia, where organized crime—particularly the "Medellín cartel"—has taken the entire country hostage. More than fifty judges, including a dozen Supreme Court justices, and twenty-four leading journalists have been murdered in Colombia since 1981. The Minister of Justice and Attorney General have also been assassinated. Corruption and intimidation have come to pervade the national society.

We do not want this to happen in Mexico. We note that the President of the Supreme Court of Mexico has warned that drug trafficking "threatens the very roots of the republic."[2] And we acknowledge the statement by Carlos Salinas de Gortari, who has expressed his own concerns with force:

> I am convinced that drug production or transportation is a threat to our national security. I am convinced that we must use all the power of the Mexican state to fight drug production and transportation, not only because it hurts some people in the United States, but mainly because of the harm it can do to the Mexican political and social system.[3]

We agree with that somber assessment.

Third, the persistence and volatility of the drug issue can inflict political damage on the conduct of *United States-Mexican relations*. Not only is it a difficult problem in itself; it also poisons the diplomatic atmosphere. This became clearly apparent in 1985, after the murder of U.S. Drug Enforcement Administration (DEA) agent Enrique S. Camarena. U.S. officials sharply denounced the Mexican government, launching accusations of corruption and complicity; Mexican spokesmen firmly defended their government's integrity.

---

1. *Bazuco* is a substance that is smoked and consists of cocaine base or coca paste mixed with marijuana or tobacco.
2. *Washington Post* Weekly Edition, March 14-20, 1988.
3. *New York Times*, January 18, 1988.

The spillover from this debate led to a general deterioration of the atmosphere of the relationship and made it all but impossible for the two governments to reach agreements on other pressing issues of the day.

Similar problems occurred in 1988 over the question of whether the U.S. government would "certify" the adequacy of Mexico's drug control efforts. Recently adopted U.S. legislation requires the President to certify annually whether drug-producing countries are cooperating in the curtailment of illicit drug production and traffic. Failure to receive certification results in suspension of U.S. foreign assistance, trade preferences, and support for international loans. In April 1988 the U.S. Senate voted by a 63-27 margin against the Administration's recommendation to certify Mexico's drug control efforts. Although the President declared his intention to veto the resolution, Mexican officials voiced outrage and frustration. The Mexican Attorney General expressed "profound shock and great displeasure," and noted that Mexico does not receive foreign assistance—except for a small amount of narcotics control funding.[4] Other Mexican officials asserted that Mexico simply does not accept certification or decertification of its conduct by another country. After extensive discussions between the Administration and members of Congress, the President's original certification was allowed to stand. However, the highly publicized debate about Mexico's performance in controlling narcotics once again inflicted severe damage on the bilateral relationship.

The Commission believes that certification has not proved useful in encouraging other governments to increase their narcotics control efforts; on the contrary, the certification process has become a highly publicized forum for criticizing other governments, and this can have adverse effects on cooperation. To date, the U.S. has failed to certify only a few countries, notably in cases where diplomatic relations are limited or non-existent—specifically Syria, Afghanistan, Laos, Iran, and, most recently, Panama. We urge the U.S. government to consider other means of public and private diplomacy that would achieve more effectively the goal of increased cooperation.

As members of the Bilateral Commission, we believe that both Mexico and the United States can increase the effectiveness of their

4. *Washington Post*, April 16, 1988.

respective anti-drug campaigns. And we issue a plea for closer collaboration in their efforts.

One of the most basic impediments to the creation of a long-term bilateral strategy for dealing with drugs has been the lack of a shared understanding of the problem. Without a common vision of the challenge, there can be no meaningful dialogue or basis for collaboration. We now attempt to address that concern.

UNDERSTANDING THE PROBLEM

Although worldwide drug production and traffic have grown steadily during the past two decades, there has been an especially rapid *expansion* during the 1980s. This simple fact fastens political attention upon the issue, forcing governments to question whether they have lost control over the narcotics problem. According to one responsible estimate, the economic value of the worldwide illicit drug traffic may now amount to more than $300 billion.

This expansion has been especially notable in the western hemisphere, where increasingly large quantities of heroin, marijuana and cocaine are produced. Drug cultivation extends from Bolivia and Peru to the Caribbean, Mexico, and the United States. The region also includes the world's largest drug consumer market, the United States, where gross income from the traffic ranges from $70 to $110 billion a year.

A second basic characteristic of the drug traffic is the structural relationship between *supply* and *demand*. Without demand there would be no supply: they are interrelated aspects of a single market. Self-evident as it seems, this observation leads to an important corollary: producer and consumer countries must share responsibility for dealing with the challenge of illicit drugs. As long as efforts to choke off the drug supply at its source are unaccompanied by simultaneous efforts to attack the factors contributing to drug demand, there will always be an overriding economic incentive to keep producing drugs somewhere in the world, and to transport and distribute those drugs to the consumers.

The global drug traffic possesses remarkable *adaptability*. Short-term fluctuations in production levels and variations in the relative contributions of different supply sources are absorbed without noticeable effect at the retail level as illicit drug networks develop new production methods and transportation routes. One source of supply can be quickly replaced by another. This ability to adapt and innovate is attributable in part to the immense resources commanded by drug traffickers, allowing them to adjust to changes in anti-drug policies.

Mexico is currently the single largest supplier of heroin and marijuana to the U.S. as well as a major transit point for cocaine produced in South America. If Mexican supplies were eliminated, the traffickers would soon develop other sources of supply, although costs might be higher because of increased transportation difficulties.

As producer and consumer countries, Mexico and the U.S. have *different problems* with regard to drugs: solution of the Mexican problem would not solve the American problem. From the U.S. perspective, drug abuse presents a pervasive problem of serious social dimensions and anti-drug campaigns display deep moral concerns. From the Mexican perspective, the drug trade has differential effects: in the short run it leads to an increase in the standard of living for peasants in the cultivation zones; in the long run it presents a challenge to political authority. In a way, the U.S. problem results from prosperity; the Mexican problem results from scarcity. This asymmetry can lead to serious difficulty in the negotiation of a joint strategy for dealing with the challenge posed by drugs.

Finally, the international drug trade bears a curiously *ambivalent relationship to legal authority*. It is the very illegality of the trade, of course, which imposes risk on participants and thus pushes up prices and profits. It is the ability to circumvent interdiction and apprehension, often through bribery of key officials, that permits the trade to continue.

Ambivalence toward drug consumption within the U.S. has contributed to an atmosphere in which occasional, recreational drug use is viewed with social tolerance more often than condemnation. This relative tolerance reinforces the strength of the U.S. market for illicit drugs.

Eradication campaigns in Mexico and other producer countries, when they are successful, have the effect in the U.S. of increasing street-level drug prices and decreasing drug purity. To the extent that drug demand is partially elastic, particularly with regard to new users, increased prices can reduce the number of users and encourage habitual users to seek treatment. Reduction in availability of drugs can provide a window of opportunity for reducing consumption until new supplies appear from other sources.

Taken together, these characteristics of the worldwide illicit drug market emphasize the enormous complexity of the problem and the obstacles to effective policy. Moreover, we anticipate that the problem is likely to get worse before it gets better. The drug traffic has expanded on every front, on both sides of the U.S.-Mexican border, in quantitative terms (levels of demand, supply, and economic worth) as well as qualitative ones (widening and deepening of the negative effects of drug production and consumption on social, cultural, economic, and political structures). This problem will be with us for years: now is the time to address it.

PATTERNS OF CONSUMPTION

Although illicit drug use in the United States and Mexico has been growing steadily since the 1960s, there are wide differences in the dimensions of its effects. While there are hundreds of thousands of regular drug users in Mexico, there are many millions in the United States. The consequence of this uneven distribution of demand is that the bulk of Mexican illicit drug production is sold to the U.S. market. Mexico's geographic proximity to the United States also makes it a key trafficking route for drugs produced in South America.

Analysis of consumption patterns in the two countries must begin with a careful distinction among the types of drugs involved. All drugs are not the same.[5] For this discussion, we differentiate among four types:

1. *marijuana:* dried leaves and flowering tops of the pistillate hemp plant that, when smoked, provide sensations of intoxication and pleasure; variants include cannabis and hashish.

2. *heroin:* a strongly addictive narcotic derived from the opium poppy, made by acetylation but much more potent than morphine; typically administered through intravenous injection.

3. *cocaine:* a crystalline alkaloid obtained from coca leaves that tends to induce sensations of stimulation and euphoria; ingested through a variety of means, including inhalation (or "snorting") and smoking.

---

5. Technically, only some drugs are "narcotics" — which induce *narcosis* (sleep, stupor); many drugs are stimulants.

4. *"dangerous drugs"*: broad categories of abusable substances, licit and illicit, which include both synthetic and naturally occurring drugs (or psychoactive substances), such as: stimulants other than cocaine, narcotics/analgesics other than opiates, psychomimetics/hallucinogens other than cannabis, depressants/sedatives other than alcohol. Examples: methamphetamine, phenyclidine (PCP), lysergic acid diethylamide (LSD or "acid"), psilocybin, methaqualone (quaalude).

Despite its role in production and traffic, Mexico does not have a major drug abuse problem. Consumption was minimal and limited until the 1960s; it spread throughout the 1970s and 80s to broad sectors of the population and juvenile drug addiction increased. Mexico is suffering more and more from the public health and social rehabilitation problems associated with expanding drug use. Areas with the highest incidence of drug addiction have become those states (Sinaloa, Jalisco, and the border states) most directly involved in the production of drugs for the North American market. Nonetheless, hard drugs such as heroin and cocaine play a relatively unimportant part in the Mexican market; consumption tends to focus on marijuana. Since the Mexican market is so modest and small, it has not in itself fostered the rise of large-scale criminal organizations.

In contrast to Mexico, illicit drug use in the United States has reached enormous proportions. Addiction to psychoactive drugs first developed as a social problem in the United States in the middle of the nineteenth century. Most of the estimated 250,000 addicts at that time were women. There were few regulations and no required labelling of drug ingredients. The turn of the century brought changes in public attitudes and new legislation. The Pure Food and Drug Act of 1906 required that manufacturers list ingredients on labels. The Harrison Narcotic Act of 1914, originally intended as a revenue measure, required that anyone producing or distributing opiates or cocaine register with the federal government; through legal interpretation, this statute came to prohibit the supply of narcotics to addicts. By 1924, the manufacture and importation of heroin was prohibited in the United States. A 1922 amendment to the Narcotics Drugs Import and Export Act also prohibited most importation of cocaine and coca leaves. U.S. laws thus drove the use of heroin and cocaine underground.

Events of the 1960s brought decisive changes in dimensions of the drug abuse problem in the United States. Drug use played a central role as American youth rejected middle-class values. Marijuana became a symbol for the counter-culture. As the revolution in drug use continued into the 1970s, experimentation with illicit drugs became a rite of passage for the nation's youth. Social tolerance was also high: respected authorities proclaimed that some drugs were relatively harmless, and popular singing groups like the Beatles extolled the pleasures of hallucinogenic experience (the hit song "Lucy in the Sky with Diamonds" was, for instance, a celebration of the benefits of LSD).

Statistical data on illicit activity are notoriously unreliable, but the application of epidemiologic techniques over the past fifteen years has made it possible to establish baseline trends and hazard responsible estimates.

By 1985, more than one-third of all teenage and adult Americans had tried an illicit drug at least once in their lives. Among young adults, 18-25 years of age, the proportion was closer to two-thirds. According to the National Household Survey, 62 million Americans reported having tried marijuana. Nearly one in ten (18.2 million) had used marijuana within the month before the survey, compared to six in ten who had used alcohol, and three in ten who had smoked cigarettes.

As shown in Table 4-1, cocaine is the most frequently used illicit drug after marijuana, with 5.8 million current users in 1985. It is estimated that the national intake of cocaine increased from 31.0 metric tons in 1982 to 72.3 metric tons in 1985. In the last three years, a smokeable form of cocaine called "crack" has gained wide popularity. Crack is potent, available, and relatively inexpensive. By late 1987, the use of crack had reached epidemic proportions in some cities, particularly among the poor, and it had spread to 46 out of 50 states.

Heroin use prevalence rates are too low to be reliably captured by sample-survey techniques. The most commonly accepted estimate, drawn from a 1981 study, is that there are about 500,000 heroin addicts in the United States, primarily in large cities. It appears that this has been a relatively stable population for the past decade. One of the most alarming drug related problems of the 1980s is the rapid spread of the Acquired Immune Deficiency Syndrome, AIDS. Intravenous drug users, particularly heroin addicts, are

TABLE 4-1. PREVALENCE OF DRUG USE IN
THE UNITED STATES, 1985

	Ever Used		Used in Past Month	
	%	Population Estimate[a]	%	Population Estimate[a]
Marijuana	33	61.9	10	18.2
Cocaine	12	22.2	3	5.8
Stimulants[b]	9	17.6	1	2.7
Tranquilizers[b]	8	14.8	1	2.2
Alcohol	86	164.4	59	113.1

a. Millions (among population 12 years of age and older).
b. Non-medical use.

SOURCE: National Institute on Drug Abuse, 1985 National Household Survey on Drug Abuse.

severely affected: in 1986, 25 percent of all AIDS cases in the U.S. involved intravenous drug users, who transmit the virus through the sharing of needles and syringes.

While no national epidemiologic studies of drug abuse were conducted in the 1960s, some indication of the magnitude of the increase in illicit drug use during the past two decades comes from retrospective data collected by the National Survey on Drug Abuse. For young adults aged 18-25, the survey estimated that, in 1962, only 4 percent had tried marijuana. Five years later, 13 percent had done so. By 1979, this figure had jumped to 68 percent. What began as a symbol of the counter-culture became the norm for American society.

Illicit drug use reached its zenith ten years ago. From 1979, the peak year for marijuana use among 18-25 year olds, the percentage of those who had tried marijuana decreased from 68 percent to 61 percent in 1985. A similar decrease has been observed for high school seniors. In 1975, the first year in which the survey was conducted, 55 percent of the seniors reported experience with marijuana. By 1979 this proportion had increased to 65 percent; by 1987 it had declined to 57 percent. Cocaine use among high school seniors also dropped from 12.7 percent in 1986 to 10.3 percent in 1987, the first drop in seven years and an indication that cocaine's popularity may have peaked within some social circles.

One of the most remarkable features of U.S. consumption is that it is so widespread. Except in the case of heroin, the user populations do not constitute readily identifiable subgroups of American society. There are relatively small differentials between the consumption patterns of males and females. There is a remarkable degree of geographic dispersion, especially in view of the common idea that illicit drug consumption is a big-city or ghetto problem. High School Senior Survey data show that current marijuana use among graduating seniors was around 27 percent in large urban areas but over 21 percent in small cities and rural zones; there was a larger variation with regard to cocaine, 9.5 percent compared to 4.3 percent. There was also noticeably less consumption in the South in comparison to other regions, but the basic point still stands: drug use is pervasive in the United States.

There may also be 2.5 million or more regular users of "dangerous drugs." The popularity of these drugs appears to have declined sharply since the 1960s, when the use of LSD reached its peak among middle-class youth. Many of the current-day consumers take other drugs as well, so it is hard to obtain a solid estimate of the total population of habitual consumers of all illicit drugs in the U.S. A responsible guess would be around 25 million people.

As a result, the United States accounts for the largest and most dynamic single market for illicit drugs in the world. U.S. consumption dominates the international trade in cocaine and marijuana, and holds a more or less equal position with Europe in the heroin trade. (Large amounts of heroin are also consumed within some producer countries, especially in Asia.) The U.S. market thus has a major impact on international flows of illicit drugs.

STRUCTURES OF PRODUCTION

Much of the tension in the bilateral relationship derives from the fact that Mexico has become the single most important source of drugs for the U.S. market. By 1986, Mexico was estimated to produce about 30 percent of the marijuana consumed in the United States and about 40 percent of the heroin. Although not itself a coca producer, Mexico serves as a transit point for approximately one-third the cocaine entering the U.S.

This situation has prompted frequent cries of outrage in the U.S., where politicians have tended to place the blame for the country's drug abuse problems on Mexico. Declarations in Washington and on campaign trails have alleged Mexican complicity in the drug trade and official corruption. But this has proved to be more than just a political spectacle: it has also been a guiding principle of U.S. policy, which has focused more on the eradication of supply than on the reduction of demand. This emphasis has further increased tensions in the bilateral relationship.

We attempt here to place the problem in proper perspective. As with all data regarding illicit activities, information is imprecise. We nonetheless hope to establish some elementary patterns and trends.

In this regard we note, first, the remarkably efficient substitutions in sources of worldwide supply. Sites for the cultivation and production of illicit drugs have shifted during the postwar period: after one source shuts down, another appears to replace it. What remains constant is the presence of demand.

Moreover, we observe that Mexico's emergence as a major producer results from a combination of structural elements: these include (1) the magnitude of demand in the United States, (2) the poverty of rural *campesinos* in some areas of Mexico (such as the states of Sinaloa and Jalisco), (3) the economic capabilities of the traffickers, and (4) geographic proximity to the consumer market.

Let us begin with marijuana. Cannabis cultivation in Mexico originated in the nineteenth century, when it was first seen as a socially useful substance with medical applications. But by 1923, the Mexican government, aware of its intoxicant properties, prohibited marijuana cultivation, and in 1927 banned its exportation. Small-scale shipments to the U.S. nonetheless continued through the 1950s, but caused little friction, despite prohibitions in the U.S., perhaps because its use was associated with the Mexican-origin population.

The 1960s changed all that. In 1969 the Nixon Administration launched "Operation Intercept," a three-week effort to search every person crossing the U.S.-Mexican border. Its most positive outcome was a joint effort known as "Operation Cooperation." In 1975 Mexico substantially increased its own interdiction efforts and reinforced its eradication campaigns. As a result, Mexico's supply declined from more than 90 percent of the U.S. marijuana market in 1975 to less than 10 percent in 1980 and only 4 percent in 1981. This did not, however, lead to a permanent decrease in U.S. supplies of marijuana. Jamaica and Colombia stepped up production to fill the vacuum. Illicit U.S. production also increased substantially, supplying 15 percent of the market by 1982.

Since 1985, according to U.S. government sources, Mexico has regained a prominent position in the production of marijuana for the U.S. market. As Figure 4-1 reveals, Mexico supplied about 32 percent of the marijuana consumed in the U.S. in 1985 and 30 percent in 1986.

Figure 4-1.   Mexican Marijuana as Share of Total
U.S. Market, 1976-86

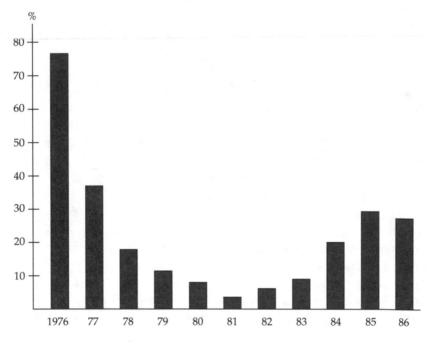

SOURCE: National Narcotics Intelligence Consumers Committee (NNICC).

With regard to heroin, Mexico began the cultivation of opium poppies in the early 1920s in the states of Sonora, Sinaloa, Durango, and Chihuahua. In 1925 the Mexican government banned its production and adopted strict legal sanctions against sellers and users. A presidential decree prohibited its exportation in 1927. In 1929 a revised penal code levied harsh penalties against growers, producers, and traffickers. Since that time, with the brief exception of a three-month period in 1940, these activities have been prohibited by law in Mexico.

In the United States, the smoking of opium (in the infamous "opium dens" of San Francisco and other cities) at the turn of the century had by the 1920s given way to heroin abuse. Imports came primarily from Italy, France, Asia, and the Middle East; the international traffic was controlled by several Mafia organizations in New York City. The Mexican supply of heroin during this period amounted to less than 15 percent of the U.S. market, a figure that increased when the outbreak of armed hostilities dried up European and Asian sources during World War II. The U.S. government then encouraged opium production in Mexico in order to assure supplies of morphine. After the war, *la Cosa Nostra* regained the control of heroin from Italian sources. When the Italian government prohibited the manufacture of heroin in 1952, the Mafia promptly replaced this supply with Turkish morphine, which was refined into heroin in Marseilles, France, and shipped to the U.S.

In the early 1970s, international collaboration led to the rupture of this "French connection." It was at this time that Mexico began to fill the gap. The supply of heroin from Mexico increased from 10-15 percent of the total U.S. supply in 1972 to 87 percent by 1975. Within three years, Mexico had replaced the Turkish-French heroin connection.

Eradication campaigns within Mexico and competition from other sources led to subsequent reductions in the Mexican share of the U.S. market. From 1982-85, the single largest source has been Southwest Asia (Afghanistan, Pakistan, Iran), which has supplied around 40 percent of the market. As Figure 4-2 reveals, Mexico now provides a nearly similar proportion. The remainder comes from the "golden triangle" in Southeast Asia (Burma, Thailand, Laos).

Although Mexico does not produce cocaine, it has recently become an important transit point for cocaine going to the U.S. from South America. Peru and Bolivia have continued to be the major cultivators of coca while Colombia, now also a significant coca cultivator, still dominates refining. It has been estimated that fully three-quarters of the cocaine reaching the U.S. comes from Colombia, and the movement of cocaine from there through Florida remains the primary smuggling route. But Colombian drug traffickers have moved into Mexico as well, and one-third of the cocaine consumed in the U.S. passes through Mexican territory.

Figure 4-2.   Mexican Heroin as Share of Total
U.S. Market, 1976-86

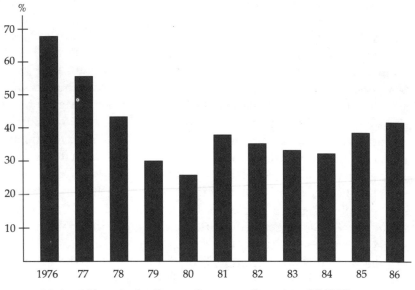

SOURCE: National Narcotics Intelligence Consumers Committee (NNICC).

TRAFFICKING AND TRANSPORTATION

The trafficking of illicit drugs is controlled by powerful criminal organizations. These are international networks that extend from production sites to retail markets. They command immense economic resources—usually in U.S. dollars, often in cash—and they have developed paramilitary capabilities. Through intimidation, violence, and corruption, they have been able to impose their will throughout the world; they have bought and bribed law-enforcement officials wherever necessary. Perhaps the most notorious of these groups is the "Medellín cartel" of Colombia.

Within the United States, the illicit drug traffic represents a major component of organized crime. According to the recent estimate of a presidential commission, the economic value of the narcotics trade in the U.S. could be as high as $110 billion per year. It is the principal source of income for organized crime, and represents nearly 40 percent of its overall economic activity.

Given such high stakes, the drug cartels use sophisticated forms of transport for gathering their cargo into the U.S. They have built vast fleets of boats and airplanes designed to evade detection. Although there are no solid data on transportation methods, seizure statistics provide some idea of commonly used methods. The vast majority of marijuana seizures (over 80 percent in 1985 and 1986) were in non-commercial vessels, mostly ships on the high seas. Cocaine seizures occurred in a variety of settings, especially general aviation aircraft and non-commercial boats. Most heroin seizures took place on commercial vessels; the largest busts were at commercial airports.

These patterns not only illustrate the inventiveness and sophistication of the drug cartels. They also make another point: very little transportation takes place by land. In other words, *undocumented migrants from Mexico have not been a major means of bringing illicit drugs into the U.S.* To be sure, some heroin has been found in the possession of individual migrants. There have also been some seizures of marijuana, which is much more bulky than heroin, on trucks that have attempted to cross the border at night. Hardly any cocaine has been found this way. A frequently repeated assertion by U.S. officials flies in the face of these seizure statistics: individual migrants are *not* significant carriers of illicit drugs. The issues of migration and narcotics should therefore be kept entirely separate for both analytical and policy reasons.

There is a long and complicated chain from cultivation to consumption, but the different links do not share equally in profitability. The costs associated with the initial stages of drug production—cultivation, refining, and transport to exit ports—account for only 8 percent of the final cost of drugs in retail markets. Data on drug prices suggest that the most profitable activities take place at the retail end of the chain. For every dollar spent on marijuana or heroin in the U.S., the drug farmer earns between seven and nine cents; cocaine producers earn even less—only one to three cents of every dollar spent by users.

The implication of these facts is clear: policies should focus on all points of this interrelated chain, not just on the supply side of the equation. Breaking a cartel in Medellín or Guadalajara alone cannot disrupt the entire network. There must be collaboration and cooperation between law-enforcement efforts in *both producer and consumer countries.*

Drug trafficking cartels have amassed huge amounts of money which have extraordinary impact in the debt-ridden economies of the 1980s. Consider the case of marijuana, which was selling at a wholesale price of $300 to $600 per pound in 1985. Mexico's production that year came to 3000-4000 metric tons, which translates into a potential wholesale market value ranging from $2.3 billion to $4.6 billion.

Contemplate even the minimum figure of $2.3 billion. This represents about one-quarter of Mexico's annual debt-service payments. It is equivalent to at least one-tenth of total gross exports. It amounts to nearly 1.4 percent of the Gross National Product. Although the Mexican cartels do not possess as much infrastructure as the Colombian rings, this kind of economic resource gives them enormous power nonetheless.

Drug revenues are liquid, mostly U.S. dollars, concentrated in the hands of a relatively small number of traffickers. In countries suffering from soaring inflation, drugs become hard currency which buys an enormous amount of political and economic leverage.

A final step in the drug traffic is the banking and laundering of money. Throughout the 1980s, banks in the Caribbean and Central America were the primary recipients of money from Latin American cocaine, marijuana, and heroin trafficking. Until 1988, Panama was the financial center most frequently used by Latin American drug traffickers. Panama's appeal was attributed to its central location, its banking and commercial secrecy laws, its political and economic stability, its use of the U.S. dollar as currency, and cultural ties with the Latin community. Recent revelations about Panamanian strongman General Manuel Noriega's role in drug trafficking and consequent political instability will probably induce the drug traffickers to search for other havens. They will have a variety of other choices. Banks in the Bahamas, the Netherlands Antilles, and the Cayman Islands have continued to provide ready repositories for *narcodólares*. Mexico, let us observe, has played a negligible role in the banking and laundering of money.

THE POLICY RECORD

Countries which have been affected by problems of illicit drug production and consumption have generally adopted policies designed to reduce both the supply and demand for illicit drugs. Supply control efforts include enforcement of laws prohibiting or restricting the availability and sale of drugs and programs to eradicate illicit drug production. The assumption behind these efforts is that reduced supply will result in reduced consumption. Disruption of illicit drug production and trafficking networks will drive up drug prices, thus reducing both the amount of consumption among current users and the numbers of new users who might otherwise try lower priced drugs.

Demand control efforts are designed to reduce drug consumption through prevention, education, and treatment programs. By working to prevent people from using drugs and to cure those who do, such strategies will presumably reduce demand for illicit drugs. The assumption is that this will lower and eventually eliminate profits from the market.

The relative emphasis which countries place on supply and demand reduction efforts vary greatly, with the result that their policies have quite different impacts both domestically and internationally. In this section we review briefly the European experience in responding to drug abuse, particularly the policies of Sweden, Great Britain, and the Netherlands. We also examine the response of the U.S. and Mexico during the past two decades and the impact these national policies have had on bilateral relations between the two countries.

THE EUROPEAN EXPERIENCE

Sweden has adopted a highly restrictive drug policy, intended to create a society free from drugs. This policy depends for its success on widespread support from the public as well as strict enforcement of very severe laws prohibiting all forms of drug possession. Sweden also provides extensive prevention and treatment resources, with particular concern for the spread of the AIDS virus among intravenous drug users. Earlier experiments in the late 1960s to give legal prescriptions of amphetamine to addicts failed. The government found that instead of reducing the spread of amphetamine addiction, a major problem at that time, new groups were drawn in because of illegal sales of prescriptions at very low prices.

Great Britain's drug control policies are similar to those of Sweden in that both countries place strong emphasis on law enforcement as well as on prevention, education, and treatment. The primary drug problem in Great Britain is heroin addiction, with some recent increase in cocaine and amphetamine abuse. Historically, the British viewed addiction more as a medical than a law enforcement problem; however, that view has changed in recent years as drug abuse became widespread. In the two decades following World War II, British doctors were permitted to prescribe heroin to addicts, a policy designed to reduce the negative consequences of addiction. Nonetheless, heroin addiction increased rapidly in the 1960s as unscrupulous doctors sold prescriptions and a black market in heroin developed. By the early 1970s, the government decided that heroin should be prescribed and dispensed only at drug clinics, where the majority of addicts were placed on methadone maintenance programs which substitutes methadone for heroin. Today, only 140 addicts are given heroin legally, while more than 7000 are given methadone.

The policies of the Netherlands have differed strikingly from those of other European countries. The government believes that drug abuse is primarily a health and social welfare problem, rather than a law enforcement matter. Treatment and prevention programs take precedence over enforcement, although severe penalties are applied to major drug traffickers. Heroin is not legally available, and methadone is widely prescribed for heroin addicts. Marijuana use is openly tolerated, although it is not legally sold. A brief experiment in selling marijuana at local youth centers ended after extensive protests from other countries in Europe, whose drug policies were not as liberal.

The trend in European countries is moving towards stricter drug laws and greater emphasis on law enforcement efforts to control the supply of illicit drugs. Consumption of heroin and especially cocaine has nonetheless increased in many European countries during recent years, as drug traffickers seek new markets to absorb the expanding worldwide production of illicit drugs. Even so, the level of drug abuse in European countries remains substantially lower than in the U.S. This difference may reflect the impact of cultural traditions and social values. The relatively low level of drug consumption (in comparison to the U.S.) may also reflect the long-term impact of the greater emphasis European countries have historically placed on drug abuse prevention, treatment and education programs compared to the U.S. focus on law enforcement efforts.

THE UNITED STATES EXPERIENCE

Supply control efforts have been particularly important in U.S. drug policies, reflecting the strong prohibitionist emphasis which has dominated U.S.control efforts since the passage of the Harrison Narcotic Act in 1914. Too little attention has been paid to reducing demand. Because the drugs of greatest concern to Americans—heroin, marijuana, and cocaine—have traditionally come from other countries, international control efforts have been a key factor in U.S. policies to reduce the supply of illicit drugs.

One of the earliest and most successful efforts to achieve international cooperation to reduce the supply of heroin coming into the U.S. was the Turkish program twenty years ago. Opium had long been an important agricultural crop in Turkey, which in addition to providing cooking oil, fuel, and seeds, was exported for the legitimate manufacture of codeine and morphine. However, as worldwide demand for heroin increased in the 1960s, heroin traffickers began buying Turkish opium for heroin refineries in France and Sicily.

Public reaction to this "Turkish-French connection" supplying heroin to the U.S. was negative and powerful. As a result, the Turkish government banned opium production. With United Nations and U.S. assistance, alternative means of livelihood were found for many of the opium growers. However, the political pressure within Turkey against the ban was too great, and in 1974 the government reinstated limited opium production in strictly controlled areas that are monitored by the U.N. Today, Turkey and India are the only licensed suppliers of opiates for U.S. pharmaceutical needs.

International efforts to control supplies at their source have continued to be a key factor in U.S. drug policy, and achieved notable success with Turkey as well as Mexico in the 1970s. During the past seven years, however, despite the public importance placed on international policies, the U.S. has in fact provided them little support. The reality has fallen far short of the rhetoric.

Although worldwide illicit drug production expanded rapidly from 1981 to 1986, the United States provided only $43 million a year on average to its international supply-control program. In the meantime the U.S. more than doubled the amount spent on drug law enforcement, from $700 million in 1981 to $1.75 billion in 1986.

This strong emphasis on law enforcement came at the expense not only of international efforts but also drug abuse prevention and education programs, which received an average of $23 million a year during the same period. In current dollar terms, total funding for demand reduction programs—prevention, education, and treatment—declined from $259 million in 1981 to only $200 million in 1986; in constant dollar terms, this amounted to a drop of 40 percent.

By 1986, the U.S. government recognized the failure of its massive emphasis on supply control efforts. The President admitted in a major speech that "all the confiscation and law enforcement in the world will not cure this plague." Widespread concern over the failure of American drug policy led the U.S. Congress to adopt a comprehensive Anti-Drug Abuse Act in October 1986, which provided more than $1.7 billion in new funds for international programs, demand reduction efforts, and law enforcement. This additional funding brought the total drug budget to over $3 billion.

The President publicly praised the new legislation and declared a "national crusade" against drugs. Two months after the congressional elections of November 1986, in which drug abuse had been a major campaign issue, the Administration quietly tried to cut 60 percent from drug prevention and education funds and to eliminate any new money for drug treatment programs. Overriding the President's action, Congress restored the funds in 1987. Several new bills appeared in both the House and the Senate by mid-1988.

There is now growing recognition in the U.S. that reducing the demand for drugs is critically important if drug abuse is to be successfully attacked. Concern about the spread of the AIDS virus has further increased public support for demand reduction programs. Because so little support has been given to demand reduction efforts since 1981, however, it will take considerable time to develop effective programs nationwide.

THE MEXICAN EXPERIENCE

Mexico has taken a firm stand against international drug trafficking since 1912 when it signed the International Opium Convention. Drug abuse has not become widespread in Mexico, though it has increased in recent years, and production did not become a major problem until the 1960s. By 1975, as we have shown, Mexico had replaced Turkey as the primary supplier of heroin to the U.S.

Responding to U.S. pressure and to national concern about the implications of expanding drug cultivation and traffic during the mid-1970s, the Mexican government with assistance from the U.S. undertook a sophisticated eradication campaign, using the most modern technology available. The impact on illicit cultivation was dramatic. By 1980, Mexican heroin comprised only 25 percent of the U.S. market, compared to 87 percent five years earlier. Mexican marijuana supplies to the U.S. also dropped, from 90 percent in earlier years to less than 10 percent in 1980.

During the 1975-1982 period, the U.S. provided $100 million in assistance to the Mexican effort. However, Mexican financial support was three to four times that amount, as well as uncounted human resources. This high level of Mexican support has continued, although illicit cultivation has nonetheless increased since 1985. The Attorney General's office, responsible for directing the campaign, now spends half its annual $36 million budget on drug control efforts. More than one quarter of Mexico's 100,000 Army soldiers are periodically deployed to conduct special missions to detect and destroy illicit cultivation.

The campaign against illicit cultivation has become more difficult as the growers have become more sophisticated in concealing their crops. New strains of poppy flowers in shades of pink, green, and brown have been developed to make them less visible to reconnaissance flights. The level of violence has also increased, costing the lives of many officials working in the campaign.

Although the Mexican Attorney General's office has increased the numbers of fields eradicated in the past three years, U.S. officials estimate that the Mexican eradication campaign is destroying no more than 40 percent of the total cultivation. Mexican officials do not agree with U.S. figures, arguing that they are intended to place blame on Mexico for U.S. drug abuse problems. This difficulty in deriving estimates that satisfy both governments further complicates the process of developing an effective bilateral program.

IMPACTS ON U.S-MEXICAN RELATIONS

Although Mexico and the U.S. have shared common concerns about illicit drug trafficking since the 1920s, the issue has had substantial impact on the bilateral relation during the past twenty years. In 1969 President Nixon declared an all-out war on drugs.

As a first step in this war, Operation Intercept effectively closed the U.S.-Mexican border. For three weeks, every person in transit was subjected to an intensive search for drugs, causing massive economic disruption on both sides. Although Operation Intercept was not continued, it called attention to U.S. concern about the increasing flow of marijuana and heroin across the border.

During the 1970s, U.S.-Mexican narcotics control cooperation increased, and the Mexican government undertook an extensive aerial eradication campaign against illicit drug cultivation. The success of the Mexican program was recognized worldwide—and especially in the United States, the primary beneficiary of the campaign. During the late 1970s, the close cooperation on narcotics control was often the bright spot in otherwise troubled U.S-Mexican relations.

By 1979, however, a new source of friction had emerged: certain groups in the U.S., including the media, objected to the Mexican government's use of paraquat to eradicate marijuana. Concern grew within the U.S. that young people who smoked marijuana exposed to paraquat spraying might suffer harmful effects. The Mexican government reacted angrily to criticism of its use of paraquat, pointing out that American concern for the health of illegal drug users seemed misplaced. The Mexican government was also angry that its successful efforts to eradicate opium cultivation were overshadowed by the paraquat protests. In late 1979, the U.S. Congress prohibited the use of U.S. funds for eradication programs using paraquat. The Mexican government turned to its own resources to support the marijuana eradication campaign, and continued using paraquat.

Despite the frictions that arose over paraquat, U.S.-Mexican cooperation on narcotics control remained positive and enhanced the strength of the bilateral relationship. As noted earlier, however, the torture and murder of DEA agent Camarena in Mexico in 1985 by people alleged to have been connected with the Mexican police set off a national furor in the U.S. Charges of Mexican government corruption at the highest levels were made publicly by U.S. officials. Relations have deteriorated further since the January 1988 indictments in San Diego, California, charging three high-ranking Mexican Army officers with drug trafficking, and since the April 1988 Senate vote on decertification.

Narcotics control concerns have on occasion severely strained U.S.-Mexican relations, particularly in the past several years. The American public now believes that drug trafficking is the single most important international problem, more serious even than arms control. Widespread frustration over the failure of U.S. drug policies has increased political pressure to develop immediate, highly visible responses, including "decertification" of foreign governments. Mexico has recently re-emerged as the single largest foreign supplier of heroin and marijuana to the U.S., after a decade of reduced production, as well as a major transit point for cocaine. This development has intensified controversy between the two countries.

CONCLUSIONS AND RECOMMENDATIONS

As members of the Bilateral Commission, we believe that there are fundamental premises that both the U.S. and Mexico can agree to support in shaping joint consideration of the problems of narcotics control.

First, both governments have a *mutual interest* in reducing illicit drug production and traffic. This mutual interest derives from shared commitments as signatories of the Single Convention on Narcotic Drugs and other international drug control treaties. It also derives from similar national concerns: both governments want to protect their citizens from the dangers of drug abuse and from the corruptive power of the drug traffickers.

Second, we believe that both governments share *joint responsibility* for responding to the narcotics problem, since it affects not only the domestic welfare of each country but also their relationship with each other. Together, the U.S. and Mexico must forge a strategy that effectively confronts their respective problems of demand and supply as well as recognizes the complex international nature of the illicit narcotics traffic.

Third, we urge adherence to principles of *proportionality* and *reciprocity* in anti-drug policies. The United States and Mexico should contribute to these bilateral efforts in proportion to their relative resources; and they should apply the same sorts of measures in both countries.

In view of our belief that the two governments have mutual interests and joint responsibility for combatting narcotics, we have developed a number of recommendations for individual government actions as well as for bilateral efforts.

For the U.S. government, the Commission recommends:

1. Recognize that demand for drugs within the U.S. is the driving force for illicit drug production and traffic in Mexico.

The U.S. has the highest rate of drug abuse of any industrialized nation. The demand for illicit drugs in the U.S., and increasingly in Europe and some Asian countries, has greatly stimulated worldwide illicit drug production in recent years. The geographic proximity of Mexico to the U.S. market has made it particularly vulnerable to the expansion of criminal networks which support illicit drug cultivation and trafficking. Since Mexico does not itself have a significant drug abuse problem, illicit Mexican drug production would greatly diminish without American demand.

2. Forge a long-term, balanced strategy with adequate funding for drug abuse education, prevention, and treatment, as well as a vigorous law enforcement and international program.

The primary emphasis of U.S. policy since 1981 has been on reducing the supply of drugs through law enforcement efforts. For most of this period very little support has been given to demand reduction programs, which have received only one-fifth as much funding as supply control programs. Recognizing the failure of this over-emphasis on law enforcement, the U.S. Congress in 1986 adopted a new Anti-Drug Abuse Act which more than tripled funding for demand reduction activities from previous levels to a total of $710 million.

However, the Commission believes that even these new funding levels will prove inadequate to carry out a successful campaign to reduce U.S. consumption of illicit drugs. Because of the lack of funding in earlier years, there have been severe limitations on research into the most effective approaches to drug abuse prevention, education, and treatment. The Commission urges the U.S. to give top priority to learning how to reduce demand and to allocate sufficient resources to move forward rapidly in attacking this critical problem.

A balanced strategy must also include a vigorous international effort, in which drug control concerns are given high diplomatic priority. If the U.S. government views international narcotics trafficking as a major national security issue—a view now expressed by high-level Administration officials—this issue must be given priority over other concerns. It cannot be subordinated or ignored, as the U.S. government appears to have done in recent years in its relations with the governments of Panama and Honduras. Such obviously selective application of its international narcotics control policy undermines U.S. credibility with other countries and with the multilateral institutions pledged to combat drug abuse.

We do *not* think the answer lies in the use of the U.S. military for interdictions and arrests, either within the United States or abroad. In particular, such a policy would wreak havoc along the U.S.-Mexican border.

3. Eradicate illicit drug production within the U.S.

Illicit marijuana cultivation in the U.S. has expanded rapidly in the past fifteen years. By 1980, marijuana had become the largest cash crop in California, Hawaii, and Oregon; by 1985 it ranked nationwide as the second largest cash crop after corn. Eradication programs using aerial herbicide spraying, similar to the Mexican eradication program, have had limited success. Local communities have forcefully resisted the spraying of herbicides because of health and ecological concerns. The manual cutting and burning method has been used in some areas, but it is too slow and costly to have much impact on marijuana acreage.

In the spirit of approaching the narcotics problem as a joint responsibility, the Commission believes that the U.S. government should undertake a vigorous campaign to eradicate illicit marijuana cultivation within its own borders. Because of the proven effectiveness of the herbicidal eradication program in Mexico, the Commission recommends that the U.S. consider ways to implement such a program, recognizing the similarity of health and ecological concerns in both countries.

4. Establish priorities among illicit drugs within the context of a balanced strategy to reduce overall supply and demand.

The Commission believes it would be useful for the U.S. government to allocate its relatively limited resources to combatting the

most dangerous drugs, especially in view of the scope of the overall problem. Despite the many harmful effects marijuana can have,
it has not yet been reported to cause fatalities, even though millions of Americans use it regularly. In contrast, both heroin and
cocaine, which together are used by less than half as many Americans as marijuana, have been responsible for numerous deaths.

By suggesting that priorities be established among drugs for the
allocation of law enforcement efforts, the Commission is recognizing the reality that resources to combat drug abuse and traffic are
not unlimited in either country. The Commission does *not* recommend the consideration of legalization of any of these drugs at this
time. Legalization of heroin, cocaine, and marijuana would violate
important international treaty obligations of both countries. We also
believe that it would result in large increases in the numbers of
users, and that it would convey the wrong social message—one of
tolerance instead of disapproval. Nor would it eliminate all drug-
related crime.

**5.   Increase support for international and multilateral efforts,
particularly the United Nations Fund for Drug Abuse Control
(UNFDAC).**

Despite the importance the U.S. attaches to international control
efforts, it has provided relatively little funding support for international and multilateral drug programs. In the period from 1981
to 1986, the U.S. allocated $43 million a year on average to its inter-
national narcotics control program, including an annual contribution to UNFDAC of about $3.2 million. In 1987, the overall
amount was increased to $118 million, of which $3.8 million was
contributed to UNFDAC. In addition, the U.S. Agency for International Development contributed $5 million to UNFDAC for devel-
opment programs in opium-growing areas of Pakistan. This
increase was a welcome recognition of the importance of these
efforts. Other industrialized countries have contributed larger
amounts to UNFDAC: in 1987, for example, Italy gave $311 million
and Sweden gave $11 million.

The Commission urges the U.S. government to increase further
its support for both international and multilateral drug control
activities. In this connection, we take note of the obvious: that
unilateral measures cannot provide adequate solutions to interna-

tional problems. The current system of certification provides a clear example; in its current form, the legislation tends to be counterproductive.

Mexico, for its part, has a strong and clearly defined national interest in the immediate reduction and eventual elimination of drug production and trafficking.

For the Mexican government, the Commission recommends:

1.   Concentrate law enforcement efforts on large drug traffickers rather than on peasants who cultivate illicit drugs.

The peasants who grow marijuana and opium poppies profit least from the drug traffic, although they earn four to five times what they could make from farming. The Commission believes that law enforcement resources can most effectively be directed at large drug traffickers who finance the illicit cultivation of crops rather than at the growers themselves. Disrupting the drug trafficking networks by arresting and convicting the leaders has greater long-term impact than using those same resources to arrest and convict drug farmers.

2.   Focus limited drug control resources primarily on heroin and cocaine.

The Commission believes that both the Mexican and the U.S. governments should place highest priority on heroin and cocaine, both because they cause the greatest damage and because they provide the largest profits to the drug trafficking networks.

3.   Strengthen drug abuse education and prevention programs.

Although drug abuse is not yet widespread in Mexico, recent studies have found that it is increasing, particularly among young people. The Commission recommends that every effort be made to educate the Mexican people about the dangers of drug abuse now before it becomes a major problem.

4.   Increase support for multilateral drug control efforts, particularly the United Nations Fund for Drug Abuse Control.

The Commission commends the recent reaffirmation by the Organization of American States of the strong commitment of its member countries to wage a vigorous war against drug traffickers. Multilateral support for a global response to the problems of drug abuse and trafficking is critically important. The Commission also commends the leadership role taken by the Mexican government both regionally and internationally in encouraging drug-producing countries to eradicate illicit cultivation. Because of the importance of developing a truly international response to these problems, the Commission recommends that the Mexican government, like the U.S. government, increase its support for U.N. activities, particularly the programs of UNFDAC.

5.   Provide economic alternatives for farmers now relying on illicit drug crops for their livelihood, while continuing to eradicate illicit drug production.

Drug cultivation has become an important source of income for many peasants who might otherwise be hard pressed to support themselves and their families. Mexico's economic crisis since the fall in oil prices has deepened the poverty of many peasants. During the 1970s, the Mexican government decided not to provide any assistance to these farmers, in the belief that illegal activities should not be rewarded. In light of current realities, and in view of the Turkish example, the Commission believes that the Mexican government should consider adopting an economic development program for drug-producing regions that will provide a realistic alternative for cultivators. One additional benefit of such an effort would be the diffusion of information to *campesinos* about the risks and dangers of drug production.

For both U.S. and Mexican governments, the Commission recommends:

1.   Lower the level of rhetoric.

To the greatest extent possible, both governments should try to address their concerns in substantive terms, rather than hurling accusations at each other. Improving real communication between the two governments and the two societies on the nature of the drug problem and programs to combat it is a vital first step in achieving increased understanding.

2.   Establish a joint mechanism for regular consultation and collaboration on drug control issues.

Such collaboration would provide a means for both countries to study and agree upon the nature of the drug problem; to establish joint priorities for action; to share intelligence and information; and to develop joint programs to combat drug abuse and traffic. This would be facilitated by the appointment of cabinet-level officers in each of the two countries with overall responsibility for their respective drug control efforts.

3.   Work together on a bilateral basis to gather and analyze information on drug consumption, trafficking, and production.

One of the most troubling obstacles to collaboration has been disputation over the statistics each goverment uses to describe the dimensions of the drug problem. The joint development of mutually agreed-upon statistics will provide a useful basis for cooperative measures to combat drug abuse. It could also contribute to reducing the intensity of the political rhetoric between the two countries on this issue.

4.   Explore the possibility of initiating a joint effort to provide alternative sources of income for peasants who are now producing illicit drug crops.

It is necessary to recognize the economic pressures that drive many peasants to cultivate illicit drug crops. Regional economic development efforts, when combined with vigorous law enforcement and eradication programs, have had substantial impact in reducing illicit cultivation in other countries, most notably Turkey.

5.   Take the lead in promoting an international campaign against illicit drugs, in keeping with principles adopted by the United Nations convention at Vienna in 1987.

Such a campaign could include the creation of an international drug agency to assist governments that request help in eradication and interdiction campaigns. This group should be located within the United Nations. It could replace the enforcement personnel associated with existing bilateral narcotic control agreements—such as those between Mexico and the United States. The performance of enforcement functions by a multilateral agency would thus help reduce conflicts in bilateral relations between consumer and producer countries. It would also reinforce the public perception that the problems of illicit drug production and consumption are truly international in nature.

And in general, the Commission urges both governments to work together to create a *model for collaboration* between producer and consumer countries. The United States and Mexico have achieved this close collaboration in the past—with beneficial results for both countries, despite frictions over such questions as certification. The Commission believes that effective bilateral cooperation is critically important. Such cooperation serves the interests of each country and, by removing a major irritant, strengthens all aspects of the bilateral relationship. It would also be a major contribution to the global struggle to combat drug abuse and trafficking.

5

Foreign Policy and
Inter-State Relations

Foreign policy is an expression of national purpose in the international system. The content of a country's external policy depends upon its relative position in the world, upon the evolution of its history, and upon its aspirations for the future. With this focus we now address the theme of foreign policy and U.S.-Mexican relations. The question is not whether two neighboring nations, such as Mexico and the United States, will sometimes disagree. The question is whether they can establish means to develop and expand their points of agreement, to comprehend their differences, and to manage them in a constructive fashion.

We begin this chapter with a brief discussion of common interests shared by Mexico and the United States in the international arena. We then describe differences in outlook and interests between the two nations, and some of the conflicts these have created. We proceed to analyze emerging foundations for a new bilateral relationship, with specific recommendations for the two governments, and we conclude with observations on the prospects for collective collaboration with regard to regional affairs.

COMMON INTERESTS/MUTUAL ASPIRATIONS

There have often been frictions and tensions between the United States and Mexico, but that cannot obscure the bedrock fact that the two countries share interests and aspirations that transcend their differences—and, as we shall argue, can provide the basis for new collaboration in the years ahead.

There is one basic symmetry. For each country the relationship is wholly unique: for neither is it accurate to describe that relationship in traditional foreign policy terms. Each deals with the other daily across a range of issues that encompasses intimate domestic questions as well as the kinds of problems that more commonly constitute traffic between states. Each is affected by the other more immediately and more intimately than by any other country. Indeed, the Commission has not been able to think of another pair of countries—including the U.S. and Canada—whose interrelationship is as penetrating as that of Mexico and the United States.

It would be a cliché to say that both countries draw major benefits from the peace and common economic development along their frontier, but for the fact that this is so taken for granted on both sides of that border. They share one of the longest frontiers in the world, as we have elsewhere said, a unique separation between an industrialized and a developing country. For more than a half century it has given rise not only to friction, but to exemplary collaboration as well. Not since 1917 has that friction had military significance; for more than seventy years, neither country has been called upon to allocate any substantial resources to border defense. This has been a blessing to both; both want to keep it that way.

Along the border, too, there is a variety of common interests. Both the U.S. and Mexico share a concern with protection of the environment and with cross-border pollution. As we have shown in Chapter 4, they have a common interest in opposition to the illegal trafficking in drugs across that line. Indeed, the border itself—potentially a most explosive issue in the bilateral relations between any two nations—has proven to be one of the most enduring and important areas of agreement between the U.S. and Mexico.

On a broader plane, the United States and Mexico are now witness to an increasing convergence of economic interests. Mexico's change in economic strategy (described in Chapter 2) means that it must now depend on continued access to outside markets—the largest and nearest also being the richest in the world. And the U.S., to meet its own economic challenges, must ensure a prosperous Mexico.

In short, each country has a direct and growing stake in the economic strength of the other. This goes beyond conventional

pieties about shared interests in the virtues of development *per se*—
true enough in any case. What it specifically means is that the
economic circumstances and the strategies of the two countries have
combined to create a special convergence of interests that will
endure until and beyond the end of this century.

DIFFERING PERSPECTIVES, DIFFERING POLICIES

Despite the many common interests between the two countries,
we have encountered—and will encounter—striking differences in
perceptions of foreign policy principles and purposes. Mainstream
United States and Mexican interpretations of recent world history
(at least as we understand them) have proven to be divergent and
resistant to reconciliation, so we have decided to set forth two
separate views of international affairs—one North American and
one Mexican.

What follows is our attempt to summarize the profoundly different perceptions of the world and of each other that have
informed and inspired U.S. and Mexican foreign relations in the
postwar era. Such generalizations can, of course, be misleading and
simplistic: not every American subscribes to the U.S. view as we
present it, nor does every Mexican citizen hold to the Mexican view.
But underlying assumptions have had a major impact on the foreign
policies of the two countries and on the conduct of the bilateral
relationship, and for that reason they require careful explication.

Comprehension does not mean acquiescence. Most members of
the Commission adhere strongly to their own country's perception
of the world, more or less as we depict it; recognizing the existence of the other country's viewpoint does not mean accepting
its validity. Our purpose here is not to resolve these differences
but to describe and understand them, since that is the key to mutual
cooperation.

U.S. FOREIGN POLICY: THE AMERICAN VIEW

American foreign policy since 1945 has responded to the perceived necessity of defending the free world from the ambitions
of the Soviet Union. Joseph Stalin retained control of Poland as
World War II came to an end. In March 1946 Winston Churchill
proclaimed that an "iron curtain" had fallen over Europe, from the
Baltic to the Adriatic, and called for the liberation of Europe. In

1948 there would be a Soviet-inspired coup in Czechoslovakia and a major crisis in Berlin.

The United States promptly came to the aid of its allies. In 1947 President Harry S Truman decided to support the government of Greece in its struggle with a leftist insurgency backed by the Soviet Union. In a ringing message to Congress, the President declared: "I believe it must be the policy of the United States to support free people who are resisting attempted subjugation by armed minorities or by outside pressures."[1] The immediate result was military aid for Greece and Turkey. The long-term result of this proclamation, the Truman Doctrine, was the assertion of U.S. support for democratic governments around the world.

As further developed by George Kennan, U.S. policy came to focus on the Soviet Union. U.S. and other western leaders saw in Soviet maneuvers an implacable tendency toward ideological and territorial expansion. The prevention of world communist domination, Kennan said, would require "the adroit and vigilant application of counter-force at a series of constantly shifting geographical and political points, corresponding to the shifts and maneuvers of Soviet policy."[2] Geostrategic concerns and military security moved to the top of the agenda.

In recognition of its new obligations, the United States—which had refused to join the League of Nations after World War I—assumed a major role in the creation of the United Nations. The U.N. immediately became a central institution in the international arena, a forum for the expression of national interests and an agency for the peaceful settlement of disputes. The U.N. established and, insofar as possible, upheld a code of conduct for the international community. With its headquarters located in New York and one-quarter of its budget coming from the United States, the U.N. also represented at that time a powerful U.S. commitment to the idea of multilateralism.

With strong bipartisan support at home, the United States assumed extensive responsibilities abroad. For Europe, the Marshall Plan in 1947 offered a massive program of aid for economic reconstruction; the creation of the North Atlantic Treaty Organization (NATO) in 1949 established a military alliance. After the revolu-

1. Quoted in Stephen E. Ambrose, *Rise to Globalism: American Foreign Policy, 1938-1980*, second revised edition (New York: Penguin Books, 1980), p. 121.
2. "The Sources of Soviet Conduct," *Foreign Affairs* 25, 4 (July 1947): 566-582, with quote on p. 576.

tionary Chinese communist victory in 1949 and the outbreak of the Korean War in 1950, the U.S. formed a network of alliances in the Pacific as well. With its economic and military might, the United States was attempting to defend its allies from the threat of communist expansion and to uphold the cause of freedom and democracy.

Within the western hemisphere, this policy found three expressions. One was the Rio Pact of 1947, a regional security system. Second was the Organization of American States, founded in 1948 as a forum for the discussion and resolution of political issues. Chapter 15 of the OAS charter asserted: "No state or group of states has the right to intervene, directly or indirectly, for any reason whatever, in the internal or external affairs of any other state." Thus did the U.S. embrace the concept of regional multilateral collaboration and confirm the ideal of self-determination.

Third was the Alliance for Progress, a collective strategy for a decade of development in the 1960s that would require at least $20 billion in capital from the U.S. As President John F. Kennedy explained it: "Latin America is seething with discontent and unrest. We must act to relieve large-scale distress immediately if free institutions are to be given a chance to work out long-term solutions."[3] The U.S. was seeking to promote the cause of democratic reform in the Americas through support for socioeconomic development. Latin Americans in general welcomed the program, though it would lose much of its momentum by the late 1960s.

During the mid-1970s President Jimmy Carter based his Latin American policy on mutual respect and the protection of human rights. One of his first decisions was to initiate negotiations for treaties on the future of the Panama Canal. And as military regimes imposed strong grip in Argentina, Chile, and Brazil, the United States came to the defense of fundamental freedoms—of speech, of press, and of dissent. This stance caused considerable friction with the dictatorial governments, which denounced the U.S. for interference; it also saved the lives of numerous dissenters and helped keep alive the prospects for democracy.

The postwar move away from the traditional isolationism that once characterized United States foreign policy for so long did not occur in a vacuum. It happened because the United States alone among the western democracies had the strength—psychological,

3. Quoted in Ambrose, *Rise*, p. 248.

economic, and military—to rebuild war-ravaged economies and defend against Soviet aggression. It was not a position the U.S. sought, but a position from which the country could not retreat. The United States had become a global power, with global responsibilities and a global perspective.

It is the global nature of United States foreign affairs that determines the country's outlook and method for dealing with the world around it. U.S. foreign policy is, and must be, concerned with a multiplicity of issues that have little interest for or impact on other countries. U.S. global responsibilities require a foreign policy sweep and a breadth of vision not called for from others. What happens in London, or Moscow, or Lagos—or Mexico City—is almost always important to the U.S., and often intimately affects Washington's security interests.

In this context, U.S. actions are often misunderstood—or not understood at all—by those nations that enjoy the luxury of a narrower focus. And in this context, the United States often fails to give proper weight and attention to issues that are, for other nations, of great importance. In a contentious world the U.S. has been forced to use a variety of strategies, from the promotion of economic development to the use of force. Americans will freely concede that their government has not always acted wisely, and that mistakes have been made. But they would argue, as well, that the United States does not have the luxury of approaching its multiplicity of challenges from the perspective of one dimension alone; a policy which makes no allowance for nuance, differing circumstances, or gradations of challenge and response, would quickly lead to chaos and *global* instability from which others, including Mexico, would suffer at least as much as the United States.

MEXICO'S FOREIGN POLICY: THE MEXICAN VIEW

Mexico's vision is different. As the United States was pursuing its grand strategy of containment in the postwar era, with commitments all over the world, Mexico was seeking to defend its central interest: the protection of national sovereignty. In view of the balance of economic and military power, both global and regional, the primary means toward this end would be support for international law. Principle became an instrument of state.

In the Mexican view, Mexico adopted a foreign policy derived from its own historic traditions as well as from the rules of international law and its multilateral orientation. This posture emerged not from short-run calculations of advantage but from long-run definitions of national purpose and need. One of the central foundations of Mexican policy has been an interpretation of the country's history, clear and sometimes painful recollections of foreign impositions and invasions. During the three main moments of Mexican history—Independence, the Reform, and the Revolution—Mexicans have had to contend with interests, pressures, and interventions from one or more world powers. In such instances Mexico has been at a serious disadvantage, largely because of the intrusion of foreign interests into its own domestic processes. Mexico has therefore had to struggle to achieve recognition and respect: independence came in 1821 with the triumph of that domestic faction that sought separation from the Spanish crown. The ultimate acquisition of recognition from major members of the international community was a paramount achievement for the newly independent nation. In this context the first U.S. envoy to Mexico, Joel R. Poinsett, was declared *persona non grata* because of his interference in domestic affairs.

From independence onward, according to the Mexican interpretation, the defense of territorial integrity and prevention of foreign interference would constitute cardinal principles for Mexico. Foreign policy became a central pillar of national identity. Thus it assumed great importance from the early years of independence, as an instrument for the protection of national interests and goals.

In keeping with its determined defense of legitimate and vital national interests, Mexico has given high priority to the articulation and observance of key principles: non-intervention, self-determination, peaceful settlement of disputes, abstention from the use or threat of military force, the juridical equality of states, and cooperation for development—principles enshrined in Article 89 of the national constitution. This emphasis reflects not only abstract norms. It also responds to a basic interest: the protection of national sovereignty. "The most effective way to uphold Mexico's right to self-determination," according to this view, "is through the defense of that right for every other country."[4]

4. Bernardo Sepúlveda Amor, "Reflexiones sobre la política exterior de México," *Foro Internacional*, 24, 4 (April-June 1984): 409.

Mexico maintains that the primary goal of its foreign policy has never been to engage in conflict with the United States. When it has occurred, conflict has been a secondary consequence. The central idea, in keeping with tradition, has been the defense of principle. Over the years, Mexico has registered firm protest not only against U.S. interventions—but also against those of other powers, including such events as the Italian invasion of Ethiopia in the 1930s. The ultimate motives behind Mexico's foreign policy therefore constitute *raisons d'etat* (*razones de estado*, or reasons of state).

In this connection, Mexico has developed a profound concern with the United States. Specialists have pointed out that proximity to the world's greatest power has led to significant historical costs—including an open and declared war, the loss of over half its original territory, several military interventions, constant interference in domestic political affairs and economic penetration at all levels. This does not mean that there are no advantages accruing from proximity to the U.S., or that they are not recognized for what they are, but that the considerable costs in terms of feelings—that Mexicans constantly keep in mind—should not be overlooked by U.S. policymakers. It would be helpful, Mexicans believe, if North Americans understood that when Mexico defends its principles it is defending more than theoretical postulates.

This explains the paramount importance that Mexicans ascribe, in their civic and historical celebrations, to those who have faced up to foreign invaders. Mexicans emphasize that this is not a cultural curiosity. It indicates reverence and appreciation for the teenage cadets who lost their lives in defense of the Chapultepec Castle against the U.S. in 1847; for the armies under General Ignacio Zaragoza that won a major battle against the French at Puebla in 1862; for Benito Juárez, who symbolized the struggles and triumphs of the Mexican people against a foreign invasion and a foreign ruler; and for President Lázaro Cárdenas, whose expropriation of foreign oil companies made him a national hero in 1938. In this regard, one of the fundamental strengths of Mexican foreign policy has derived from its reflection of the historic and cultural experience of its people and its acute concern about the neighbor to the north.

Mexicans believe that the current international order continues to be dominated by relations of force, and that the prevailing economic order is inequitable. They consider that the global economy is likely to plunge into severe crisis if paths to development are closed to those nations that represent more than 75 percent of the world's population.

Mexico's apprehensions about the United States continued during the era of the "special relationship," briefly mentioned in Chapter 1. Mexicans believe that this occurred within the context of a "special relationship" that the U.S. had already granted to Latin America as a whole for security reasons. Never clearly defined, the term alluded to both economic and political aspects of the relationship: on the one hand, preferential U.S. treatment of Mexican exports and cooperation in dealing with economic problems, especially along the border; and on the other hand, a sort of unspoken understanding that the U.S. would permit Mexico to take independent positions on foreign policy matters that did not greatly affect U.S. security interests.

In accord with the principle of non-intervention, Mexico refused to support a U.S. proposal before the OAS condemning the administration of Jacobo Arbenz in Guatemala in 1954 (a CIA-sponsored movement would overthrow him later that same year). In 1961 Mexico condemned the U.S.-supported invasion at the Bay of Pigs by anti-Castro elements, and later refused to yield to what it saw as U.S. pressure to break diplomatic relations with Cuba—although President Adolfo López Mateos supported the U.S. during the missile crisis of 1962. In 1965 Mexico refused to support the U.S.-led occupation of the Dominican Republic.

These episodes entailed profound disagreement between the concept of regional security (as espoused by the U.S.) and the idea of self-determination and non-intervention (as interpreted by Mexico). But the conflicts proved to be manageable within the spirit of the "special relationship"—partly, some Mexicans surmise, because they dealt with third-country issues, and partly their country's position was not new: Mexico had been expounding its principles ever since the nineteenth century.

Finally, Mexicans regard support for multilateral institutions as a logical corollary to their stress on international law. The United Nations assumes particular importance in this conception, not only because of its peacemaking capacities—now reasserted in the late 1980s—but also because of its commitment to socioeconomic progress. Such organizations as the U.N. Development Program, UNESCO, and the Economic Commission on Latin America have all made important contributions. But in the words of one Mexican expert:

> the performance of the United States in both systems has been oriented towards the principle of safeguarding what its directors consider to be vital interests, independently of whether these interests coincide closely with the precepts defined by said bodies [the OAS and the U.N.], while Mexico has maintained a policy derived from its historical experience with strict adherence to the norms and principles of international law.[5]

CONTRASTING WORLDVIEWS

Differences in perspective between Mexico and the United States derive at least in part from their positions in the international arena: as the most powerful nation on earth, the U.S. assumed responsibility for the defense and protection of its allies; still emergent from its Revolution, Mexico wanted mainly to protect its national integrity and its social reforms. Such differences in posture and interpretation continue to pervade the bilateral relationship. We here attempt to highlight some of the sharpest discrepancies in outlook.

First, there is asymmetry in the significance of the one for the other. For Mexico, the United States has been a constant concern; for the United States, Mexico is an afterthought. From the North American standpoint the United States has been preoccupied ever since the end of World War II by numerous international issues: by the claims of the Soviet Union to first rank among the world powers and its ideological and imperial ambitions, by the conflict in the Middle East, by the Vietnam War, by the openings to and in China and by the revolutionary alteration of the world's economic structures. The tensions created in U.S. foreign policy by these developments have not primarily involved Mexico. Mexico has not been a major participant in the great military conflicts of the modern era. The two nations in short have not shared a common experience or common challenges in the international arena in this century.

---

5. Jorge Montaño, "Mexican and United States Participation in the United Nations and the Organization of American States," paper presented to the workshop on inter-state relations of the Bilateral Commission (February 1988), p. 2.

Second, Mexico and the United States have developed sharply differing perceptions of the international system, and these perceptions have had a profound impact on their respective foreign policies. Let us take some examples to illustrate the point. In schematic and simplified form:

IN THE BILATERAL ARENA,

- Americans tend to see their government, save on those rare occasions like Irangate when it acts out of character, as limited in power and constrained by constitutional checks; Mexicans tend to view the U.S. government as manipulative, willful, and secretly powerful in working its will abroad.

- Americans assume that the United States has relatively little impact on Mexican development and policies; Mexicans see the United States as a primary factor in their personal and national lives.

- Americans take their own national sovereignty and identity as a given and so tend to ignore the importance of the issue for others; Mexicans regard their own sovereignty as under threat and their national identity assaulted by the language, culture, and values of the North.

- Many Americans regard Mexico's political system as inefficient, corrupt, and elitist; Mexicans consider, first, that such a judgment constitutes an intervention in domestic affairs, and, second, that North Americans have yet to resolve some of their own problems and internal difficulties. Moreover, many Mexicans argue that if their political system indeed requires change in order to strengthen its democracy, these transformations should occur in keeping with its own historical traditions and sociocultural realities.

IN THE HEMISPHERIC ARENA,

- Americans believe that the ambition of U.S. policy should be to protect the weak and vulnerable republics in the Americas; citing the history of military interventions, Mexicans tend to think that U.S. behavior has reflected the national self-interest of the United States, and that, with some exceptions, it has been self-serving and imperialistic.

- Americans see violent revolution in the Americas as more than likely to provide an opening to radical authoritarianism; from their own experience, Mexicans conclude that revolution is an understandable, natural, and sometimes inevitable response to repression and inequity.

- Americans sometimes charge that Mexico's public solidarity with revolutionary causes is a transparent attempt to coopt leftist opposition at home; Mexicans contend that revolution arises in response to poverty and oppression and foreign domination, as their own experience has shown.

- Americans see Mexico's emphasis on non-intervention in the hemisphere as a policy adapted to Mexico's national interests rather than a policy of "principle," and often criticize it as hypocritical and narrow-minded, since it fails to deal with problems of dictatorship and poverty; Mexicans retort that such judgments ignore the difficult historical processes of Mexico's emergence and the numerous interventions it has suffered in the past, that their government has provided socioeconomic assistance within the limits of its resources (especially in Central America, as in the Pact of San José), and that non-intervention is a universal principle that would serve the hemisphere well if only the U.S. would respect it.

IN THE GLOBAL ARENA,

- Americans see their foreign policy as driven by the global nature of their country's responsibilities and supportive of the political ideal of democracy; Mexicans tend to regard the underlying goals of U.S. policy as the economic promotion of capitalism and the preservation of advantage over other nations.

- Americans see themselves generous, their attitude to the world typified by the Marshall Plan, the Alliance for Progress, and forty years of foreign aid in general; Mexicans see such programs in large part as reflections of self-interest.

- Americans are reluctant to resort to force in international relations—but they tend to see force as occasionally necessary to protect human rights, to vindicate the inherent rights of individual and collective self-defense recognized in the U.N. Charter, to stop terrorist acts and to support self-determination, and they believe that it can, if employed with caution, obviate a need for greater force at a later time and under more dangerous circumstances; Mexicans repudiate the resort to force as a matter of principle and they consider that, except in those instances contemplated by the U.N. Charter, the unilateral use of force violates international law and endangers world peace and security.

- Americans believe it essential to global peace and stability to restrain Soviet imperialism; Mexicans want to protect themselves and other countries from the expansionist tendencies of both the superpowers—and they are painfully aware that the United States is the more proximate of the two.

In short, though Mexico and the United States are neighbors and the United States is separated from its Western allies by oceans, it is patent that the United States' view of the world has far more in common with that of Europe and Japan than with Mexico. There are understandable reasons in history and current reality for these contrasts in outlook. They are fruits of differing national experiences, different cultures, different language, and different stages of development. But they speak volumes about the difficulties for both nations in their efforts to conduct their global relations in the years to come.

In addition, the United States and Mexico entertain profoundly different views on national security. Territorial independence and political integrity, after all, are the ultimate tests of a nation's foreign policy. For the United States, its national security, and the security of those nations where it conceives its essential national interests are at stake, are the ultimate determinants of its global behavior. No sacrifice is too large, for there is no nation of last resort to which the United States can look for ultimate protection. The great debates of American foreign policy of the past forty years have been instrumental—not whether, but how to maintain an effective defense of its vital interests.

For Mexico, the contrast could hardly be more striking. National security is not the dominant foreign policy issue in Mexico that it is to the north. There is no active domestic debate on defense, and no need to focus on military matters in the conventional sense with anything like the intensity those questions command in other nations in the Middle East, Asia, Africa and even South America.

It is highly indicative that Mexico assigns less than 1 percent of its national budget to defense expenditures. (U.S. Commissioners applaud that policy.) There is currently no external menace to Mexico's territorial integrity.

Nor can Mexico hope to match American military power. Thus the enduring dilemma of Mexican foreign policy: while the United States sees itself as a guarantor of Mexican security, Mexico perceives the United States as the one realistic threat to its sovereignty and independence. This is the reason that U.S. concern for, and engagement in, the turbulence in Central America causes such acute concern in Mexico. What is true today for Central America could be so for Mexico tomorrow. To live next to a giant is both a comfort and an anxiety, particularly if that giant has used its power against one's own territory before.

PATTERNS OF CONFLICT

Such differences in worldview can, as history shows, generate considerable tension. And so they have.

Friction between Mexico and the United States has increased in frequency and intensity, and changed in form as well. Whereas the disputes of the past proved to be more or less manageable, conflicts of the current era create profound disagreements and recriminations. The discovery of massive petroleum deposits during a period of instability in the Middle East made Mexico a matter of strategic concern to the U.S. Mexico's positions in international forums and its stance on Central America also contributed to the atmosphere of conflict and to U.S. preoccupations with regional security.

Mexico began pursuing a somewhat more active foreign policy beginning in the early 1970s. Under President Luis Echeverría, Mexico expressed itself in support of Third World interests. He provided material and diplomatic support to the government of Salvador Allende in Chile; launched the Charter of Economic Rights and Duties of States in the United Nations, which the U.S. eventually voted against; cast Mexico's vote at the U.N. in favor of the "Zionism is a form of racism" resolution, prompting a strong reaction in the U.S. Jewish community; and promoted the creation of the Latin American Economic System (SELA), which does not include the United States.

Under José López Portillo, Mexico continued to expand its international influence, largely as a result of what it took to be the negotiating power of petroleum. One of the most serious conflicts between the two countries occurred in 1979 when Mexico did not provide a new entry visa for the Shah of Iran after cancer treatment in the United States. This development took place in the midst of the hostage crisis.

Central America has been a source of continual difference. Mexico severed relations with Nicaragua's Somoza in May of 1979, withdrew its Ambassador from El Salvador in 1980, and joined with France in recognizing the insurgent coalition as a "representative political force" in El Salvador. It played an important part in the Contadora process in January of 1983, when President Miguel de la Madrid met with the presidents of other Latin countries to begin the multilateral search for peace within the region. U.S. policymakers saw Mexico's actions in El Salvador as intervention in the internal affairs of that state and took an ambiguous view of the Contadora initiative, where some became deeply troubled by what they took as an absence of balance in Mexico's attitude toward the peace talks. The Mexican government did not agree with this view. Others in Washington were convinced that Mexico had embarked on an independent foreign policy for its own sake.

At the same time, the United States was continuing a foreign policy, most obviously in the Caribbean and Central American region, which Mexico saw as insensitive and interventionist. Chile in 1973, strong support for the central government of Salvador against the insurgents beginning in 1981, U.S. support for the United Kingdom in the Malvinas conflict, Grenada in 1983, the crescendo in the conflict in Nicaragua and the recent dispute with Panama—all served to heighten Mexico's apprehensions about U.S. interventionism.

Mexico would become concerned about its own sovereignty as well. The ominously-timed articles in the *Washington Post* by Jack Anderson claiming that the CIA had intelligence of high-level corruption in Mexico and of Mexican political instability, and the blatant attack by Senator Jesse Helms on the legitimacy of Mexican presidential elections during Senate Foreign Relations Committee hearings in 1986, although of little significance in the U.S., led Mexico to believe that it was not exempt from these ambitions. Some even took the occasional waverings by the United States with respect to Mexico's debt crisis as confirmation of their darkest suspicions that Washington was prepared to punish Mexico financially for its behavior in Central America.

In recent years, too, there has developed considerable acrimony over disagreements in international forums. U.S. spokesman have been sharply critical of Mexican pronouncements in the Organization of American States and especially in the United Nations. They have expressed open frustration with the positions Mexico has taken on Third World issues, and they have intimated the suspicion that Mexico has taken the lead in organizing anti-U.S. stances and coalitions. Mexico has a "right" to do this, one top U.S. official has admitted, but it is a "mistake" that poses unspoken dangers to "the quality of the bilateral relationship." It was not hard for Mexicans to see this as a threat.

In reply, Mexican representatives have asserted that they indeed have a right to vote as they please, that a vote in favor of Mexico is not a vote against anyone else, and that the open expression of disagreement represents the essence of democratic practice. Mexico has not been automatically opposing the United States. It has been upholding longstanding traditions of its foreign policy. With pride, Mexico asserts that its votes in international forums adhere to the spirit of the U.N. Charter.

It is inevitable that U.S. policymakers will react negatively if they perceive a persistent pattern of votes in the U.N. against what they consider to be important U.S. interests. This is a fact which, whether considered to be appropriate or not, Mexican policymakers need to recognize (and ignore if they wish). On the other hand—and on this both Mexican and U.S. Commissioners agree—for the United States to "punish" Mexico for the free exercise of its sovereign right to vote as it sees fit within the U.N. is both shortsighted and counterproductive. Shortsighted in the sense that it confirms to Mexicans their view of the "imperial" aspects of U.S. policy; counterproductive in the sense that a proud nation intent on demonstrating its independence is not likely to change its ways under such pressure.

It is essential for the United States to accept—in meaningful ways—Mexico's sovereign right to its own foreign policy. It is equally essential for Mexico to engage in direct and candid discussions with the United States to further common understanding of the foreign policy views and positions of both countries.

THE FUTURE OF THE BILATERAL RELATIONSHIP

Given these discrepancies and differences, how should each nation conduct its diplomacy in the decade ahead? One thing is plain: the interaction of the two countries will be far more intense in the decades ahead even than it has been in the recent past. We believe that this reality presents both countries with new challenges and opportunities.

Moreover, the management of U.S.-Mexican relations will require new instruments. It is time to look for new ways of dealing with each other. From the U.S. perspective, as former secretaries of state Henry Kissinger (Republican) and Cyrus Vance (Democrat) have said,

> Mexico may well represent the most challenging problems for the United States in the western hemisphere. Most Americans appreciate the importance of Mexico to the United States. However, it is very difficult to know how to deal with the complex relationship.
>
> Traditional foreign policy approaches are of little use: the usual levers of diplomacy, military power and international economic policies, do not apply to a close and friendly neighbor, with which we are connected by so many intangible ties. The issues that we face in Mexico are almost all domestic in character: the flow of people, cross-border trade, energy, culture, education, financial and fiscal matters, drugs.[6]

It is further our conviction that the areas for bilateral cooperation are expanding steadily as the two nations become linked more intimately. This is so whether one considers the consequences of the technological and scientific revolution of our age, the monumental needs of education in the two countries, the control of illicit substances or environmental measures. By the same token, the levels of government and the number of agencies within each level that will find themselves treating issues affecting both nations is constantly increasing.

BORDER RELATIONS

One of the most successful chapters in the history of U.S-Mexican relations has been the border. For nearly one hundred years, a bilateral commission has quietly and competently resolved disputes

---

6. "Bipartisan Objectives for American Foreign Policy," *Foreign Affairs* 66, 5 (Summer 1988): 899-921, with quote on p. 917.

about the precise location of the boundary (usually caused when the Río Grande changes course). In 1944 this agency was renamed the International Boundary and Water Commission (IBWC) and it has dealt with issues arising from allocation of water, from contamination of rivers, and from the location of border crossing-points. It is currently grappling with complex questions of underground water deposits and transboundary aquifers.

To be sure, there are unresolved border issues: one of them is the maritime limits in the Gulf of Mexico, about which a treaty awaits confirmation by the U.S. Senate. But the bilateral management of border questions stands in remarkably good shape. There are various reasons for this happy outcome. One might be the very specific nature and definition of the issues; another might be the preeminent role of technicians on the commission. In addition, the spirit of collaboration and cooperation we have observed among local authorities, from mayors to county officials to governors, no doubt contributes to the maintenance of a congenial and supportive atmosphere. Whatever the case, the handling of the border presents a worthy model for other parts of the world—and for other aspects of the U.S.-Mexican relationship.

At the same time, we believe that border issues do not receive sufficient attention from the U.S. and Mexican national governments. In the past, "benign neglect" may have permitted local officials to manage problems on their own, and this may have assisted the resolution of difficult issues. We do not believe that this formula will be appropriate in the years ahead. Border and regional problems, and the management of local cooperation, should receive greater attention from the national governments.

THE QUESTION OF STYLE

The style of the relationship will be central in the future, as it has been in the past. The weighty substantive issues on the U.S.-Mexico agenda for the rest of this century should not obscure this fact.

The United States tends to express itself to other nations directly, even bluntly. It has certainly done so in the case of Mexico. In recent years there has been an increasing tendency, or so Mexicans have seen it, for U.S. policymakers, both in the Congress and the Executive Branch, to use the medium of mass communication to deliver messages to Mexico City—with questionable results.

Both countries would be advised to consider amending the manner of their discourse. Without compromising its interests and principles, the United States must learn to work with more prudence and subtlety with Mexico, recognizing that Mexico has its own national interests and rational objectives. Without compromising its interests and principles, Mexico needs to look with greater understanding on the global nature of the U.S. role and on the limitations and complications that imposes on the conduct of U.S. foreign policy. Mexico could, as well, take greater advantage of opportunities deriving from its relationship with the United States by using the impressive legions of Mexicans who know the idiom and style of the United States in a more vigorous effort to bring Mexico's interests and needs to the attention of American policymakers.

Foreign policy differences can give rise to public controversy. Precisely because the two nations are locked in such an intimate embrace, public differences can have a particularly wounding effect for both the United States and Mexico.

This leads to three points. First, both countries must learn to accept the reality that controversy will result from disagreements on foreign policy. Its very occurrence is a sign of the increasing importance each has achieved for the other. Second, there is a difference between controversy and punishment. The emergence of a controversy itself does *not* mean that either government should impose penalties against the other. Third, we believe that both governments should strive to prevent foreign policy differences from contaminating the bilateral relationship.

ADMINISTRATIVE ADJUSTMENTS

Both countries will want to consider how they can refashion their foreign policy machineries to manage the delicate but intense relationship in the coming decades.

For the government of Mexico, the Commission recommends:

1.   Creating a "specialized cabinet" for foreign affairs—

along the lines of the ones now in place for agriculture, health, foreign trade, and economics, to be led by the Secretary of Foreign Relations and to include other appropriate ministries such as Treasury, Trade, Planning and Budget, Interior, Defense, and Justice;

   2. Strengthening the role and resources of the Mexican Embassy in Washington;

   3. Strengthening the roles and resources of selected consulates in key cities throughout the United States; and

   4. Promoting systematic dialogue between the Mexican and U.S. legislatures with respect to foreign policy and bilateral matters.

In this connection, we add a word with respect to a unique element in the relationship, one which has a limited but important bearing on the way American decisionmaking affects Mexico—the presence in the United States of a large, growing, and increasingly activist population of Mexican-Americans. This could provide a useful resource for Mexico on a few specific issues such as the rights of immigrants. But as one expert has explained to us, as to the efforts of Mexican officials to create a "Mexican-American lobby":

> If the effort is defined narrowly and limited to the issue of immigration rights, there is no question that the government's initiative will be successful. There are no other significant foreseeable issues, however, on which there is likely to be so much agreement between Mexican-Americans and Mexican officials.[7]

In short, the Mexican government would be well advised to comprehend the diversity, complexity, and sophistication of the Mexican-American population in the U.S. It would no doubt be useful and appropriate for the Mexican government to expand its communication with this segment of American society. But it should cultivate contact with a representative spectrum of Mexican-American leaders in the U.S., not only those who lend automatic support to Mexican positions. It should not expect the considerable population of Mexican-Americans to act as a built-in, all-purpose lobby which can be automatically mustered in support of any Mexican national interest.

There are other ways Mexico may enhance its capacity to exercise a beneficent effect on the U.S. policymaking process. Mexico has traditionally pursued a formally correct diplomacy. The nation's commitment to nonintervention has led it to eschew opportuni-

---

7. Rodolfo de la Garza, "The Changing Political Role of the Mexican-Origin Population in U.S.-Mexican Relations," paper presented to the workshop on inter-state relations of the Bilateral Commission (February 1988), pp. 30-31.

ties for making its voice heard and its influence felt in the decisionmaking process in Washington. Communications still tend to be largely concentrated through the Department of State.

But Washington has become inordinately more complex than it once was. Policy involves far more than the Department of State. Other Executive Branch agencies assert a role; Congress is more than ever a full partner in the management of relations abroad, and it is enveloped in a horde of staff aides. Think tanks, the press and TV, church groups—all influence foreign policy.

Mexico is behind other nations—Canada, conspicuously—in equipping itself to communicate with the new, complex structures in Washington. We recommend that the Mexican government deploy its diplomatic instruments to strengthen its presence in the U.S., especially in view of the open quality of American society. The historic policy of abstention has been based in part on a sense of the proprieties, in part on the fear that engagement in the decisionmaking process in Washington would invite intervention by the U.S. in Mexico. Mexico should make the distinction between making itself heard through various channels in U.S. society, in order to pursue its interests and defend its point of view, and intervening in the U.S. political system. Washington regards it as entirely appropriate for foreign governments to bring their views to the attention of lawmakers, and has rules to govern the process. Others do it; Mexico should as well. This will require a greater maturity on the part of both nations, of course, to know how to operate under the rules of the other without failing to continue to respect one's own.

Turning to the U.S. management of foreign policy, the Commission quickly encountered long-known axioms: decisionmaking in the United States government on issues relating to Mexico tends to be fragmented, disjointed, and focused on other concerns. What might be done? Good process is no substitute for good policy, of course, but there can be no good policy without good process.

As organizing principles, we urge that U.S. government give high-level priority to relations with Mexico; that the President pay special and appropriate attention to Mexico, communicating this concern to all levels of the governmental bureaucracy; that there should be continuous planning and evaluation of U.S. policy toward Mexico at the highest levels; and that the U.S. should make every effort to harmonize its official activities which touch Mexico.

Moreover, we think the U.S. should make special efforts to understand and appreciate the complexity of the decisionmaking process in Mexico, just as Mexico should improve its understanding of the U.S.

For the U.S. government, the Commission recommends:

1. Appoint a high-level coordinator for U.S. policy toward Mexico.

The coordinator should, we believe, be located in the Department of State and subordinate to the Secretary of State—but with good access, through the Secretary, to the President. The coordinator should head an interdepartmental group made up of representatives of *all* the departments and agencies of government dealing with Mexican-U.S. matters and should, through this group, be responsible for the preparation of policy recommendations for the appropriate cabinet-level officials and the President. The coordinator should also be responsible for overseeing the implementation of policy under the direction of the Secretary of State.

2. Appoint individuals of stature and dignity to key positions with regard to Mexico.

The American Embassy in Mexico is a showpiece appointment. It deserves the best representation the United states can muster— a person from the public or private sector with experience, sensitivity, prominence, knowledge of Mexico, and command of Spanish. Too often in the past that has not been the case.

3. Strengthen contact and communication between the legislative branches of the two governments.

In particular, we urge strengthening of the U.S.-Mexican parliamentary group that now meets on a semiannual basis.

4. Appoint an outside advisory group to consult on a regular basis with key decisionmakers in the U.S. government with regard to Mexico.

Mexico and the United States interact as intensively and intimately as any other pair of nations in the world. Issues of common concern will emerge in the course of the next decade, therefore, which call for more intense cooperation between the U.S. and Mexico. The new challenges will exceed the capacities of either government acting alone. We therefore perceive in the remaining years of this century the need for more formal mechanisms to energize, channel, and advance the mutual interests of the two nations.

For both the U.S. and Mexican governments, the Commission recommends:

1. Intensified activity and cooperation at the level of the summit.

The President of Mexico and the President of the United States meet regularly. The Commission applauds this custom. It has considerable symbolic value. Such meetings provide useful opportunities for each nation to pay its respects to the other. We believe, however, that the presidential summit process in this instance should assume more substantive meaning, perhaps drawing inspiration from the model of the summit meetings of the Group of Seven. The agendas of the Mexico-U.S. presidential meetings could be prepared in advance of the meetings and thoroughly staffed by representatives of both Presidents (in the case of the U.S., under the direction of the high-level coordinator) prior to the meeting. In this way it should be possible for the meetings to encompass, *inter alia*:

- a careful and detailed review of the economic relationship between the two nations, including transborder activities affecting agriculture, migration, services, and capital flows;
- an analysis of the cooperative activities undertaken by the two governments;
- a review of the work of all subordinate binational agencies, and issues of common foreign policy concern.

Within this context we encourage regular meetings between the foreign ministers and other high officials of the two nations.

2. Creation of a permanent cabinet-level binational economic commission.

As we have said in our chapter on economics, this group would have a significant mandate. It would:

- conduct regular and intensive consultations with regard to the respective macroeconomic policies of the two countries;
- review the record of trade and investment cooperation within the Framework Agreement, with a view to recommending additional measures to open up trade and investment opportunities;
- monitor the international financial posture of each country as it affects the economy of the other;
- maintain an early warning surveillance system to monitor economic challenges to the relationship and recommend responses.

The work of this binational commission would enjoy the assistance and support of an adjunct body of private Mexican and American business leaders, labor leaders, bankers, and academics. The binational economic commission should have a permanent secretariat. It would report to the Presidents.

At the outset, the economic commission would have a consultative, investigative, and advisory mandate only. In our vision, the commission would be endowed with an instructional influence on the body of public opinion in the two countries, particularly if it is constituted, as it should be, by respected senior statesmen from both.

3.   Movement toward the establishment of binational authorities on border affairs, consistent with the exercise of national sovereignty.

These authorities would be composed of representatives of the two nations and staffed with binational experts. They would assume regulatory responsibility for specific matters of common concern. We conceive that such authorities could usefully undertake the management and regulation of a number of discrete activities. These include:

- environment and salinity problems;
- customs procedures;

- transborder infrastructure projects such as bridges, ports and rail junctions.

These authorities would function for the most part on the local level.

THE NEW DIPLOMACY

As we have said more than once, the U.S.-Mexican relationship does not exist in a vacuum. To a great and increasing extent, it is affected by events and developments in other parts of the world—especially within the western hemisphere. Both Mexico and the United States have profound interests in Latin America.

In view of these prospects, the Commission recommends the adoption of a basic principle: *mutual respect*. In practice, this understanding rests on several related postulates: that both Mexico and the United States have the inalienable right to devise their own foreign policy, that they can each disagree with the other, that neither country should in any way attempt to interfere in the domestic affairs of the other. In addition, we believe that neither country should allow foreign policy disagreements on multilateral or third-party issues to contaminate the bilateral relationship.

In general, the United States and Mexico should renew their tacit accord of the 1960s: to respect the right to disagree. And they should continually recognize the importance of the bilateral relationship itself. We also believe that it is time for the United States and Mexico not only to consolidate the bilateral agreement to disagree—but also to pursue a new vision of collaboration and cooperation in the international arena. Such a partnership must be based on the idea of mutual respect and diplomatic equality. This is not a call for either nation to surrender its sovereignty, but an appeal for constructive and voluntary collaboration on the basis of mutually shared interests.

As Commissioners, we see several reasons for optimism in this regard. First are far-reaching changes in the international arena itself. The policies of Mikhail Gorbachev may have opened unprecedented possibilities with and within the Soviet Union. These shifts could pave the way for a durable *détente* between the U.S. and the USSR, as shown by the intermediate nuclear force (INF) treaty of late 1987. It is our hope that we are at the beginning of a truly new phase in East-West relations. We find additional encouragement in the apparent reduction of regional conflicts in Southern Africa, Afghanistan, and the Persian Gulf.

We see changes in the hemisphere as well. The transition from military dictatorship to electoral democracy in many parts of Latin America offers new possibilities for constructive cooperation at the regional level. This has already become evident in the diplomatic collaboration (or *concertación*) shown by such initiatives as Contadora and Cartagena. Mexico has played a leading role in these developments, and we look forward to further activity of this character.

In addition, of course, change is imminent within both Mexico and the United States. Both countries are about to inaugurate new Presidents. Both countries are undergoing considerable transformation. In the future, both nations should be able to show a new readiness to collaborate on matters of mutual interest.

This vision of diplomatic partnership will require adjustments from both countries. As Henry Kissinger and Cyrus Vance have together observed, unilateralism no longer provides a feasible approach to hemispheric questions:

> It is no longer possible for the United States to pretend that it alone can determine events from within or deter hostile forces from without in the western hemisphere. Since its own independence, the United States has felt a special concern for developments in the New World, although there has often been too much ignorance and arrogance in our policies and attitudes. The past presence of our missionaries, corporations and, on some occasions, U.S. gunboats and troops, in many of these countries are all part of a difficult heritage for Latin and North Americans.

And the challenge, according to the former Secretaries of State, is to find a new approach:

> Recent troubles in these relations have made it clear that we must deal with the problems of our region differently than before, and also differently from the way we defend our interests on other continents. While it may be necessary to retrench American commitments in more distant places, it is unthinkable that we should now pay less attention to the western hemisphere.[8]

We firmly agree with that conclusion.

8. Kissinger and Vance, "Bipartisan Objectives," 916-917.

The Commission recommends that the governments of Mexico and the United States create a mechanism for discreet and regular consultation and information-sharing on bilateral and regional issues.

An efficient early warning system would eliminate unnecessary frictions and conflicts. It would be a new instrument for a new relationship.

MULTILATERAL STRATEGIES

We believe that Mexico and the United States can take the lead in promoting new multilateral approaches to regional issues. A challenge for the 1990s will be to find practical means for multilateral approaches.

The Commission recommends that the governments of Mexico and the United States initiate a frank and open dialogue on the concept of regional security.

These discussions must go beyond the limited focus that has so far emerged from the Organization of American States and the Rio Pact. We are urging the governments of both countries to take a new and fresh look at the subject.

What constitutes a genuine threat to the hemisphere? On what issues might Mexico and the U.S. find common ground?

For many Americans, Mexico has customarily shown considerable reluctance to address the problem of regional security. This reluctance has meant that the United States has had to act in the hemisphere under conditions when greater Mexican (and other Latin American) involvement might have obviated this necessity. Too often, according to many Mexicans, the United States has utilized the concept as a justification for military and/or diplomatic intervention in the hemisphere.

According to one Mexican expert, the security of Latin America "is not to be confined to the military-strategic arena, but rather should encompass the political, economic, and social substratum that has been at the root of the various conflicts in the region."[9]

9. Claude Heller, "U.S. and Mexican Policies toward Central America," paper presented to the workshop on inter-state relations of the Bilateral Commission (February 1988), pp. 81-82.

The Commission agrees with this concept, in the belief that a country's national security derives from its own social and economic development.

All Commission members regard socioeconomic development as a major component of regional security. There can be no progress without social justice, and no social justice without progress. Growth and development offer the keys to peace (and peaceful change) throughout the region. Long-term campaigns against poverty, hunger, illness, and ignorance can provide the eventual basis for domestic and international security in Latin America.

In the United States, even now, we anticipate an increased understanding of, and a willingness to accept and cooperate with, Latin American initiatives toward the peaceful resolution of Latin American difficulties. There is a growing awareness that America's security concerns are coincident with those of Mexico, and that Latin America's diplomatic efforts can authentically coincide with the interests of the United States.

We also see a strong convergence of national interests. We believe that both Mexico and the United States would oppose the installation of long-range missiles in the hemisphere, and that both oppose the proliferation of nuclear weapons. The Caribbean Basin, a region of vital interest to both Mexico and the United States, remains a focus of conflict, turmoil, and tension. The U.S. and Mexico both look forward to the early and peaceful resolution of these conflicts. Both will benefit when the nations of Central America are firmly on the road to economic and political development. Both stand to gain when chaos in Haiti is arrested, when Cuba can be fully reintegrated in the hemispheric community, and when the other Caribbean islands find access to the resources they need for growth. These shared objectives are bound to be achieved more rapidly and effectively if Mexico and the United States can work together rather than at cross-purposes.

MULTILATERAL INSTRUMENTS

We have already expressed our view that the formal institutions of multilateralism within the hemisphere are not working well. We believe that this situation requires urgent and immediate improvement.

Specifically, we have given careful consideration to the role of the Organization of American States. While we do not anticipate that the OAS will have a predominant role in arbitrating the future links between the two countries, the OAS can be significant.

The recent record has been uneven. The Organization has made only a modest contribution to the peace process in Central America; its Council has not contributed much to the public understanding or practical resolution of the region's debt and other economic difficulties. But the Inter-American Commission on Human Rights and the Human Rights Court are flourishing institutions, and they deserve the cooperative support of Mexico and the United States. The OAS can still play important roles in the settlement of future regional problems. In such instances, we would hope that the United States and Mexico could work closely together in shaping and supporting the efforts of the organization.

In view of these considerations, we believe that the Organization of American States could play an important role within the region in the future. The practical question is how to achieve a meaningful reinvigoration of that institution.

The Commission recommends that the United States and Mexico collaborate in the search for effective measures to strengthen the OAS.

We also encourage support for such institutions as the Latin American Parliament. This is potentially an extremely useful forum for the exchange of views by legislators throughout the region. An active and vigorous parliament would serve the interests of all nations in the hemisphere.

At the same time, we recognize that many hemispheric issues will be of such a nature that they will not fit within the current problem-solving structure of formal multilateral institutions. There will be a constant need for informal mechanisms as well.

And new forms of cooperation are constantly appearing outside the traditional molds. Through such organizations as the Group of Six (for disarmament), Contadora and its Support Group, the Group of Eight, and the Economic System of Latin America (SELA)—which have enjoyed support from the secretariats of both the OAS and the U.N.—Mexico has established close working relations with other nations of the region. A practice by which nations can form *ad hoc* groupings to merge their strengths and wisdom to deal with common problems is a positive development. The United States should make clear that it welcomes this practice. Mexico should continue it. And both nations should take full advantage of this new development to forge collaborative efforts in the international arena.

Indeed, we suspect that hemispheric security in the long run might be best served by a series of interlocking and regional networks. After all, those closest to the problems will be in the best position to find workable solutions. These arrangements might vary in membership and composition. The United States might belong to some but not all; Mexico might belong to some but not all. But both countries should play an active role in hemispheric institutions.

For as far as the eye can see, the foreign policy of both countries will be tugged by contradictory forces. For Mexico, there will be the need to nurture its independence on the one hand and the imperative of finding avenues of economic and diplomatic cooperation with the U.S. on the other. United States policymakers will be forced to recognize the long-term importance of relations with Mexico and the possibilities of fruitful collaboration on regional and international matters.

It should be possible for the statesmen of the two nations to resolve these twin dilemmas. As we suggest, much will turn on style, on expanding Mexico's influence in the United States, on refashioning the foreign policy machineries of both countries and ultimately on building a binational authority for border affairs to cope with problems of truly binational dimension.

These are far-reaching proposals. They cut against the grain of habit, but we think they speak to real needs. For it is certain that until and beyond the end of this century there will be no more important relationship in the world for either nation than this one.

6

Education for New Understanding

Misunderstanding complicates relationships. As we have already suggested, some differences of interest and policy may be inevitable in relations between Mexico and the United States. The problems of economic interdependence, migration, drugs, and foreign policy pose serious and enduring challenges to the management of the relationship. These issues are needlessly complicated, however, by cultural stereotypes that cloud public understanding, by ignorance and misperception that affect policymakers and the media as well as ordinary citizens, by the failure to inform and educate, and by the dearth of scholars and researchers needed to produce new knowledge and expert analysis.

Conversely, mutual awareness can enhance the prospects for cooperation. Reciprocal respect for cultural values, greater knowledge, better communication, and ready sources of accurate information can contribute decisively to improving relations and expanding collaboration. The point, as we have said before, is not to minimize the importance of societal and cultural differences between Mexico and the United States; it is to *understand* them. Only then can the two countries have a realistic basis for the management of the bilateral relationship.

As we look toward the future, we think it is of utmost importance to strengthen public understanding. This will require an improvement in education—not only through the formal learning that takes place in schools, but in the informal inculcation of attitudes through the mass media. Our children, and the children of our children, will face the challenge and the responsibility for conducting U.S.-Mexican relations in the century to come. The least we can do now is to give them the tools.

Such an effort will have special meaning for the United States, which is just beginning to witness a flourishing of Hispanic culture within its own borders. The number of Hispanics in the U.S. has increased by 30 percent since 1980, to 19 million, nearly 8 percent of the total. Over three-fifths are of Mexican origin. By the year 2000 the Hispanic population is likely to reach 30 million, or 12 percent of the whole. Partly as a result of these demographics, Hispanic popular culture and fine arts are coming of age. Latina music has moved to the top of the popular charts; successful films signify a new respectability and poignancy in Mexican-American themes; Latin American and Mexican novels have achieved literary stature and widespread popularity. For mainstream America, learning about Mexico thus has a dual significance; it also means learning about the newly emergent U.S.

We begin this chapter with a review of public opinion in the two countries—about each other and about the state of the relationship. Next we explore the sources of public attitudes: teaching in the schools and messages of the mass media, especially news coverage and the entertainment media. We turn to the need for investment in high-level expertise about the United States and Mexico, in academia and elsewhere, and we then focus on the need to strengthen scientific and cultural exchange. Recommendations come after that.

IMAGE AND OPINION: HOW WE SEE EACH OTHER

The opinions and perceptions of ordinary citizens in Mexico and the United States help to shape not only official policies but also the myriad informal interactions that bring the citizens and institutions of the two countries into increasing contact. Widely-held and deeply-rooted images tend to impose limits on the acceptable range of governmental policies. Consistently high levels of public tolerance for compromise and cooperation can encourage helpful initiatives. Negative or hostile perceptions, on the other hand, can provide serious obstacles to the improvement of bilateral relations. Of course, no amount of good will and effort could ever eliminate all the potential sources of friction and stress in the bilateral relationship. Each of our two countries will always find grounds to criticize the other.

As the number and diversity of interactions between the United States and Mexico multiply, the potential for both negative and positive public perceptions will grow apace. Both societies contain groups that oppose better relations and seek to mobilize sentiment against closer ties. Some interest groups and politicians in the United States have argued that the United States should isolate itself from Mexico's problems by closing the border. In Mexico, nationalist sentiments are occasionally used to reject any form of cooperation. Efforts to improve relations will continue to remain hostage to such appeals unless major efforts are undertaken in both countries to improve public understanding of the bilateral partner.

PUBLIC OPINION

We have touched on general features of public opinion in Chapter 1. Perceptions of the United States in Mexico show a much greater awareness of the bilateral partner than in the United States, but they also reflect a high degree of ambivalence. In two opinion polls, published almost simultaneously in 1986, majorities of respondents described the United States as an "enemy," but characterized Mexico's relations with the United States as "friendly" or "very friendly." In United States Information Service (USIS) polls of urban, educated Mexicans from 1956 to 1985, between 39 percent (1972) and 65 percent (1985) of respondents held a "favorable" or "very favorable" view of the United States. The problem, as we have already noted, lies not in American society; it concerns U.S. treatment of Mexico. Overwhelming majorities of educated Mexicans polled (between 60 and 71 percent since 1979) believe the United States treats Mexico "unfairly." And while most Mexicans believe that their country should work closely with the United States for economic reasons (82 percent in 1985), many believe that U.S. economic policies have been "harmful" to Mexico (56 percent in 1984, 44 percent in 1985).

Educated Mexican opinion has been consistently more favorable in its view of the chief economic competitors of the United States. In a poll conducted for USIS in June 1984, for example, the United States received a "favorable" or "very favorable" rating from 78 percent of respondents, but Japan (94 percent), France (91 percent) and Spain (83 percent) all ranked higher. The Soviet Union, just below the United States, was viewed favorably by 69 percent of those polled. In a poll conducted in late 1984 and early 1985, when 60 percent of Mexican respondents said they felt the United States treated their country "unfairly," only 9 percent held that view of Japan. And in June 1984, when asked which countries Mexicans would prefer as sources of future investment in Mexico, 69 percent named Japan while 49 percent mentioned the United States.

In the 1986 *New York Times* poll of 1,576 Mexicans throughout the country, a minority of respondents, 47 percent, expressed a "favorable" opinion of the people of the United States. While respondents thought U.S. citizens enjoy greater political freedom, they also expressed the belief that Mexicans are closer to their children, have stronger values, and are more religious. People in the U.S., they believe, have more opportunities to become rich without working hard. By a small margin, they concluded that people in the U.S. are happier with their lives.

While such opinion polls provide snapshots of Mexican views, they do not yield much information on how the opinions are formed. In the *New York Times* poll, one-half of all respondents stated that at least one close relative was living in the United States, one-third had visited the United States, and one-quarter knew a U.S. citizen. Two-fifths of all respondents said they would go to live in the United States if they had the opportunity. Mexicans better acquainted with the United States thus tended to have somewhat more positive view of its people and institutions. The *New York Times* poll did not contain questions designed to test empirical knowledge of the United States or to determine the sources of the information and analysis from which Mexicans form opinions about their neighboring country.

Other sources, however, suggest that Mexican leaders and citizens know relatively little about diverse aspects of U.S. politics and society. Mexican citizens are largely unfamiliar with U.S. domestic and international history unrelated to Mexico, and particularly with the history and culture of working-class, minority, or rural North Americans. U.S. television programs and movies fail to inform Mexicans about U.S. history and institutions and tend to reinforce stereotypical images of the United States as a rich nation beset by widespread crime, promiscuity, and violence.

Mexican perceptions about U.S. policymaking often fail to take into account the decentralized structures and competitive nature of U.S. governing processes or to recognize the complex ways in which public officials interact with private interests and the news media. Mexicans often interpret loosely connected, contingent events as though they represented orchestrated campaigns or well-organized conspiracies. This tendency can have a counterproductive result: Mexican criticisms of U.S. policy and behavior are often dismissed in the United States because they are ill-informed about the U.S. political system, when they should be examined carefully for their substance and content.

In the United States, popular perceptions of Mexico often reflect deep-rooted prejudice and ignorance. Most North Americans are unaware that the first mass social revolution of the twentieth century occurred in Mexico and, as a result, they cannot comprehend the profound effects of this experience on Mexican society and political culture. They do not realize that, as a result of the Revolution, Mexico has enjoyed more than a half century of uninterrupted constitutional rule; next to the United States and Canada, it is the most stable polity in the western hemisphere.[1] U.S. commentators and policymakers have been prone to miscalculate the effects of policy initiatives designed to exert pressure on the neighboring republic.

U.S. citizens find it difficult to understand why the Mexican public and policymakers often fail to share U.S. perceptions and interests in foreign policy. Still less do they understand the significance of the broad consensus on foreign policy issues that stretches across the political spectrum in Mexico, a consensus that embraces strict adherence to doctrines of non-intervention and respect for international law. The United States, with its global interests and commitments, has tended to view Mexico's defensive and strict construction of foreign policy principles with impatience, most recently in response to Mexico's criticism of U.S. activities in Central America.

---

1. In another recent U.S. poll, 62 percent of respondents cited "political instability" in Mexico as the "most important" (32 percent) or "second most important" (30 percent) issue affecting U.S. relations with that country. See Christine E. Contee, "U.S. Perceptions of United States-Mexican Relations," paper presented to the cultural relations workshop of the Bilateral Commission (October 1987), p. 20, Table 13.

Though fairly widespread throughout the U.S., positive images of Mexico usually refer to the exotic and unusual (by North American standards) in Mexican life rather than to the modern and familiar. Americans see Mexico as an inexpensive and hospitable tourist haven, as an object of entertainment and a source of spicy cuisine. U.S. citizens are largely unaware of Mexican cultural and scientific achievements.

Indeed, recent surveys have yielded remarkable findings. First is the chronic inattention to international affairs within the American public. Second, American citizens acknowledge but do not fully appreciate the significance of U.S.-Mexican relations: only 40 percent rated Mexico as "very important" to the United States (compared with 48 percent for China and 60 percent for the Soviet Union).

And third, U.S. respondents often hold negative views about Mexico's political performance and institutions. In mid-1986, as controversy was swelling over narcotics and immigration, 69 percent declared that Mexico was "poorly governed"; 79 percent described illegal immigration as a serious problem requiring stronger law enforcement; 60 percent said that drugs from Mexico contributed "a great deal" to the problem in this country. "In brief," one analyst writes, public-opinion surveys

> show that while Americans believe that what happens in Mexico is important to the United States, the public has a generally negative image of Mexico. Americans see Mexico not only as a poor country but also as a poorly governed and corrupt country. They think tougher actions should be taken to keep illegal aliens from Mexico from entering this country and often blame Mexico for this country's drug problems. Most fundamentally, Americans think that Mexico's problems are largely self-inflicted . They do not believe that Mexicans can or will work out their problems, and they do not favor giving increased American aid [sic] to Mexico.[2]

2. Hal Quinley, "United States Public Opinion of Mexico," paper presented to the cultural relations workshop of the Bilateral Commission (October 1987), pp. 1-2. Opinion about U.S. aid to Mexico was tested in the Yankelovich Clancy Shulman poll for *Time* magazine (July 7-9, 1986). Despite the fact that Mexico does not receive U.S. aid (except for a small U.S. contribution to the costs of Mexico's large-scale effort against narcotics trafficking), the survey question asked, "Do you think the United States should *increase its level of foreign aid* to Mexico to help Mexico deal with its economic problems?" (italics added). The wording of this question seems to imply that the United States is already providing aid to help Mexico deal with its economic problems, an implication that is empirically false. See Quinley, "Public Opinion," Table 10.

In general, U.S. citizens show more interest in domestic than in international issues, and they tend to judge Mexico and other Third World countries through the prism of domestic concerns.

In both countries opinion surveys and other data have also shown that people harbor negative images of government authority on the other side of the border. Mexicans frequently see the United States as a great power whose high officials are given to exerting undue pressure. U.S. local officials, courts, and police, together with the border patrol and the *migra* (agents of the U.S. Immigration and Naturalization Service) are widely viewed as hostile to Mexicans and Mexican-Americans. On the U.S. side, negative perceptions are focussed on the issue of corruption and on allegations of electoral fraud and narcotics trafficking by local and national officials.

Negative images and stereotypes coexist with more contradictory and even positive impressions. Increasing contacts, particularly between populations living along the border, have led to greater mutual understanding. Polls have repeatedly demonstrated that people who have visited or resided in the other country hold more positive and complex opinions about it. Familiarity, in U.S.-Mexican relations, at least, breeds respect. Negative stereotypes, especially virulent in the United States some decades ago, are far less common in the media and in public discourse than they once were. However, these positive trends are in danger of being overwhelmed by new sources of friction as the bilateral relationship becomes more complex.

Ignorance not only has an impact on public opinion; it also affects public policy. The bilateral relationship suffers not only because public opinion in the two countries is often prejudiced or ill-informed, but also because leaders in public and private life—including journalists, businessmen, labor leaders, and public officials on both sides of the border—frequently lack knowledge and first-hand experience of the other country and are too often forced to rely on half-truths and distorted images. Media reports, business behavior, and public policies have at times inadvertently reinforced cultural antagonisms and exacerbated tensions unnecessarily.

In part, such failures in communication reflect weakness in the training and deployment of experts, scholars, and teachers in both countries. The United States and Mexico have failed to invest adequately in the development of the expertise needed to produce and

disseminate knowledge about each other. And even when experts
have been available, key policymakers and private actors may not
seek their advice. In Mexico, the acute shortage of expert personnel is compounded by a widespread though flawed and partial
awareness of North American affairs. Advice and information
sometimes fail to reach decisionmakers because they do not know
they lack it. In the United States, key policymakers and private
sector leaders are able to call upon a larger community of experts
but often fail to do so, especially in making the most critical, high-
level decisions. U.S. decisionmakers are by tradition knowledge-
able about Europe and the Soviet Union; most know less about
Mexico than their Mexican counterparts know about the
United States.

IMPROVING PUBLIC KNOWLEDGE AND UNDERSTANDING

We attribute much of this public misunderstanding to inadequate
sources of information. With regard to the United States, we believe
three factors have been instrumental:

- first, a conspicuous neglect of Mexico in the nation's educational
  institutions, especially the primary and secondary schools;
- second, the episodic and altogether inadequate coverage of
  Mexican affairs in the U.S. news media; and
- third, the persistence of cultural stereotypes in the entertainment media, particularly films and television.

In the case of Mexico, as we have already pointed out, awareness of the United States is nearly universal. But Mexican perceptions of the bilateral partner nonetheless come from sources and
experiences that impart a partial or one-sided image:

- first, though the United States receives balanced treatment in
  the free primary school textbooks produced and distributed by
  the Ministry of Public Education, secondary school commercial textbooks used in Mexico frequently contain factual errors
  and one-dimensional portraits of the United States;
- second, at the university level only a handful of courses on the
  United States (mostly on U.S. literature) are taught because

Mexico has so few scholars trained at the doctoral level in U.S. history, society, politics, economy, or culture;

- third, the images of the United States which Mexicans acquire from film and electronic media come largely from the United States itself; these images display U.S. efficiency and wealth but they also emphasize violence, crime, and promiscuity;

- fourth, reporting on the United States in the Mexican news media is taken largely from U.S. commercial news services and television networks. U.S. public television news and documentaries are seldom carried. Few Mexican correspondents are stationed permanently in the United States and little effort is made to interpret the news in ways that might enhance knowledge and understanding of U.S. society and politics.

Let us begin at the beginning, with consideration of the elementary schools.

PRIMARY AND SECONDARY SCHOOLS

The Commission believes that both countries need to make a major effort to increase and improve primary-, secondary-, and university-level teaching about each other. Since the educational structures of the two countries are as different as the problems to be overcome, the steps to be taken will necessarily be different.

In Mexico, supervision of primary and secondary is centralized in the Ministry of Public Education, though recent efforts have been made to decentralize. School attendance is obligatory through the sixth grade. Free primary school textbooks (*textos gratuitos*) through the sixth grade in required subjects are published and distributed nationwide by the ministry, though private schools often prefer to use commercially produced texts. After sixth grade, only commercially produced textbooks have been available (until the 1988-89 school year, when the Ministry of Public Education produced textbooks for optional use at the secondary level). The free primary school social studies textbooks emphasize learning about Mexican history and culture. Material on foreign countries and cultures in the free texts is introduced mainly in the sixth grade. There are no special curriculum units on the United States, though the 1846-48 war with the United States as well as other interactions with the

United States are briefly (and objectively) covered in the fourth-year social sciences textbook; aspects of U.S. politics, culture, science and international behavior receive extended treatment in the sixth-grade social sciences text.

At both the primary and the secondary levels, a variety of texts in history and social studies produced by commercial publishers compete for adoption in the schools. Coverage of the United States in these texts ranges from no mention at all in many primary texts to lengthy, but occasionally one-sided and inaccurate, treatment in the secondary texts. Mexican school children also learn about the United States from sources outside the classroom, including television, movies, and popular music. Mexican students are thus aware of the United States, but the quality and balance of the information they absorb from these diverse sources leave room for much improvement.

For Mexico, the Commission recommends review and revision of school textbooks.

This effort should specifically include:

- the incorporation of a special unit on Mexico's neighbors, perhaps in the sixth-year social studies free textbook used throughout the country;
- the revision of secondary school history texts to incorporate more accurate materials on the United States;
- systematic study of the U.S. content of commercially-produced primary and secondary school textbooks as a further means of assisting private publishers in making needed revisions.

In the United States, by contrast, the educational system is highly decentralized. State and local school authorities receive federal funds for specific programs, but retain control over the content and administration of local schools. School attendance is generally obligatory through the age of sixteen. Textbooks are produced entirely by commercial publishers who compete with each other to get their works adopted. In some cases, this competition results in debilitating self-censorship, as publishers adjust their works to conform to local tastes.

With regard to international studies, the performance of the U.S. system has been equivocal at best. Study after study has decried the "pervasive ignorance" that American students have shown toward other parts of the world.[3] Educators and others have decried the lack of emphasis on foreign languages. Business executives and government officials throughout the United States have expressed constant anxiety about the country's preparation for the twenty-first century. An interdependent world will require an ability to communicate and to understand alien cultures.

Like the rest of Latin America, Mexico receives precious little emphasis in the U.S. pre-university curriculum. And the exposure, such as it is, remains superficial and biased. Textbooks on world civilization make passing reference to the pre-Columbian era and then move on to Europe and the United States: the impression, one critic reports, is "that other than the glories of the Maya and the Aztecs, Mexico has little importance in or impact on the course of world events."[4] A survey of U.S. history textbooks concludes: "The perspective of the Latin American countries is given little attention in most books and cultures of the regions are ignored . . . they fail to reveal the hostility and distrust built up in Latin America towards the United States as a result of our policies there over the past century or more."[5]

While Mexico's school textbooks on history and social studies devote considerable attention to the 1846-48 war with the United States and to U.S. interventions in Mexico's 1910 Revolution, U.S. textbooks barely mention these events or treat them as minor incidents in the country's inexorable march through territorial expansion to world power.

Supplementary teaching materials appear to be even worse. One study of elementary school readers with Hispanic motifs reports that only one-third are noteworthy; some are acceptable but not outstanding; fully one-third are grossly unbalanced and deemed unacceptable. Another evaluation of grade-school readers reveals a series of stock themes: a poor boy from a poor village, wearing sandals and a sombrero, accompanied by (or looking for) his

3. The phrase is from Robert Leestma's introduction to Lewis Pike and T.S. Barrows, *Other Nations, Other People: A Survey of Student Interests, Knowledge, Attitudes, and Perceptions* (Princeton: Educational Testing Service, 1979), p. xii.

4. Gerald Greenfield, "Mexico in U.S. Primary and Secondary Schools," paper presented to the cultural relations workshop of the Bilateral Commission (October 1987), p. 10.

5. Dan B. Fleming, "Latin America and the United States: What Do United States History Textbooks Tell Us?" *The Social Studies* (July-August 1982): 168-171.

beloved burro; in the typical plot, kindly Americans come to his rescue.

U.S. school children are not exposed to information or images of Mexico in their daily lives, except in areas along the U.S.-Mexican border. Negative cultural stereotypes, in reference to Latin American or Hispanic groups in general as well as to Mexicans or Mexican-Americans, have diminished in intensity since earlier in this century, but they remain a potent force within the U.S. educational establishment.

To deal with these problems, U.S. educational policymakers need more information. While research has been published on the image of Mexicans or Hispanics in selected U.S. textbooks, there has been no systematic study of the Mexico-related content of U.S. primary and secondary textbooks. And to our dismay, U.S. federal as well as state education authorities do not know how much information reaches U.S. school children nor how much time is devoted to teaching about Mexico in U.S. schools. A telephone survey showed that about half the state-level officials in the U.S. are unaware of modules or programs on Mexico within their own school systems.

For the United States, the Commission recommends:

1.   The investigation and improvement of teaching materials and practices regarding Mexico.

This should specifically include:

- a major effort to survey U.S. local school districts to collect data on teaching about Mexico in U.S. schools;
- a thorough study of the Mexico-related content of U.S. primary and secondary school textbooks;
- the incorporation into primary and secondary textbooks on U.S. history of special units on Canada and Mexico (or Canada, Mexico, and Central America); and
- the development of special units on neighboring countries for inclusion in other secondary as well as primary school textbooks.

2.   Creation of national and regional clearinghouses to develop inventories of curricular and extra-curricular materials on Mexico for use by teachers and schools.

This step should be coordinated with efforts to promote the development of new supplementary curriculum materials, including guides and manuals for teachers, as well as the creation of a special fund in the federal Department of Education to support the development of special units, exhibits, and other traveling programs on Mexico for primary and secondary schools.

3. Initiation of a large-scale effort to enhance and enrich awareness of Mexico in U.S. schools.

Mexican private and public agencies could contribute to these efforts by organizing a series of traveling exhibits and media presentations suitable for use in U.S. schools, with financing for the circulation and distribution of these materials from the Department of Education as well as from private foundations and state and local education authorities.

We urge a special effort to combat negative cultural stereotypes in the United States. Accordingly, we support the preparation of special supplementary teaching materials that illustrate this problem with examples drawn from feature films and television videos commonly used in U.S. classrooms. Such materials have proven useful in other contexts for reducing racial and ethnic bias among children.

For both countries, the Commission recommends intensified communications between educators and increased opportunities for student visits and exchanges.

Such programs should include:

- special efforts to promote bilateral consultations and exchanges between Mexican and U.S. educators;
- short-term travel or study-abroad seminars and workshops for Mexican and U.S. school teachers;
- an expansion of supervised field trip opportunities for Mexican and U.S. school children, especially at the secondary level.

Exchanges of individual secondary students, such as those sponsored by the Experiment for International Living and similar nongovernmental organizations, provide unique opportunities for young people to experience the culture and family life of their counterparts. The Commission calls for a major expansion of such exchanges with the support of public and private agencies in both countries, and with scholarships for students who now lack the financial resources to participate.

In addition, the Commission believes that universities and research centers in both countries could play a major role in the continuing education of primary and secondary school teachers and in the development of curriculum materials. The Commission urges private foundations and public agencies in both countries to provide greater support for university outreach programs, with particular emphasis on special centers of U.S. and Mexican studies.

NEWS COVERAGE

News coverage of the bilateral partner in Mexico and the United States provides another example of the asymmetry and inequality that produce avoidable misunderstanding. The United States is a global superpower; Mexican news media feature stories on the United States every day, ranging from coverage of diplomatic and political events to economic policy and baseball scores. By contrast, U.S. news media do not carry daily reports on Mexico. Coverage is episodic and uneven; only major events—such as earthquakes or national elections—receive substantial attention.

The structure and organization of the news media differ between the two countries. In Mexico, the print media are dominated by a small number of Mexico City daily papers distributed throughout the country. Local and regional papers (often weeklies) generally cover only local news and are designed to supplement the national and international coverage provided by the Mexico City dailies. News of the United States consists largely of dispatches from U.S. wire services. On Mexico's electronic media, much of the coverage of the United States (as well as a major portion of other foreign news) is taken directly from U.S. commercial television networks with Mexican stations translating in voice overlays. U.S. public radio and television news does not reach Mexico. Except for rare instances of open conflict between the Mexican and U.S. governments, and infrequent news and feature stories by the small number of Mexican correspondents in Washington, the news Mexicans receive about the United States is identical to the national news

U.S. citizens get. Indeed, some 300,000 middle- and upper-income families, including most of Mexico's intellectual and political leaders, receive U.S. commercial network news programs directly in English by cable.

In the United States, by comparison, news from Mexico is reported by regular correspondents and part-time "stringers" employed by a number of U.S. newspapers, wire services, and television networks. For major stories, U.S. news media send in additional reporters and crews. Virtually no news on Mexico printed or broadcast in the United States originates with Mexican reporters or media. Coverage by both print and electronic media is episodic at best.

Some Spanish-language television stations in the U.S. carry the commercial news programming of Mexico's major privately-owned network or the Spanish International Network news programs that cover Mexico. Most Spanish-language stations are primarily oriented toward local news coverage, however, and carry little news of Mexico. Mexico's public television network does not reach the United States. Since few North Americans and still fewer U.S. officials and opinion leaders speak Spanish (in contrast to the many Mexican leaders who understand English), Mexican news broadcasts in the United States attract small audiences outside Hispanic minority communities.

Most U.S. citizens subscribe to a single newspaper, local or regional, which carries no more than two or three foreign news stories each day, seldom on Mexico. Most therefore get their international news from the evening television network news, in which stories on Mexico appear infrequently. Occasional documentaries or talk shows treat Mexican affairs, but often from the perspective of U.S. preoccupations (immigration, drugs, debt). While Mexican newspapers and television stations regularly carry commentary by U.S. editorialists and columnists, their Mexican counterparts are virtually unknown in the U.S. media. At its best, U.S. news media coverage of Mexico provides balanced coverage of individual stories, but intermittently and with close attention to U.S. tastes and interests. At its worst, coverage of Mexico reflects a keen competition for air time and print space that puts a premium on disasters, conflicts, and scandals.

In short, there is ample ground for criticism of the U.S. media's treatment of Mexico. As a careful observer has written, concerns about inadequate, superficial, and unbalanced reporting have considerable basis in fact. This suggests a discouraging bind: either Mexicans should care less or learn to endure criticism more gracefully, or the U.S. media should adjust their tone and method. None of these is likely to happen.[6]

By the same token, he adds, there is no evidence at all to support the accusation, commonly heard in Mexico, that the U.S. media undertake deliberate campaigns to discredit or destabilize Mexico. The American press operates according to its own incentives and criteria. To Mexican eyes the repetition, pursuit, and elaboration of a single "hot" story by various papers and networks might *look like* an orchestrated conspiracy, and North Americans would do well to take note of this resemblance; but in fact this activity actually reflects the imperatives of journalistic competition, which (according to this analyst) Mexicans might do well to acknowledge.

Despite this judgment, many Mexicans nonetheless believe that it would be naive to assume that politics does not include the manipulation of images and atmospheres.

Mexico has received growing attention from the U.S. media in recent years. The quantity of coverage has increased over the past decade, partly as a result of highly publicized tensions in Mexican-U.S. relations. Media focus on Mexico mounted during 1985, as a result of the murder of a U.S. anti-drug agent and of the Mexico City earthquake, and reached a peak in 1986, largely because of U.S. congressional hearings on corruption and fraud within Mexico. Because of its immediacy and drama, the killing of DEA agent Enrique Camarena attracted special attention from the TV network news.

Nevertheless, most local news editors outside the border states remain convinced that their listeners and readers lack interest in Mexican news. It will be virtually impossible to improve the situation so long as they share this conviction. The first step in improving U.S. media coverage, therefore, as for the editors themselves to realize the long-term importance of Mexico and Mexican affairs to the United States. The next step should be a concerted educational effort to provide U.S. media personnel with more

6. John Bailey, "Mexico in the U.S. Media, 1979-86: Implications for the Bilateral Relation," paper presented to cultural relations workshop of the Bilateral Commission (October 1987), p. 5.

intimate knowledge of Mexican society, culture, and politics. In part, this could be accomplished by enlisting the aid of scholars and policy experts in U.S. universities.

The Commission recommends:

1.   Closer contacts between Mexican and U.S. journalists and exchanges of personnel between news organizations in the two countries;

2.   The development of a service to provide English translations of Mexican news and commentary to U.S. print media;

3.   Efforts sponsored by Mexican private or public agencies to provide more continuous and instantaneous information services to the U.S. media;

4.   That steps be taken to make news and cultural programming from the Mexican educational television networks readily available to Spanish-language stations in the United States.

Reporting by U.S. journalists in Mexico would also improve through a concerted effort on their part, and on the part of Mexican officials, to understand and adjust to the difficulties that arise from divergent standards and expectations. U.S. journalists often expect Mexican officials to respond to their queries quickly and forthrightly. Mexican officials are generally unaware of how the U.S. press operates. Often they fail to respond to queries as quickly as U.S. deadlines require and sometimes refuse to respond at all. In these circumstances, U.S. reporters often come to the conclusion that Mexican officials are concealing unfavorable information. Mexican officials, at the same time, are apt to feel they are being pursued or persecuted for failing to provide information they do not possess or do not feel authorized to divulge.

The Commission recommends that the government of Mexico undertake a concerted effort to promote understanding of U.S. and international media expectations among policymaking officials.

Such an effort would help to improve the quality of reporting on Mexico in the United States and elsewhere; it could also prove beneficial to relations between the Mexican government and the third estate. We believe, as well, that U.S. journalists in Mexico should face their difficulties with greater patience and sensitivity.

The Commission also recommends the development, in both countries, of specialized outreach programs organized and staffed by university-based experts as well as the creation of in-country workshops by independent, non-governmental organizations specifically directed at serving the needs of editors and journalists.

ENTERTAINMENT MEDIA

Specialists have shown that the propagation of negative stereotypes in the mass media, particularly in television and films, has diminished steadily over the past several decades in both countries. In Mexico, negative images of the United States stem almost entirely from electronic media programming that originates in the United States. As a result of this strange paradox, entertainment media in Mexico therefore reflect U.S. attitudes, biases, and self-images, including persistently negative portrayals (and lack of positive roles) of ethnic minorities, including Hispanics.

In the United States, the motion picture industry has long promoted pejorative images of Mexico. From the making of *The Greaser's Gauntlet* (1908) to such fine works as *The Treasure of the Sierra Madre* (1947) and beyond, the Mexican "greaser"—besotted, ruthless, violent, amoral—has been a stock figure in Hollywood films. The Mexican Revolution has also provided a common theme for American films, from *The Life of General Francisco Villa* (1915)—starring the general himself—to *Guns of the Magnificent Seven* (1968).

Over time, there have been many different Mexicos in Hollywood screenplays. As a leading expert has summarized:

> These many Mexicos have straddled a series of dimensions—geographical, temporal, ethnic, gender, psychic, and metaphorical. Geographically, Hollywood's Mexico consists of the U.S.-Mexican border and the rest of Mexico as an undifferentiated mass. Temporally, there is historical Mexico, usually portrayed with escapist equanimity, and contemporary Mexico, often treated with ethnocentric alarm. In terms of ethnicity and gender, Hollywood's Mexico consists of "greasers" (usually men) and romantic, occasionally sophisticated, sometimes hot-blooded Spaniards (often women). Psychologically, movie Mexico has alternated between being a good neighbor and a neighboring menace. Finally, while Hollywood occasionally treats Mexico as a historical and cultural reality on its own terms, more often it uses Mexico as a

metaphor: a backdrop for American activity; a stage on which Americans conduct their own personal morality plays; and sometimes a surrogate for political and ideological struggles within the United States.[7]

Except for the brief emphasis on "good neighborhood" during the 1930s and World War II, none of these portrayals is either responsible or positive. One of the high points of the prewar period was *Juárez* (1939), a film that likened the Mexican hero to his contemporary Abraham Lincoln.

On numerous occasions Hollywood's depiction of Mexico has prompted official rebukes. In 1919 the Mexican government sent a formal protest to American filmmakers, denouncing their negative portrayals and threatening to restrict their work in Mexico; after this warning failed, the government decided to prohibit the showing of anti-Mexican films. Authorities applied this ban to such movies as *The Girl from Rio* (1932), especially for its characterization of Señor Tostado, a thoroughly despicable greaser; and to *They Came to Cordura* (1959), which depicted General Pershing in triumph over General Villa—in a battle that never occurred.

Perhaps the most positive (and accurate) portrayals of Mexico came during the 1950s. The crowning achievement of this period was *Viva Zapata!* (1952), directed by Elia Kazan from a screenplay by John Steinbeck. A complex film with a variety of subtle messages, *Viva Zapata!* conveyed a thoughtful picture of the Mexican peasantry and of the Mexican Revolution.

In recent years the Hollywood image of Mexico has become ambiguous at best. Films with Mexican motifs frequently emphasize themes of Anglo-American superiority; of the pathology of Latin America in general; and of the Latino menace *within* the United States. Just as *La Bamba* (1987) may represent the arrival of a new era in Mexican-American filmmaking, so does the controversial *Colors* (1988) stress the theme of gang warfare and violence in the Los Angeles *barrios*.

U.S. television plays upon similar themes. According to one study, TV Hispanics fall into three categories: law breakers, law enforcers, and comic characters. Two-thirds of the Latino characters are involved in law breaking or enforcing, both roles emphasizing violence. Another survey shows that Hispanics comprise

7. Carlos Cortés, "To View a Neighbor: The Hollywood Textbook on Mexico," paper presented to the cultural relations workshop of the Bilateral Commission (October 1987), p. 4.

only one percent of the educated professionals or business executives portrayed on television.

Such imbalances in imagery and characterization have an ultimately corrosive effect on U.S.-Mexican relations, and we strongly urge the U.S. media to accept responsibility for the improvement of this situation. On this point we make an appeal to those in charge of the film and TV industries to make room for high-quality programs on the cultural and historical legacy of Mexico. We think the ministries of public education and of foreign affairs in Mexico should play an active role in this area.

In addition, we suggest that U.S. public educational television programs, including entertainment and cultural features as well as documentaries and news programs about the United States, be made more accessible to the Mexican public. This could be accomplished by direct agreement between Mexican networks and U.S. public television; it could be facilitated by support from private foundations or public agencies.

The U.S. film and television industries would benefit from careful scrutiny and close study by professional researchers who would be able to call attention to patterns of bias and stereotyping and recommend steps to correct them. Accordingly, we believe it would be useful for independent studies to be undertaken, in cooperation with managements where practicable, with a view to assisting these U.S. industries in efforts to rid themselves of unwarranted assaults on the sensitivities of Mexican and other Hispanic audiences.

INVESTING IN EXPERTISE

Throughout its deliberations over the past two years, our Commission has relied on expert analysis and judgment in the process of defining issues, searching out and analyzing vast quantities of information, and formulating recommendations. In so doing we have discovered that both the United States and Mexico have failed to invest adequately in the development of the expertise needed to produce and disseminate knowledge about each other. This failure has been compounded in recent years by the effects of fiscal and financial constraints on support for higher education on both sides of the border. Thus, as the two nations approach the twenty-first century, neither country possesses adequate human and institutional infrastructure to address common problems. Major efforts are required in both countries to correct this deficiency.

Despite continuing debates about the roles of higher education, each of our two nations is proud of its great universities and centers of learning. Newspaper editors and journalists, policymakers and diplomats, lawyers and businessmen, labor leaders and school teachers all rely to some extent on the knowledge and expertise embodied in institutions of higher education. But those who need this expertise on Mexico in the United States or on the United States in Mexico find themselves relying upon a small number of researchers and scholars who are unable to meet the demand.

In both countries, this scarcity is compounded by the highly skewed age distribution of the specialist community. In the United States, a period of rapid growth in the 1960s was followed by a sharp decline in the number of doctorates awarded to Mexican specialists during the 1970s and early 1980s; by the end of the 1990s, more than half of all the scholars now working on Mexico will be retiring. The United States is not educating enough younger specialists to replace them. In Mexico, U.S. specialists—much smaller in number to begin with—were largely trained during the oil boom years of the 1970s. Because of Mexico's economic difficulties in the 1980s, which caused an abrupt decrease in support for foreign graduate study, the training of U.S. specialists in the United States declined sharply. Advanced training in U.S. studies in Mexico scarcely exists. Having laid a promising foundation, Mexico has been unable to construct a solid edifice.

Out of more than 2,500 colleges and universities in the United States, only a handful of major centers and programs are devoted to Mexican studies or to relations between Mexico and the United States. In Mexico, there is not one major center for U.S. or North American studies; research and teaching about the United States is centered in four or five small programs, most of them in Mexico City. In most of the institutions of higher education in both countries, students cannot even find courses on the history, culture, politics or economic conditions of the bilateral partner. Very few institutions in the United States—such as the Center for U.S.-Mexican Studies at the University of California, San Diego (UCSD)—offer regular seminars or other outreach programs directed at journalists. In Mexico, such programs do not even exist, except for the UCSD-El Colegio de México summer seminars for nonacademic professionals held alternately in San Diego and Mexico City.

The Commission recommends a major expansion of training and research centers on the United States in Mexico and on Mexico in the United States coupled with national programs of support for graduate training and postdoctoral research.

Some resources for this enterprise could come from the respective governments, either alone or in collaboration. Much will have to be supported or undertaken by public agencies and private initiative separately in each of the countries.

In the United States, the Commission suggests that support for independent centers and programs on Mexican studies and U.S.-Mexican relations be expanded not only through grants from private foundations, as at present, but also through an expansion of the Title VI international studies program of the Department of Education. Such an increase should come only from new funding, however, and not from a reallocation of current resources of this already underfunded federal program. Without wishing to engage in micro-management of this effort, we would envision an increase in support for existing Mexican studies or Mexican-U.S. relations centers in the West and Southwest plus the creation of several new programs in other regions of the country. We believe the United States should have at least a dozen first-class major centers for the study of Mexico and U.S.-Mexican relations.

In Mexico, as well, we urge a major public commitment to the support and development of centers of research and instruction. Existing centers are largely devoted to policy research on Mexican-U.S. relations. These centers should be supported in their efforts to expand their activities, and several new centers for basic research and training on the United States *per se* should be created. A firm foundation for policy research will not exist until Mexico develops an independent capacity to produce new knowledge in the fields of U.S. history, culture, social life, and economic conditions.

In promoting both basic as well as policy research, Mexico should make full use of existing human and material resources. There is no point in creating new centers without sufficient trained specialists to staff them. We therefore suggest encouragement of opportunities for collaboration and cooperation among scholars already working on the United States or on U.S.-Mexican relations.

In a number of Mexican institutions, research and teaching on the United States are dispersed in various faculties and administrative units that have little contact with each other. In these institutions, new academic units could serve to coordinate existing scholarly and teaching resources and to undertake various outreach and collective professional activities. Such units could also offer services unavailable at present to both scholars and students including documentation, bibliography, access to U.S. publications, and information about fellowship opportunities. To function as effective points of contact and collaboration, however, these new academic units must receive substantial financial support from the institutions they serve as well as from external sources. This observation underlines the more general point we as Commissioners feel obliged to emphasize: *without new resources, both human and material, Mexico's effort in this field will necessarily remain inadequate.*

The Commission recommends the strengthening and support of efforts to coordinate U.S. studies programs by the Asociación Nacional de Universidades e Institututos de Educación Superior (ANUIES).

An effective consortium of U.S. studies programs could serve to promote the development of new U.S. studies programs at institutions where they do not now exist and to meet the diverse needs of existing programs. It could channel support, including foreign fellowships, to scholars at participating institutions, promote conferences and lecture series by both Mexican and U.S. scholars, and provide support services such as documentation and information.

Both countries have failed to provide adequate support for the training of new specialists. In the United States, the most pressing need is for fellowships to support dissertation and postdoctoral research on Mexico. Less than ten dissertation grants and no more than twenty or so postdoctoral awards are made in national (public and private) competitions each year. We think these numbers should be doubled. Twenty Ph.D.s per year seems like a modest and prudent investment. A major portion of this expansion could be funded through private agencies.

In Mexico, an important initial contribution to the development of U.S. studies could come from the creation of a fellowship program for those established scholars who are already teaching courses on the United States in Mexican universities, those whose research interests have recently shifted toward U.S. topics, and those who have specialized in U.S.-Mexican relations but now wish to expand the range of their expertise to related topics in U.S. studies. To meet this need, we would support the creation of five to ten research awards per year for individuals who wish to pursue advanced or postdoctoral research on U.S. topics in the United States. In addition, fellowships for M.A. and Ph.D. candidates at Mexican universities for thesis research in the United States should also be developed, beginning with one or two per year and rising thereafter as the size of the applicant pool increases. While various U.S. and Mexican government fellowship programs could be adapted to these purposes, a non-governmental program administered by respected scholars would be likely to encourage the largest and most qualified pool of applicants.

Until the field of U.S. studies has achieved a greater degree of development and institutionalization in Mexico, the training of scholars expert on the United States will continue to take place mainly in U.S. universities. Mexico's long-run goal should be to develop its own M.A. and Ph.D. granting capacities both in separately organized "U.S. studies" programs as well as in U.S.-focussed concentrations within the various disciplines of the social sciences and humanities. An important contribution to that goal could be made by a fellowship program for Mexicans that would award five to ten fellowships per year for graduate study on the United States at U.S. institutions over the next decade.

We furthermore encourage a significant increase in scholarly exchanges. In the United States, an expanded number of Mexican studies centers should be granted the resources to act as hosts for Mexican visitors, as some do already. Visits by Mexican scholars who work on Mexico as well as those who specialize on the United States or Mexican-U.S. relations are of immense benefit to U.S. experts and students. Similarly, increased support for U.S. visiting professorships at Mexican institutions would benefit both the U.S. scholars and Mexican host institutions. Efforts should also be made to bring U.S. scholars who are specialists on the United States to Mexico. While such scholars do not generally speak Spanish and would thus not be useful for undergraduate teaching at Mexican institutions, they could play an important role in the training of graduate students in diverse aspects of U.S. culture, history, society, and economy, especially in a period of transition when Mexican specialists in U.S. studies remain scarce and new specialists have not yet completed their training. We thus call for public and private support for at least ten new visiting professorships per year in U.S. and Mexican studies at appropriate institutions in each country.

Over the years, such modest efforts could make a long-run difference in levels of mutual comprehension between the United States and Mexico.

EDUCATIONAL AND CULTURAL EXCHANGE

The Commission recommends the development, intensification, and expansion of cultural exchanges between Mexico and the United States.

A full-scale program of cultural exchange is needed to enhance public awareness and understanding of the history, culture, and social life of our two nations. We look forward to exchanges that are varied, broad, and sustained. They should emphasize popular culture as well as fine arts, they should challenge stereotypes, and they should reach out to large numbers of people in both countries. They could focus on everything from literature to film, from private portraiture to public graffiti, from historical recollections to futuristic anticipations, from life in the cities to life on the borders. The sad fact is that the peoples of Mexico and the United States do not know each other very well, and a sustained series of exhibits, festivals, and exchanges—throughout the decade of the 1990s—could make an important contribution to the improvement of mutual understanding.

Such a program will require cooperation as well as support from public agencies of the two governments. Private institutions can also play an important role in this effort. In the United States, with its well-developed tradition of private, voluntary initiative, the creation of a non-governmental association to promote cultural exchange with Mexico, led by civic and cultural figures of national reputation, and supported by contributions from public agencies, foundations, and the private sector could make a major contribution in this field. In Mexico, private support for cultural exchange should also play a greater role alongside that of public institutions and agencies.

The 1980s have taken a heavy toll on student exchange. One of the largest costs of Mexico's economic austerity measures over the past six years has been the dramatic decline in spending on higher education and on support for Mexican students studying abroad. Since 1981 the number of Mexican students studying in the United States has fallen *by 40 percent,* from 7,890 to just over 5,000, while the number of U.S. study-abroad programs in Mexico has also declined. Many exchange programs between universities and research institutions in the two countries have been abandoned or fallen into disuse through lack of funds and support.

The most serious effects have been apparent in the critical area of graduate and professional training, where the number of Mexican graduate and professional students in U.S. universities has fallen from nearly 2,500 to just over 1,800 since 1981. In effect, an entire generation of Mexico's future leaders now is reaching maturity without having experienced travel or study outside the country and without having established the kind of international contacts and friendships that build understanding and facilitate cross-cultural communication.

The Commission recommends a major effort to restore the 1981 level of 2,500 Mexican graduate students in U.S. universities.

We estimate that the annual additional cost of these 700 fellowships will come to approximately $15 million, and we believe the financing should come largely from U.S. public and private sources. The vast majority of Mexican students now on financial aid in the U.S. receive support in the form of scholarships, fellowships, and assistantships provided by the colleges and universities they attend. These institutions, already under financial pressure in recent years, should be commended for their extraordinary contributions to Mexican-U.S. relations and should not be expected to shoulder additional costs. Funding from the U.S. government to realize this goal should be channelled through academic institutions in Mexico and the United States.

We would also like to see mutual support of university and other academic and scientific exchanges. Bilateral collaboration could lay the groundwork and provide funding commitments for exchanges of faculty, students, publications, exhibitions and performing artists. U.S. private and public agencies must also be convinced of the need for new efforts to assist in the maintenance and improvement of Mexico's academic and scientific infrastructure through support for library acquisitions of U.S. newspapers, periodicals, and books, enhancement of computing facilities, and related items. U.S. private foundations, whose support for research in Mexican institutions has expanded in the past few years, could make an important contribution to meeting these needs. One step that could be taken immediately would be the adoption of more flexible rules concerning the use of grant funds for equipment purchases.

The Commission recommends the creation of a non-governmental binational U.S.-Mexican Council for Advanced Research to facilitate a wide range of scholarly collaborations and exchanges between the United States and Mexico.

This new Council could be composed of representatives of leading research institutions in both countries. Its purpose would be to support individual as well as institutional programs of research and scholarship that involve the two countries. It could assist Mexican and U.S. scholars who wish to pursue training or research in the neighboring country with information about institutions, fellowship and grant opportunities, visa regulations, fieldwork sites, and sources of data. It could raise and administer fellowship and grant funds, organize and promote conferences, act as a clearinghouse and documentation center, help select works for translation, and facilitate cultural and academic exchanges of all kinds.

We have a special concern about scientific and technological exchange. Always valuable in its own right, scientific exchange is especially vital to Mexico at this particular juncture, as the country is revising its economic structure and seeking international competitiveness. To achieve success in the 1990s, Mexico will have to strengthen its scientific and technological capability.

And Mexico will have to overcome a slow start. Traditionally, Mexico has made only modest investments in research and development (R&D). During the decade of the 1970s R&D expenditures increased from 0.1 percent of GDP to 0.5 percent. By the mid-1980s the figure was around 0.6 percent of GDP (about $600 million in total), at a time when advanced industrial countries were spending

2 percent or more. (The rate for Japan was 2.8 percent.) Among developing countries 1 percent generally constitutes a benchmark for commitment, and Brazil and India have stood out within this group. Mexico has a long way to go.

Part of the problem has stemmed from the country's prolonged economic crisis. The R&D budget for CONACYT, the national agency for science and technology, declined from $20 million in 1981 to $6 million in 1987. CONACYT-sponsored fellowships for study abroad plummeted from 3,000 in 1982 to 880 in 1986. In the meantime, salaries for researchers have skidded from about $2,000 per month in 1981 to $500 in the mid-1980s. Many of the country's leading scientists have been forced to take other jobs—or to go abroad.

This situation has dire implications for Mexico—and it is not good for the United States. We believe that the two countries should form a constructive partnership in the area of science and technology, as distinct from a unidirectional program of aid, and we offer three suggestions:

- U.S. governmental agencies, such as the National Science Foundation, should set aside funds to promote and support collaborative research projects in science and technology;
- the National Academy of Sciences should establish a Latin American Science and Technology Board, which should make special efforts to establish close links with the scientific community in Mexico; and
- together, the United States and Mexican governments should take immediate steps to strengthen and reinvigorate the Mixed Commission on Science and Technology.

Established in 1972, the Mixed Commission has never lived up to its full potential. The U.S. and Mexican governments have held several discussions on the subject, but there has been no substantive action thus far. We urge immediate attention to this matter.

Under one or more of these auspices, we urge an increase in the number of visits and exchanges of professors and postdoctoral research fellows. Such non-governmental agencies as the U.S. National Science Association and the Academia Mexicana de Investigación Científica can play an active role in this regard.

Finally, we believe that the restoration of the post of Scientific Advisor in the Mexican Embassy in Washington would also facilitate scientific exchange.

A special opportunity for some of these initiatives will come in 1992, the quincentennial anniversary of Christopher Columbus' voyage to America—and, as such, a landmark celebration of the benefits of applied technology. It will also be the occasion for the International Space Year. We urge both U.S. and Mexican governments to take advantage of these celebrations in order to promote bilateral programs in science and technology.

CONCLUSIONS AND RECOMMENDATIONS

Throughout this chapter we have offered numerous recommendations, large and small, for the improvement of cultural relations and communications between Mexico and the United States. We have called for further research on three subjects: (1) a study of the U.S. content of Mexico's commercially produced primary and secondary textbooks in history and the social sciences; (2) a survey of the content as well as the time and resources devoted to Mexico in U.S. primary and secondary schools; and (3) studies of cultural stereotypes of Mexicans, Mexican-Americans, and Hispanics in U.S. film and television.

We have suggested the creation of three new institutional initiatives: (1) creation of a national clearinghouse (or regional clearinghouses) to make curricular and extra-curricular materials on Mexico available to primary and secondary schools throughout the United States; (2) strengthening of the ANUIES organization of U.S. studies programs in Mexico to facilitate the development of research and training on the United States; and (3) formation of a new binational U.S.-Mexican Council for Advanced Research to organize, coordinate, and promote scholarly and scientific exchanges between our two countries.

In addition, we have set forth a variety of recommendations for increasing and improving what school children in Mexico learn about the United States, and vice versa; for expanding and improving the quality of news coverage in the two countries; and for developing human and institutional resources devoted to university-level teaching and research on the United States in Mexico and on Mexico in the United States. We conclude with our most important proposal:

The Commission recommends the implementation, expansion, and development of the recent Bilateral Agreement on Cultural Exchange and Scientific Cooperation between Mexico and the United States.

Signed in June 1987, the Agreement itself establishes a series of categories and themes for cultural cooperation, and it offers a promising framework. But previous agreements, for all their good intentions, have languished for lack of commitment.[8] The challenge will reside in the implementation: in the allocation of funds and in the practical execution of cultural programs. A formal agreement between the two countries will improve relations only if both sides recognize the importance of making it work.

Of course, all of our objectives could be achieved piecemeal outside the framework of the formal document. None should be set aside or scaled down by either government merely for a lack of support through a treaty.

Implementation of the Bilateral Agreement should recognize that the disparities in power and resources that characterize other aspects of the U.S.-Mexican relationship find their counterparts in the fields of cultural promotion and educational development. The United States should thus be prepared to contribute the major share of the financial resources needed to assure the success of the new agreement. Such a commitment was lacking when the two countries recently agreed to a new "program" which incorporated plans to enlist private support for cultural exchanges between the two countries. The Commission endorses such efforts and recommends that they be continued and expanded. The Commission also believes, however, that strengthening cultural and scientific exchange and cooperation between the two countries is a goal of such importance that both governments, in proportion to their capacities, must be prepared to contribute significant new resources to the effort.

To enhance public understanding, the two governments should agree (a) to promote and finance, through appropriate public as

8. The first formal agreement on cultural cooperation took effect in 1949; it was amended in 1972, 1979, and 1987. Its governing board, a United States-Mexican Commission on Cultural Cooperation, has met *only six times* since 1949. The 1987 agreement does not entail any specific commitment of resources by either country.

well as non-governmental bodies, a vastly increased program of exchanges involving the performing and fine arts, television, and film as well as other cultural resources. The Bilateral Agreement should also undertake (b) to provide support, channelled through appropriate non-governmental bodies, for the timely translation of literary, journalistic, and scholarly works to make them accessible to the general publics of the two countries.

The agreement should include a commitment on the part of the United States government to appropriate the resources needed for many of the activities we have already recommended:

- to provide scholarship and fellowship opportunities for Mexican students in U.S. universities on a much larger scale than in the recent past, especially in science and technology;

- to expand existing programs of support for the research of U.S. and Mexican scholars through the Fulbright program as well as other, non-governmental programs;

- to facilitate and support exchanges of students, researchers, and other personnel as well as publications and other materials between cultural institutions, universities, and scientific laboratories;

- to make U.S. books and periodicals available to Mexican institutions;

- to provide support for the designation and operation of at least one Mexican depository for U.S. federal government publications, and vice versa;

- to support public and private efforts to create and promote short in-country educational programs on historical and cultural themes;

- to promote exchanges for occupational and professional bodies, civic associations, public interest organizations, local officials, and other private groups; and

- to establish a program of grants for travel to conferences and seminars in the United States, for purchases of scientific equipment including computing facilities, for the enhancement of research facilities such as libraries, archives and museums, and for U.S. training of Mexican personnel at the technical and vocational level in such skills as electronics and machine operation.

The U.S. government should also commit itself to a revision of existing visa regulations that restrict issuance of student or exchange visitor visas for certain kinds of scholars, such as degree candidates at Mexican universities pursuing M.A. or Ph.D. thesis research, postdoctoral fellows supported by Mexican institutions or private grants, and students or scholars who are not degree candidates but wish to engage in formal study in U.S. institutions.

For its part, the government of Mexico should undertake to promote and support cultural and scientific exchanges (a) by contributing to the local-currency costs they generate and (b) by eliminating bureaucratic obstacles to visits by foreign students, scholars, and scientists, and to the importation of scientific equipment.

The Commission also wishes to make clear its recognition that an expanded program of cultural and scientific exchange cannot, by itself, overcome the effects of the consistent failure of governments in both countries to give sufficient priority to educational reforms. In the United States, for example, repeated studies of education at all levels have pointed to serious and persistent deficiencies, from the high dropout and low achievement rates of inner-city minorities (including Mexican-Americans) to the lack of support for training in foreign languages and international studies. In Mexico, the long-term, historic failure to devote sufficient resources to education from primary schooling through postgraduate training and research (in comparison with other countries at similar levels of development) has been compounded by the fiscal constraints of the 1980s.

At the same time, we also believe that this kind of program represents a solid investment in the future of the relationship. According to our preliminary estimates, the total costs for U.S. contributions to all the activities we have recommended would come to less than $100 million per year. Contributions on the Mexican side might come to an additional $10-to-$15 million. These are substantial sums, but we firmly believe that they represent sound investments.

To a large degree, the future shape of the bilateral relationship between Mexico and the United States is being determined, here and now, by the magnitude and quality of the cultural relations between our two peoples. The future is now being shaped:

- by the information and images available in the media;
- by what our children are taught (or not taught) in school;
- by the number and quality of cooperative contacts among individual citizens, private institutions, and public agencies of the two countries;
- by the extent to which the people of the two countries are coming to know about and learn to respect each others' cultural and scientific achievements; and
- by the investment each country is making in training and employing scholars and experts on the history, economy, politics, culture, and society of the other.

Improved knowledge of each other's past history, of current situations, and of the complexity of the relationship will not eliminate differences of opinion or points of friction. But it will, undoubtedly, help give citizens of our two countries a realistic basis for judging and appreciating one another. How successful Mexico and the United States will be in managing their relations in the twenty-first century will be determined to a large degree by what they do to enhance communications and cultural relations right now.

Conclusion:
Toward A Bilateral Approach

Like its topic, this report is unwieldy. We have covered a great deal of material, and we have offered a substantial number of recommendations to the governments of both Mexico and the United States. We do not have a single or simple solution to problems the two countries face. The bilateral relationship is delicate and complex. Its management must be thoughtful, careful, constructive.

The issues that we analyze in this report—economics, migration, drugs, foreign policy, culture—lie at the core of the relationship. They will persist through the 1990s and into the next century. A sensible approach to these questions will make an important contribution to the betterment of the relationship as a whole.

Our recommendations are designed to do just that. Having reviewed our proposals time and again, from the perspectives of both nations, we believe that our suggestions should be acceptable to the governments in Mexico City and Washington. We think our measures will have significant and positive results. We regard our suggestions as feasible and effective.

Our deliberations have left us with several strong impressions. We have been struck, first, by the scarcity of information on some basic issues in the relationship. The lack of a reliable estimate on the stocks and flows of Mexican migrants to the U.S. is but one example of the problem. There are too many unknowns.

Second, we have seen, time and again, profound differences in general attitudes and outlooks. Mexicans and Americans simply see the world in different ways. There are misperceptions about each other on both sides of the border, and our recommendations for public education are intended to address some of these problems. But there are fundamental differences in worldviews as well: even with the same facts in hand, Mexicans and Americans are likely to forge differing interpretations. This situation calls for flexibility and understanding, not just more information.

Third, and perhaps most important, we have discovered a remarkable range of agreement. On economics, drugs, foreign policy—and other issues that have given rise to so much controversy throughout the 1980s—we have found that, notwithstanding unavoidable differences in national interest, basic goals for Mexico and the United States are highly compatible. The two nations have every reason to be able to get along with each other. Our appeals for cooperation are based not on wishful thinking but on practical assessments of national realities and purposes.

We also recognize that the U.S.-Mexican relationship is constantly evolving, that new issues will arise in the future. People and governments in both countries should be ready for such transformations. As the bilateral agenda changes, there will be a need for continual evaluation and innovation in the policy process.

What we offer in this report is not only a series of specific recommendations, but an overall approach—a bilateral approach to bilateral problems. Common challenges call for cooperative responses.

This is more easily said than done. Collaboration demands more than good will. The formulation of a truly bilateral approach requires patience, understanding, and determination. It demands a willingness to discard preconceptions and to search for innovations. At times this can be hard.

Our experience on this Commission has been instructive. The discussions have on the whole been amiable, but on occasion they have been tense. We have talked past each other more than once. At one point some even thought we might have to abandon the project altogether.

We persisted. In retrospect, it appears that we owe much of our success to several key factors. First was our mandate: we were focusing on long-term questions, not immediate crises or headlines, so our discussions could aim beyond short-term vexations. Revealingly enough, our most serious difficulty arose only when we were unable to avoid the temporary pressure of headlines and events.

Second, we had time on our side. With a two-year work schedule we had ample opportunity to work things out, to correct misunderstandings, to rethink our positions and start anew. We have all changed our minds on some subjects.

Third was the composition of the Commission itself. Since we did not participate as official representatives of our nations or governments, we could express independent and personal views. This proved to be a special advantage as presidential campaigns were taking place in the two countries.

Fourth was our conviction—about the importance of U.S.-Mexican relations and about the need for action, especially at this rare moment of opportunity. By common agreement we have managed to reach a bilateral consensus on virtually all of our recommendations; to achieve this goal some of us have sometimes refrained from pursuing ideas to their logical conclusions. In the end, we persisted because we cared enough to do so.

This report is one result.

Another result is procedural. In a sense, our *process* is our most important product. We believe that the kind of dialogue we have undertaken—open, flexible, unencumbered by short-term pressure—can serve as a model for private leaders and public officials in the two countries. In particular, we urge representatives of both Mexico and the United States to focus upon both the *nature* and the *potential* of the relationship, to take a long-term view of national interests, to discard preconceptions and to explore the possibilities of collaboration and cooperation. Working together and respecting each other, Mexico and the United States can create a remarkable future.

Appendices

I. Biographies of Commission Members

Héctor Aguilar Camín

Héctor Aguilar Camín is director of the magazine *Nexos*. Born in Chetumal, Quintana Roo, he studied at the Universidad Iberoamericana and obtained a doctorate in history from El Colegio de México.

A historian and journalist, Mr. Aguilar Camín has written works of fiction and non-fiction. His latest book, a novel, is entitled *Morir en el Golfo*. He was one of the founding editors of the newspaper *La Jornada*.

Gilberto Borja Navarrete

Gilberto Borja is president of the Grupo ICA, a consortium of 137 member companies in construction, engineering, tourism, cement, automobile parts, electronics, mining, and petrochemicals.

Born in Mexico City, Mr. Borja received a degree in engineering from the National Autonomous University of Mexico. He began his career as an engineer with ICA (Ingenieros Civiles Asociados) in 1950 and became president of the ICA group in 1984.

He belongs to various corporate boards—including those of the Banco Nacional de México, the Fundación Mexicana para la Salud, and the Banco Obrero. Mr. Borja is also an adviser to the IEPES (Instituto de Estudios Políticos, Económicos, y Sociales) of the PRI, a member of the Patronato del Sistema Nacional para el Desarrollo Integral de la Familia, and a board member for the Colegio de Educación Profesional Técnica.

Yvonne Brathwaite Burke

Now in the practice of law, Yvonne Brathwaite Burke was born in Los Angeles. She graduated from UCLA in 1953 and received her law degree from the University of Southern California in 1956.

A Democrat, Ms. Burke won election to the California Assembly and later to the U.S. House of Representatives, where she served as chairwoman of the congressional Black Caucus. She is also a member and has been vice chairwoman of the Women's Democratic Forum.

She sits on numerous boards and has received many honors, including the designation by *Time* magazine as one of 200 Future Leaders in 1974. She has been a fellow at the John F. Kennedy School at Harvard and a Chubb Fellow at Yale University. In 1987 Ms. Burke became a member of the Board of Regents at the University of California and a trustee of the Ford Foundation.

Juan José Bremer Martino

Juan José Bremer is Mexico's Ambassador to the Soviet Union. Born in Mexico City, he obtained his law degree from the National Autonomous University in 1967.

Mr. Bremer has served as private secretary to the President (1972-75), Undersecretary of the Presidency (1975-76), and director of the National Institute of Fine Arts (1976-82). He has been Ambassador to Switzerland (1982) and Undersecretary of Public Education (1982-85). At the time of his appointment to the Bilateral Commission he was a federal deputy from the Federal District in Mexico and chairman of the Foreign Relations Committee.

Fernando Canales Clariond

Mr. Canales Clariond is director of the Grupo IMSA, an industrial group in the Mexican north.

Born in Monterrey, he earned a degree from the Free Law School (the Escuela Libre de Derecho). He also earned a master's degree in business from the Instituto Tecnológico de Monterrey and specialized in the study of industrial relations at the Institute for Social Studies in the Netherlands.

He has been a professor at the Autonomous University of Nuevo León and president of the Confederation of Chambers of Commerce of Nuevo León. A member of the PAN (Partido de Acción Nacional), he was elected to the national Chamber of Deputies in 1979-82 and ran for the governorship of Nuevo León in 1985. He is currently a member of the national executive committee of the PAN.

Henry G. Cisneros

Henry Cisneros is the mayor of San Antonio, his native city. He obtained bachelor's and master's degrees from Texas A&M University and received a master's degree from the Kennedy School of Government. In 1975 he earned the doctoral degree from George Washington University in public administration. He has been on the faculty of the University of Texas at San Antonio since 1974 and in 1982 he published a book on *San Antonio's Role in the Technology Economy*.

He was first elected Mayor in 1981. A Democrat, he is currently a member of the President's Federalism Council and of the National Council for Urban Economic Development. He has received the Jefferson Award from the American Institute of Public Service and the Torch of Liberty Award from the Anti-Defamation League of the B'nai B'rith. In 1983 he served on the Bipartisan Commission on Central America.

Socorro Díaz Palacios

Socorro Díaz has been a federal Senator from Colima, her native state, and is now a federal deputy. She received a degree in journalism in 1970 and has pursued an active career in that field, becoming director of the newspaper *El Día* in 1981.

She has been active in the PRI since 1969. In the Senate she served on a wide variety of committees and was president of the chamber.

Ms. Díaz has written numerous articles and essays and she has taught at the national university.

Lawrence S. Eagleburger

Lawrence Eagleburger is president of Kissinger Associates, Inc. Born in Milwaukee, he earned bachelor's and master's degrees from the University of Wisconsin and entered the U.S. Foreign Service in 1957.

Early in his career Mr. Eagleburger served in embassy posts in Tegucigalpa and Belgrade. He subsequently became a staff member of the National Security Council (1966-67), special assistant to the Under Secretary of State (1967-69), political adviser to the U.S. Mission to NATO (1969-71), department assistant to the President for National Security Operations and executive assistant to the Secretary of State (1975-77).

Mr. Eagleburger was Ambassador to Yugoslavia. In 1982-84 he was Under Secretary of Political Affairs. He received the President's Award for Distinguished Federal Civilian Service in 1973 and the Presidential Distinguished Service Award in 1983.

Ernesto Fernández Hurtado

Mr. Fernández Hurtado is currently director of the Banco de Comercio (BANCOMER). Born in Colima, he studied economics at the National Autonomous University and did post-graduate work at Harvard University.

A distinguished public servant, Mr. Fernández Hurtado joined the Bank of Mexico in 1948 and rose through the ranks to become its director from 1970 to 1976.

He has taught at the national university and at the Instituto Tecnológico de México (ITAM), and he is the author of *50 años de banca central*. He is a member of the Colegio de Economistas and other professional organizations.

Carlos Fuentes

Carlos Fuentes is a playwright, essayist, novelist, professor, and critic. The son of a Mexican diplomat, Mr. Fuentes was born in Panama City and attended schools in Washington, D.C., Santiago de Chile, Buenos Aires, Geneva, and Mexico City. Mr. Fuentes has also served on numerous governmental commissions, and was Mexico's Ambassador to France from 1974 to 1977.

His novels include *La región más transparente, Las buenas conciencias, La muerte de Artemio Cruz, Zona sagrada, Terra nostra,* and *El gringo viejo.* His works have been translated into twenty-five languages and reached a worldwide audience. He has lectured at such institutions as Harvard, Columbia, Princeton, and Cambridge. He has received honorary degrees from Harvard and Wesleyan and, in 1982, was made a Literary Lion of the New York Public Library.

Roger W. Heyns

Roger Heyns is president of the William and Flora Hewlett Foundation, a position he has held since 1977.

A native of Grand Rapids, Michigan, he earned the Ph.D. in social psychology from the University of Michigan and joined the faculty of that institution. There he became dean and vice-chancellor before moving to the University of California, Berkeley as chancellor in 1965.

From 1972 to 1977 Mr. Heyns was president of the American Council on Education. He has received numerous awards for teaching and for service to education, including the Clark Kerr Award in 1967. He has also been a trustee of the Brookings Institution and of the Center for Advanced Studies in the Behavioral Sciences.

Nancy Landon Kassebaum

Nancy Kassebaum is a U.S. Senator from Kansas. Born in Topeka, she obtained a bachelor's degree from the University of Kansas and a master's degree from the University of Michigan.

A member of the Republican Party, she was first elected to the Senate in 1978 and is now in her second term. Her assignments there have included a post on the Foreign Relations Committee.

Ms. Kassebaum was a radio journalist before moving to Washington as a senatorial staff member. She is a recipient of the Matrix Award for Women in Communications.

Hugo B. Margáin

Hugo Margáin has been most recently a Senator from the Federal District of Mexico. Born in Mexico City, he studied law at the National Autonomous University of Mexico and practiced law from 1939 to 1980. In 1947 and 1951-56 he was a professor at the national university.

Mr. Margáin has had a long and distinguished public career. From 1964 to 1970 and again from 1976 to 1980 he served as Mexican Ambassador to the United States. He was Secretary of the Treasury in 1970-73 and co-founder of the National Institute of Housing (INFONAVIT) in 1971. He was also Ambassador to the Court of St. James in 1973-76.

He is a past president of the special group of governors of the Inter-American Development Bank and he has been a governor of the International Monetary Fund. Mr. Margáin has received honorary degrees from several universities in the United States.

Hugo Margáin has served as Co-chairman of the Bilateral Commission.

Robert S. McNamara

Born in San Francisco, Robert S. McNamara graduated from the University of California in 1937 and received a master's degree from the Harvard Business School in 1939. He was on the Harvard Business faculty from 1940 to 1943, served in the U.S. Air Force from 1943 to 1946, and joined the Ford Motor Company in 1946.

From 1961 to 1968 he was Secretary of Defense. From 1968 to 1981 he was president of the World Bank.

Mr. McNamara has written several books and served on numerous committees, including the boards of the California Institute of Technology and of the Ford Foundation. His many awards include the Albert Einstein Peace Prize and the Franklin D. Roosevelt Freedom from Want Medal.

Mario Ojeda Gómez

Mario Ojeda is president of El Colegio de México. Born in Jalapa, Veracruz, he studied at the national university and at Harvard.

Mr. Ojeda joined the faculty of El Colegio de México in 1962. A leading analyst of Mexican foreign policy and international relations, he has published two major books, *Alcances y límites de la política exterior de México* and *México: el surgimiento de una política exterior activa*. He serves on numerous academic boards and has been a visiting researcher at the Brookings Institution and the Royal Institute of International Affairs and a visiting professor at the Massachusetts Institute of Technology.

Charles William Parry

Charles W. Parry is the former chairman and chief executive officer of the Aluminum Company of America. He was born in Pittsburgh, and after serving in the U.S. Army earned a bachelor of science degree in electrical engineering from the University of Pittsburgh in 1948.

That same year he went to work for Alcoa. He became a vice president in 1974, president in 1981, and chairman/CEO in 1983. He is a member of the board of trustees of Carnegie-Mellon University and Carlow College. He is also a director of Alcoa, the Aristech Chemical Corporation, the Goodyear Tire and Rubber Company, and the Nalco Chemical Company.

William D. Rogers

William Rogers is a partner in the Washington law firm of Arnold & Porter. He entered the firm after graduating from Princeton University and the Yale Law School and after serving as a clerk on the United States Supreme Court.

In 1962 he became Special Counsel and later Deputy U.S. Coordinator for the Alliance for Progress, eventually receiving the Agency for International Development's Medal of Honor. In 1974 he became Assistant Secretary of State for Inter-American Relations, and in 1976 he became Under Secretary of State for Economic Affairs. He returned to private practice with Arnold & Porter in 1977.

Mr. Rogers currently sits on numerous panels and boards, including the Board of Directors of the Council on Foreign Relations and the Executive Committee of the Overseas Development Council. He was president of the American Society of International Law from 1972 to 1974. He was a member of the law faculty of Cambridge University, England in 1982-83 and senior counsellor to the National Bipartisan Commission on Central America in 1983. He also serves as a member of the Board of Directors of Kissinger Associates, Inc.

William Rogers has served as Co-chairman of the Bilateral Commission.

Glenn E. Watts

Glenn Watts is recently retired president of the Communications Workers of America and a former vice-president of the AFL-CIO. Born in Stoney Point, North Carolina, he went to work for the Chesapeake & Potomac Telephone Company in 1941 and joined the Communications Workers Union in 1942.

A member-at-large of the Democratic National Committee since 1974, Mr. Watts served on the President's Commission on Mental Health in 1977-78 and on the President's Commission on the Holocaust in 1978-79. He has been a member of the Labor Council for Latin American Advancement. He has been a board member of Common Cause and of the Ford Foundation. He also serves on the Trilateral Commission, on the Helsinki Watch, and on the Aspen Institute of Humanistic Studies.

STAFF DIRECTORS:

Rosario Green

Rosario Green is director of the Matías Romero Institute of Diplomatic Studies. She studied economics and international relations at the National Autonomous University of Mexico, at El Colegio de México, at Columbia University in New York and at the Instituto para la Integración Latinoamericana (INTAL) in Buenos Aires.

She has been a professor at El Colegio de México since 1968. Ms. Green has published ten books, including a prescient analysis of Mexico's foreign indebtedness—*El endeudamiento público externo de México: 1940-1973; Estado y banca transnacional en México*; and, most recently, *La deuda externa de México de 1973 a 1988: de la abundancia a la escasez de créditos*. She has written articles for academic reviews and journalistic media in various languages. Ms. Green has also been a consultant to the United Nations and to the Sistema Económico Latinoamericano.

Peter H. Smith

Peter H. Smith is professor of political science and Simón Bolívar professor of Latin American studies at the University of California, San Diego. Born in Brooklyn, New York, he graduated from Harvard College in 1961 and earned a Ph.D. from Columbia University in 1966.

A specialist on long-run processes of political change, Mr. Smith has written books on Argentina and on empirical methodology. His best-known work on Mexico is *Labyrinths of Power*, a study of elite recruitment and mobility. He has also co-authored a textbook entitled *Modern Latin America*.

Mr. Smith has served as a department chair and academic associate dean at the University of Wisconsin and at MIT, and he is past president of the Latin American Studies Association. He was professor of history and political science at the Massachusetts Institute of Technology before joining the faculty of UC-San Diego.

II. Inventory of Commissioned Papers

ECONOMICS: DEBT, TRADE, AND INVESTMENT

I. Linkages

Living with Macroeconomic Imbalance
Barry Bosworth (Brookings Institution)

Today's Dilemma in U.S.-Mexican Economic Relations: Cooperation or Aggravation of the Crisis
Mauricio de María y Campos (Secretaría de Hacienda)

The Challenge of United States-Mexican Interdependence
Clark W. Reynolds (Stanford University)

Medium- and Long-Term Problems in U.S.-Mexican Economic Relations
and
Underlying Problems of the Mexican Economy and Their Impact on U.S.-Mexican Relations
Francisco Gil Díaz (Secretaría de Hacienda)

II. Debt

Mexico and the U.S. Banks
Rosario Green (Instituto Matías Romero)

Implications of Alternative Debt Strategies for Mexico
William R. Cline (Institute of International Economics)

Mexico's Foreign Debt: Scenarios for the Future
Francisco Suárez Davila (Secretaría de Hacienda)

III. Trade

Mexico's Foreign Trade Policy and Commercial Relations with the United States
Luis Bravo Aguilera (Secretaría de Comercio y Fomento Industrial)

U.S.-Mexican Trade Issues
Guy F. Erb and Joseph Greenwald (GFE Associates)

IV. Investment

The Role of Foreign Investment in the 1990s
Manuel Armendáriz (Secretaría de Comercio y Fomento Industrial)

Foreign Investment in Mexico: A Statistical Note
Guy F. Erb (GFE Associates)

THE PROCESS OF MIGRATION

I. Patterns

The United States Demand for Mexican Labor
Wayne Cornelius (Center for U.S.-Mexican Studies, University of California, San Diego)

The Mexican Labor Supply
Manuel García y Griego (El Colegio de México)

II. Effects

Looking to the 1990s: Mexican Immigration in Sociological Perspective
Marta Tienda (University of Chicago)

Social Change and International Labor Migration: An Overview of Four Agrarian Regions in Mexico
Guillermo de la Peña (El Colegio de Jalisco)

III. Options

The Immigration Policy Debate: A Critical Analysis and Options for the Future
Kitty Calavita (Center for U.S.-Mexican Studies, University of California, San Diego)

Undocumented Immigration: Policy Options for Mexico
Jorge Bustamante (El Colegio de la Frontera Norte)

THE PROBLEM OF DRUGS

I. Issues

Changing Patterns of Drug Abuse in the United States
    Ann J. Blanken (National Institute on Drug Abuse)

The Supply of Illicit Drugs: International Flows and the Changing Role of Mexico
    Miguel Ruiz-Cabañas I. (Columbia University)

II. Policies

United States Anti-Drug Policy with Mexico: Consequences for American Society and U.S.-Mexican Relations
    Richard B. Craig (Kent State University)

Control Perspectives for the Drug Market: United States and Mexico
    Samuel I. del Villar (El Colegio de México)

III. Lessons

The Historical Record: U.S. Narcotics Control Collaboration with Turkey, Mexico, and Colombia
    Mathea Falco (Hunter College/CUNY)

The European Experience: Programs for Prevention and Control in Sweden, Britain, and the Netherlands
    Hans Lundborg (Coordinator of Drug Programs, Social Department, Government of Sweden)

FOREIGN POLICY AND INTER-STATE RELATIONS

I. Issues

U.S. and Mexican Policies toward Central America
    Claude Heller (Secretaría de Relaciones Exteriores)

Mexican and United States Participation in the United Nations and the Organization of American States
    Jorge Montaño (Secretaría de Relaciones Exteriores)

Collaboration and Cooperation along the Border
    Marco Antonio Alcazar (Secretaría de Relaciones Exteriores)

The Changing Political Role of the Mexican-Origin Population in U.S.-Mexican Relations
    Rodolfo de la Garza (University of Texas)

II. Foundations

Mexico: Traditions and Premises in Foreign Policy
   Guadalupe González (Instituto Latinoamericano de Estudios
   Transnacionales)

United States: Traditions and Premises in Foreign Policy
   Lars Schoultz (University of North Carolina)

III. Processes

The Making of U.S. Policy toward Mexico
   Bruce Bagley (University of Miami)

The Making of Mexican Policy toward the U.S.
   Jorge Chabat (El Colegio de México)

IV. Capacities

*Mexico and the United States: Mutual Interest in the Development of a
Good Neighborhood*
   José Juan de Olloqui (Secretaría de Relaciones Exteriores)

Potential for Mexican Influence on the United States
   Carlos Rico (El Colegio de México)

*Potential for United States Influence on Mexico: Will Administrative
Reform Help?*
   Cathryn Thorup (Overseas Development Council)

U.S.-Mexico: A Modest Proposal
   William H. Luers (Metropolitan Museum of Art; former U.S.
   Ambassador)

EDUCATION AND PUBLIC OPINION

I. Public Opinion

United States Public Opinion of Mexico
   Hal Quinley (Yankelovich, Skelly and White/
   Clancy, Shulman, Inc.)

U.S. Perceptions of United States-Mexican Relations
   Christine E. Contee (Overseas Development Council)

Mexican Public Opinion of the United States: A North American View
   Barbara G. Farah (New York Times)

II.   Society and Media

Change in Mexico and United States Potential Consciousness
    Sergio Aguayo (Universidad Nacional Autonóma de México)

Mexico in the U.S. Media, 1979-86
    John Bailey (Georgetown University)

To View a Neighbor: The Hollywood Textbook on Mexico
    Carlos E. Cortés (University of California, Riverside)

III.   Education

Mexico in U.S. Primary and Secondary Schools
    Gerald Greenfield (University of Wisconsin, Parkside)

The Image of the United States in Mexican Textbooks
    Josefina Vázquez (El Colegio de México)

Student, Academic, and Cultural Exchanges between Mexico and the United States
    John H. Coatsworth (University of Chicago)

The Status of Mexican Science and Technology Research: Potential Avenues for Collaborative Programs with the United States
    José Sarukhan (Universidad Nacional Autonóma de México)

Mexican Studies in the United States
    Peter H. Smith (University of California, San Diego)

U.S. Studies in Mexico
    Carlos Rico (El Colegio de México)

III. Selected Bibliography

Alduncín Abitia, Enrique. *Los valores de los mexicanos*. México: Fundación Cultural Banamex, 1986.

Ambrose, Stephen E. *Rise to Globalism: American Foreign Policy, 1938-1980*, second revised edition. New York: Penguin Books, 1980.

Bean, Frank, Allan King, and Jeffrey Passel. "The Number of Illegal Migrants of Mexican Origin in the United States: Sex-Ratio-Based Estimates for 1980." *Demography* 20, 1 (1983): 99-109.

Bjerke, John A., and Karen K. Hess. "Selected Characteristics of Illegal Aliens Apprehended by the U.S. Border Patrol." U.S. Border Patrol and Immigration and Naturalization Service, 1987.

Connor, Walker (ed.). *Mexican-Americans in Comparative Perspective*. Washington: The Urban Institute, 1985.

Conover, Ted. *Coyotes: A Journey through the Secret World of America's Illegal Aliens*. New York: Vintage/Random House, 1987.

Cornelius, Wayne A. "Impacts of the 1986 Immigration Reform and Control Act: A Second-Year Assessment," presentation to the Eighth Annual Briefing Session for Journalists. La Jolla, CA: Center for U.S.-Mexican Studies, University of California, San Diego, June 1988.

_____ et al. "Mexican Immigrants and Southern California: A Summary of Current Knowledge," Research Report 36. La Jolla, CA: Center for U.S.-Mexican Studies, University of California, San Diego, 1982.

Cosío Villegas, Daniel. *Historia mínima de México*, seventh edition. Mexico: El Colegio de México, 1983.

_____. *Historia moderna de México. La República restaurada: vida política*, third edition. México: Editorial Hermes, 1973.

Cross , Harry E., and James A. Sandos. *Across the Border: Rural Development in Mexico and Recent Migration to the United States.* Berkeley: Institute of Governmental Studies, University of California, 1981.

Current, Richard N., T. Harry Williams, and Frank Friedel. *American History: A Survey,* third edition. New York: Alfred A. Knopf, 1971.

Díaz del Castillo, Bernal. *Historia verdadera de la Conquista de Nueva España,* fifth edition. Madrid: Espasa-Calpe, 1982.

Felipe Leal, Juan. *La burguesía mexicana y el estado mexicano,* fifth edition. México: El Caballito, 1972.

Fleming, Dan B. "Latin America and the United States: What Do United States History Textbooks Tell Us?" *The Social Studies* (July-August 1982): 168-171.

Fulbright, J. William. *The Arrogance of Power.* New York: Random House, 1967.

Grayson, George W. *The United States and Mexico: Patterns of Influence.* New York: Praeger, 1984.

Green, Rosario. *La deuda externa de México de 1973 a 1988: de la abundancia a la escasez de créditos.* México: Secretaría de Relaciones Exteriores/Nueva Imagen, 1988.

Greenberg, Bradley S. and Pilar Baptista-Fernández. "Hispanic Americans—The New Minority on Television," in Bradley S. Greenberg et al., *Life on Television: Content Analysis of U.S. TV Drama.* Norwood, NJ: Ablex Publishing Corporation, 1980.

Harper, Gregory. "Profiles of Illegal Aliens Apprehended by the U.S. Border Patrol." Statistical Analysis Branch, Immigration and Naturalization Service, 1987.

Harris Survey Press Release 44 (August 11, 1986).

Hartz, Louis (ed.). *The Founding of New Societies.* New York: Harcourt, Brace, and World, 1964.

_____. *The Liberal Tradition in America: An Interpretation of American Political Thought since the Revolution.* New York: Harcourt Brace, 1955.

Hill, Kenneth. "Illegal Aliens: An Assessment," in Daniel B. Levine, Kenneth Hill, and Robert Warren (eds.), *Immigration Statistics: A Story of Neglect.* Washington: National Academy of Sciences, 1985.

Inter-American Working Group. *Collective Security in the Americas: New Directions.* Boston: World Peace Foundation, 1988.

Keys, Donald, and Astrid Koch. "Voting in the General Assembly of the United Nations: 1970-1985." San Anselmo, CA: Planetary Citizens, 1985.

Keely, Charles B. "Immigration Composition and Population Policy." *Science* 185 (1982): 587-593.

Kissinger, Henry, and Cyrus Vance. "Bipartisan Objectives for American Foreign Policy." *Foreign Affairs 66*, 5 (Summer 1988): 899-921.

Kleiman, Mark A. "State and Social Drug Law Enforcement: Issues and Practices." Program in Criminal Justice Policy and Management, John F. Kennedy School of Government, Harvard University, 1987.

Lang, James. *Conquest and Commerce: Spain and England in the Americas.* New York: Academic Press, 1975.

Lee, Rensselaer W. III. "The Latin American Drug Connection." *Foreign Policy*, (Winter 1985-86): 142-159.

Lichter, S. Robert, Linda S. Lichter, Stanley Rothman, and Daniel Amundson. "Prime-Time Prejudice: TV's Images of Blacks and Hispanics," *Public Opinion* (July-August 1987): 13-16.

México. *IX censo general de población*, 1970. Mexico City: Talleres Gráficos de la Nación, 1971-1973.

_____. *Cuaderno de Información Oportuna*, nos. 150 and 160 (1985 and 1986).

_____. *Política exterior de México: 175 años de historia*, vol. I. México: Secretaría de Relaciones Exteriores, 1985.

_____. *Procuraduría de la República. Campaña contra el narcotráfico y la farmacodependencia: el esfuerzo de México.* México: Talleres Gráficos de la Nación, 1987.

Meyer, Lorenzo, and Josefina Vázquez. *México frente a Estados Unidos: un ensayo histórico 1776-1980.* México: El Colegio de México, 1982.

Millard, William. "Better-Educated Mexican Opinion on Key Political and Economic Issues." Research Report R-2285. Office of Research, United States Information Service; decontrolled 30 September 1986.

Moore, Mark H. "Drugs: The Problem and the Options." Program in Criminal Justice Policy and Management Working Paper 87-01-09, John F. Kennedy School of Government, Harvard University, 1987.

Muller, Thomas, and Thomas Espenshade. *The Fourth Wave: California's Newest Immigrants.* Washington: The Urban Institute Press, 1985.

Nadelmann, Ethan A. "U.S. Drug Policy: A Bad Export." *Foreign Policy* 70 (Spring 1988): 83-108.

National Narcotics Intelligence Consumers Committee (NNICC). *The NNICC Report, 1976-77* through *1986-87*.

Ojeda, Mario. *Alcances y límites de la política exterior de México.* México: El Colegio de México, 1976.

_____. *México: el surgimiento de una política exterior activa.* México: Secretaría de Educación Pública, 1986.

Paz, Octavio. *Sor Juana Inés de la Cruz o las trampas de la fe*, third edition. México: Fondo de Cultura Económica, 1983.

_____. *The Labyrinth of Solitude: Life and Thought in Mexico*, trans. Lysander Kemp. New York: Grove Press, 1961.

Perkins, Dexter. *A History of the Monroe Doctrine*, revised edition. Boston: Little Brown, 1963.

Pike, Lewis, and T.S. Barrows. *Other Nations, Other People: A Survey of Student Interests, Knowledge, Attitudes, and Perceptions*. Princeton: Educational Testing Service, 1979.

Portes, Alejandro, and Robert L. Bach. *Latin Journey: Cuban and Mexican Immigrants in the United States*. Berkeley and Los Angeles: University of California Press, 1985.

Rabasa, Emilio. *La Constitución y la dictadura: estudio sobre la organización política de México*, third edition. México: Editorial Porrúa, 1956.

Reilly , John E. (ed.). *American Public Opinion and U.S. Foreign Policy 1987*. Chicago: Chicago Council on Foreign Relations, 1987.

Reuter, Peter. *Eternal Hope: America's International Narcotics Efforts*. Washington, DC: The Rand Corporation, 1983.

_____ and Mark A. Kleiman. "Risks and Prices: An Economic Analysis of Drug Enforcement," in Michael Tonry and Norval Morris (eds.), Crime and Justice: *An Annual Review of Research 7* (July 1986).

Reyes Heroles, Jesús. *El liberalismo mexicano*, vol. II (*La sociedad fluctuante*). México: Universidad Nacional Autónoma de México, 1958.

Riding, Alan. *Distant Neighbors: A Portrait of the Mexicans*. New York: Alfred A. Knopf, 1985.

Rouse, Roger. "Changing Patterns of Migration: A Case Study of Mexican Migration to the United States." Paper presented to the Commission for the Study of International Migration and Economic Development (March 1988).

Rubio Mañé, José Ignacio. *El virreinato: Introducción al estudio de los virreyes de Nueva España, 1535-1746*, vol. I. México: Fondo de Cultura Económica, 1955.

Schlesinger, Arthur M., Jr. *The Cycles of American History*. Boston: Houghton Mifflin, 1986.

Schoultz, Lars. *National Security and United States Policy toward Latin America*. Princeton: Princeton University Press, 1987.

Schon, Isabel. *A Hispanic Heritage, A Guide to Juvenile Books about Hispanic Peoples and Cultures*. Metuchen, NJ: Scarecrow Press, 1980.

Sepúlveda Amor, Bernardo. "Reflexiones sobre la política exterior de México." *Foro Internacional*, 24, 4 (April-June 1984): 407-414.

Siegal, Jacob S., Jeffrey S. Passel, and J. Gregory Robinson. "Preliminary Review of Existing Studies of the Number of Illegal Residents of the United States." Report of the U.S. Bureau of the Census, 1980.

Smith, Peter H. "Uneasy Neighbors: Mexico and the United States." *Current History* 86, 518 (March 1987): 98-100, 130-132.

Tucker, Robert W. *Intervention and the Reagan Doctrine.* New York: Council on Religion and International Affairs, 1985.

Warren, Robert, and Jeffrey S. Passel. "A Count of the Uncountable: Estimates of Undocumented Aliens Counted in the 1980 United States Census." *Demography* 24 (August 1987): 375-398.

United Nations. *Statement by President of International Conference on Drug Abuse and Illicit Trafficking.* United Nations, Press Release ICDAIT/ MISC/3. June 17, 1987.

_____. UNFDAC. *Status of Cash Contributions and Pledges as of December 31, 1987.* January 1988.

_____. *Annual UNFDAC Report to the U.N. Commission on Narcotic Drugs.* December 1987.

United States. Bureau of the Census, U.S. Department of Commerce. *The Hispanic Population in the United States: March 1985,* Current Population Reports, Series P-20, No. 422 (March 1988).

_____. Department of Health and Human Services. *National Household Survey on Drug Abuse.* Washington: National Institute on Drug Abuse, 1985.

_____. Department of State. *Report to Congress on Voting Practices in the United Nations.* Washington, April 1987.

_____. Department of State. Bureau of International Narcotics Matters. *International Narcotic Control Strategy Report.* March 1988.

_____. General Accounting Office. *Drug Abuse Prevention.* Report to the Select Committee on Narcotics Abuse and Control, House of Representatives. Washington, December 1987.

_____. General Accounting Office. *Drug Control: U.S.- Mexican Opium and Marijuana Aerial Eradication Program,* Report to the Congress. January 1988.

_____. House of Representatives. Select Committee on Narcotics Abuse and Control. *Annual Report for the Year 1985.* Washington: U.S. Government Printing Office, 1986.

_____. President's Commission on Organized Crime. *America's Habit: Drug Abuse, Drug Trafficking and Organized Crime.* Washington: U.S. Government Printing Office, 1986.

_____. *The Cash Connection: Organized Crime, Financial Institutions and Money Laundering.* Washington: U.S. Government Printing Office, 1985.

_____. United States Information Service. Research Memoranda, Office of Research, 28 February 1985; 13 February 1986.

Van Wert, James. "El control de los narcóticos en México. Una década de institucionalización y un asunto diplomático," in Gabriel Székely (ed.), *México-Estados Unidos, 1985*. México: El Colegio de México, 1986.

Weinberg, Albert K. *Manifest Destiny: A Study of Nationalist Expansion in American History*. Baltimore: Johns Hopkins University Press, 1933.

Wellhausen, Edwin J. "The Agriculture of Mexico." *Scientific American* 235, 3 (September 1976): 128-150.

Wood, Bryce. *The Making of the Good Neighbor Policy*. New York: W.W. Norton/Columbia University Press, 1967.

Woll, Allen. *The Latin Image in American Film*. Los Angeles: Latin American Center, University of California at Los Angeles, 1977.

IV. Additional Participants in Meetings and Workshops

In addition to contracting papers on a wide variety of topics from leading specialists, as listed in Appendix II, the Bilateral Commission has received oral testimony and informal statements from numerous other individuals, many of them government officials (in which case we identify position held at the time of their meetings with the Commission). With this listing we acknowledge our gratitude.

MEXICO

Government Officials:

Aspe, Pedro (Secretary of Programming and Budget)
Escobar, Javier (Consul General in San Diego)
Espinosa de los Reyes, Jorge (Ambassador to the U.S.)
Farías, Luis (Mayor of Monterrey)
García Ramirez, Sergio (Attorney General)
González, Raúl (Mayor of Ciudad Acuña)
Gurría, Angel (Director General of Public Credit)
Hegewisch, Adolfo (Undersecretary of Industrial Development)
Herrera Lasso, Luis (Adviser to Undersecretary of Finance)
Mendoza, Héctor (Consul General in San Antonio)
Oropeza, Antonio (Adviser to Undersecretary of Commerce)
Pellicer, Olga (Ambassadress to Greece)
Petricioli, Gustavo (Secretary of Finance)
Salas, Federico (Ministry of Foreign Affairs)
Sepúlveda Amor, Bernardo (Secretary of Foreign Affairs)

Private Citizens:

Bátis, Humberto (Unomásuno)
Bueno, Gerardo (El Colegio de México)
Castro, José Luis (El Colegio de la Frontera Norte)
Elizondo, Everardo (Index de Economía Aplicada)
García Soler, León (Excélsior)
González Arechiga, Bernardo (El Colegio de la Frontera Norte)
Meyer, Lorenzo (El Colegio de México)
Morales, Cesáreo (Universidad Nacional Autónoma de México)
Toro, Celia (El Colegio de México)
Treviño Westendarp, Raúl (Grupo Visa)
Valdez de Villalba, Guillermina (El Colegio de la Frontera Norte)
Verea, Mónica (Universidad Nacional Autónoma de México)
Zenteño, René (El Colegio de la Frontera Norte)

UNITED STATES

Government Officials:

Abrams, Elliott (Assistant Secretary of State for Inter-American Affairs)
Bradley, William (U.S. Senator/New Jersey)
Carlucci, Frank (National Security Advisor to the President)
Dodd, Christopher (U.S. Senator/Connecticut)
Eliason, Alan (Chief of San Diego Section, U.S. Border Patrol)
Fascell, Dante (U.S. Representative/Florida)
Latell, Brian (National Intelligence Council)
Lugar, Richard (U.S. Senator/Indiana)
Nelson, Alan (Commissioner of Immigration and Naturalization
    Service)
Pilliod, Charles (Ambassador to Mexico)
Rennek, Gary (Deputy Director, INS in San Antonio)
Ruiz, Edgar (County Judge, Edinburgh, Texas)
Schultz, George (Secretary of State)
Trott, Stephen (Deputy Attorney General)

Former Government Officials:

Krueger, Robert (former Special Assistant to the President for
    Mexican Affairs)
Linowitz, Sol (former Ambassador to the OAS)
Pastor, Robert (former director of Latin American and Caribbean
    Affairs/National Security Council)
Shankle, Perry (former Director/Mexico Desk, Department of State)
Téllez, Raymond (former Mayor of El Paso, Texas)
Vaky, Viron P. (former Assistant Secretary of State for Inter-
    American Affairs)

Private Citizens:

Camp, Roderic Ai (Central College)
Cárdenas, Blandina (UNAM/San Antonio Project on U.S.-Mexican
  Policy Studies)
Catugno, Catanzo (Catholic Services/San Antonio)
Chisti, Muffazar (International Ladies Garment Workers Union)
Ellis, Patricia (The McNeil-Lehrer Report)
Hernández, Antonia (Mexican American Legal Defense/MALDEF)
Lowenthal, Abraham (University of Southern California)
Manning, Vesta (University of Florida)
Migdail, Carl (syndicated columnist)
Oswald, Rudy (AFL-CIO)
Purcell, Susan Kaufman (Council on Foreign Relations)
Robinson, Alan (International Correspondents Association/Mexico City)
Roett, Riordan (SAIS/Johns Hopkins University)
Ronfeldt, David (Rand Corporation)
Rosenfeld, Steve (The Washington Post)
Sánchez, Laura (Proyecto Hospitalidad)
Sewell, John (Overseas Development Council)
Sinkin, Richard (Strategies International)
Smith, Clint (William and Flora Hewlett Foundation)
Stockton, William (The New York Times/Mexico City)
Treviño, Jesse (Syndicated columnist)
Vázquez, Juan (CBS/Miami)
Zysman, John (University of California/Berkeley)

V. Individual Statements by Commissioners

Only one member of the Commission has chosen to submit an individual statement about the report:

The invitation to join the Bilateral Commission on the Future of United States-Mexican Relations came to me as an honor and an opportunity to serve my country, so I immediately accepted with pleasure. The chance to work together with the other Commissioners, with scholars and experts on the various facets of U.S.-Mexican relations, offered the opportunity to apply both knowledge and experience to this important theme.

I have always believed that the achievement of a better relationship between Mexico and the United States, more mature and less emotional, would provide great benefits for both societies. Encouraged by this conviction, I have taken active part in the work of the Commission that culminates in the publication of this book.

One of the first problems we encountered was in the definition of our basic subject matter. We analyze, in this document, issues of vital importance for our two countries. But in my opinion there is one missing: the question of democracy. To be sure, the form of government is a sovereign decision that every nation should take in conformity with its culture and with the aspirations of its people, without any foreign intervention. It is also true, however, that a government's political ideas, and its procedures for defining its structure and action, have an impact on international relations in general—and particularly, in our case, on relations between Mexico and the United States.

The governments of Mexico and the United States conceive of democracy in different ways, and this is a source of bilateral problems. This study would be more complete if it had taken up this theme.

The majority of Mexican Commissioners considered this as an internal matter, not an international one. On this subject, and on some others that we covered, I formed the impression that the official position of the Mexican government was being followed. I respect that opinion but I do not share it.

Among all my Mexican colleagues I recognize their good faith, their great personal capacity, and their dedication to the improvement of U.S.-Mexican relations. I can say the same of the U.S. Commissioners.

— **Fernando Canales Clariond**